First World War
and Army of Occupation
War Diary
France, Belgium and Germany

27 DIVISION
Divisional Troops
20 Brigade Royal Field Artillery
28 September 1914 - 30 January 1915

WO95/2257/5

The Naval & Military Press Ltd
www.nmarchive.com
Published in association with The National Archives

Published by

The Naval & Military Press Ltd

Unit 10 Ridgewood Industrial Park,

Uckfield, East Sussex,

TN22 5QE England

Tel: +44 (0) 1825 749494

www.naval-military-press.com

www.nmarchive.com

This diary has been reprinted in facsimile from the original. Any imperfections are inevitably reproduced and the quality may fall short of modern type and cartographic standards.

© **Crown Copyright**
Images reproduced by permission of The National Archives, London, England, 2015.

Contents

Document type	Place/Title	Date From	Date To
Heading	WO95/2257/5		
Heading	27th Division Divl Artillery 20th Brigade R.F.A. Nov 1914-Dec 1915		
Heading	27th Division 20 Brigade R.F.A. Vol I 16.11-23.12.14		
War Diary	Devonport	16/11/1914	16/11/1914
War Diary	Winchester	19/11/1914	23/12/1914
Heading	27th Division 20th Brigade R.F.A. Vol II 6-31.1.15		
War Diary		06/01/1915	30/01/1915
Map	Sketch 1		
Heading	27th Division 20th Brigade R.F.A. Vol III 1-28.2.15		
War Diary		01/02/1915	28/02/1915
War Diary		14/02/1915	15/02/1915
Diagram etc	Communications-20th Bde R.F.A.	28/02/1915	28/02/1915
Diagram etc	Communications-20th Bde R.F.A.	12/02/1915	12/02/1915
Heading	27th Division 20th Brigade R.F.A. Vol IV 1-31.3.15		
War Diary		01/03/1915	31/03/1915
War Diary		14/03/1915	15/03/1915
Diagram etc			
Heading	27th Division 20th Bde R.F.A. Vol V		
War Diary		01/04/1915	30/04/1915
Heading	27th Division 20th Bde R.F.A. Vol VI 1-31.5.15		
War Diary		01/05/1915	31/05/1915
Heading	27th Division 20th Bde. R.F.A. Vol VII 1-30.6.15		
War Diary		01/06/1915	30/06/1915
Heading	27th Division 20th Bde R.F.A. Vol VIII 1-31-7-15		
War Diary	Armentieres	01/07/1915	31/07/1915
Heading	27th Division 20th Bde R.F.A. Vol IX Aug Vol 1.15		
War Diary		01/08/1915	31/08/1915
Heading	27th Division 20th Bde R.F.A. Vol X Sept 15		
War Diary		01/09/1915	30/09/1915
Heading	27th Division 20th Bde. R.F.A. Dec 15 Vol XI		
War Diary	Cerisy	01/10/1915	07/10/1915
War Diary	Chuignolles	07/10/1915	25/10/1915
War Diary	Cerisy	26/10/1915	26/10/1915
War Diary	Boves	27/10/1915	27/10/1915
War Diary	Bricquesmesnil	28/10/1915	31/10/1915
Operation(al) Order(s)	81st Infantry Brigade Group Operation Order No.62		
Miscellaneous	March Table		
Diagram etc	Billet Area		
Miscellaneous	Areas		
Heading	20th Bde R.F.A. Nov Dec Vol XII		
War Diary	Bricquesmesnil	01/11/1915	25/12/1915
War Diary	Conde Folie	30/12/1915	30/12/1915
Heading	27th Division 67th Battn R.F.A. Vol I 26.11-31.12.14		
Heading	War Diary of 67th Battery Royal Field Artillery 26-11-14 To 31-12-14 (Volume I)		
Miscellaneous			
War Diary	Winchester	26/11/1914	26/11/1914
War Diary	Winchester Southampton	19/12/1914	19/12/1914
War Diary	Havre	20/12/1914	21/12/1914

War Diary	Arques		22/12/1914	22/12/1914
War Diary	Wallon Capelle		23/12/1914	31/12/1914
Heading	27th Division 67th Battery R F A Vol II 1-31.1.15			
Heading	War Diary of 67th Battery Royal Field Artillery From 1-1-15 To 31-1-15 (Volume II)			
Miscellaneous				
War Diary	Wallon Capelle		01/01/1915	06/01/1915
War Diary	Strazeele		07/01/1915	07/01/1915
War Diary	Zevecoton		08/01/1915	09/01/1915
War Diary	Dickebusch		10/01/1915	19/01/1915
War Diary	Westoutre (Heksken)		18/01/1915	23/01/1915
War Diary	Dickebusch		24/01/1915	31/01/1915
Heading	War Diary of 67th Battery Royal Field Artillery 27th Division From 1.2.15 To 28.2.15 Volume III			
Miscellaneous				
War Diary	Dickebusch		01/02/1915	27/02/1915
Heading	67th Batty R.F.A. Vol IV 1.31.3.15 27th Division			
Heading	War Diary Of 67th Battery Royal Field Artillery From 1-3-15 To 31-3-15 (Volume IV)			
Miscellaneous				
War Diary	Dickebusch		01/03/1915	14/03/1915
War Diary	Ouderdom		15/03/1915	25/03/1915
War Diary	Poperinghe		26/03/1915	26/03/1915
War Diary	Ouderdom		27/03/1915	27/03/1915
War Diary	Dickebusch		28/03/1915	31/03/1915
Heading	27th Division 67th Batty R.F.A. Vol V 1-30.4.15			
Heading	War Diary of 67th Battery Royal Field Artillery From 1-4-15 To 30.4.15 (Volume V)			
Miscellaneous				
War Diary	Dickebusch		01/04/1915	01/04/1915
War Diary	Poperinghe		02/04/1915	05/04/1915
War Diary	Hooge		06/04/1915	30/04/1915
Heading	27th Division 67th Battery R.F.A. Vol VI 1-31.5.15			
Heading	War Diary of 67th Battery Royal Field Artillery From 1-5-15 To 31-5-15 (Volume VI)			
Miscellaneous				
War Diary	Hooge		01/05/1915	03/05/1915
War Diary	Vlamertinghe		04/05/1915	08/05/1915
War Diary	Kruisstraat		09/05/1915	22/05/1915
War Diary	Zillebeke		23/05/1915	26/05/1915
War Diary	Armentieres		27/05/1915	31/05/1915
Heading	27th Division 67th Batty R F A Vol VII 1-30.6.15			
Heading	War Diary Of 67th Battery Royal Field Artillery From 1-6-15 To 30.6.15 (Volume VII)			
Miscellaneous				
War Diary	Armentieres		01/06/1915	30/06/1915
Heading	27th Division 67th Batty R.F.A. Vol VIII 1-31.7.15			
Heading	War Diary Of 67th Battery Royal Field Artillery From 1-7-15 To Vol VIII			
Miscellaneous				
War Diary	Armentieres		01/07/1915	18/07/1915
War Diary	Bois Grenier		19/07/1915	31/07/1915
Miscellaneous				
Heading	21st Division 67th Battery R.F.A. Vol X From 1-31.8.15			

Heading	War Diary Of 67th Battery Royal Field Artillery From 1-8-15 To 31.8.15 (Vol IX)		
Miscellaneous			
War Diary	Bois Grenier	01/08/1915	31/08/1915
Heading	27th Division 67th Batty R.F.A. Vol X Sept 15		
Heading	War Diary Of 67th Battery Royal Field Artillery From 1-9-15 To Vol X		
Miscellaneous			
War Diary	Bois Grenier	01/09/1915	14/09/1915
War Diary	L'Hallo Beau	15/09/1915	15/09/1915
War Diary	Oultersteen	16/09/1915	18/09/1915
War Diary	In The Train	19/09/1915	19/09/1915
War Diary	Cerisy	20/09/1915	24/09/1915
War Diary	Cappy	25/09/1915	25/09/1915
War Diary	Cerisy	26/09/1915	30/09/1915
Heading	27th Division 99th Batty R.F.A. Vol I 28.9-31.12.14		
War Diary	Neemuch India	28/09/1914	10/10/1914
War Diary	Rutlam	11/10/1914	11/10/1914
War Diary	Phagoda Bombay	12/10/1914	12/10/1914
War Diary	Bombay	13/10/1914	16/10/1914
War Diary	At Sea	17/10/1914	18/10/1914
War Diary	Portsuez	23/10/1914	23/10/1914
War Diary	Port Said	24/10/1914	24/10/1914
War Diary	At Sea	25/10/1914	07/11/1914
War Diary	Gibraltar	08/11/1914	11/11/1914
War Diary	Plymouth	16/11/1914	17/11/1914
War Diary	Winchester	18/11/1914	18/11/1914
War Diary	Morn Hill Camp	19/11/1914	26/11/1914
War Diary	Winchester	27/11/1914	15/12/1914
War Diary	Morn Hill	16/12/1914	20/12/1914
War Diary	Southampton	20/12/1914	20/12/1914
War Diary	Havre	21/12/1914	22/12/1914
War Diary	On Train	23/12/1914	23/12/1914
War Diary	Nr. Sercous	24/12/1914	31/12/1914
Heading	27th Division 99th Batty R.F.A. Vol II 1-31.1.15		
War Diary	Sercous	01/01/1915	06/01/1915
War Diary	Strazeele	07/01/1915	07/01/1915
War Diary	Dickebusch	08/01/1915	17/01/1915
War Diary	Westoutre	18/01/1915	31/01/1915
Heading	27th Division 99th Batty (20th Bde) R F A Vol III 1-28.2.15		
War Diary	Dickebusch	01/02/1915	28/02/1915
War Diary	Dickebusch	14/02/1915	15/02/1915
Heading	27th Division 99th Batty. R.F.A. Vol IV 1-31.3.15		
War Diary	Dickebusch	01/03/1915	31/03/1915
Heading	27th Division 364 Batty R F A Vol I 26.11-31.12.14		
War Diary	Winchester	26/11/1914	31/12/1914
Heading	27th Division 364th Batty. R.F.A. Vol II. 1-31.1.15		
War Diary		05/01/1915	31/01/1915
Miscellaneous	War Diary 364th Battery R.F.A.	31/01/1915	31/01/1915
Heading	27th Division 364th Battery R F A Vol III 1-28.2.15		
War Diary		01/02/1915	28/02/1915
War Diary	Dickebusch	28/02/1915	28/02/1915
Miscellaneous	War Diary For February 1915 364th Battery R.F.A.		
Heading	27th Division 364th Batty R F A 20 Bde Vol IV 1-31.3.15		

Type	Description	Start	End
War Diary		01/03/1915	06/03/1915
War Diary	(5th Omitted In Error Appears On Sheet 20)	06/03/1915	06/03/1915
War Diary	Omitted In Proper Place	05/03/1915	31/03/1915
Miscellaneous	364th Battery R.F.A. War Diary March 1915 Appendix VI		
Miscellaneous	364th Battery R.F.A. War Diary March 1915 Appendix VII	31/03/1915	31/03/1915
Miscellaneous	364th Battery R.F.A. War Diary March 1915 Appendix VIII	31/03/1915	31/03/1915
Heading	27th Division 364th Batty R.F.A. 20 Bde Vol V 1-30.4.15		
War Diary		01/04/1915	30/04/1915
Heading	27th Division 364th Batty RFA 20 Bde Vol VI 1-31.5.15		
War Diary		01/05/1915	31/05/1915
Heading	27th Division 364th Batty. R.F.A. 20 Bde Vol VII 1-30.6.15 27th Division		
War Diary		01/06/1915	30/06/1915
Heading	27th Division 364th Batty R.F.A. 20 Bde Vol VII 1-31.7.15		
War Diary		01/07/1915	31/07/1915
Heading	27th Division 364th Batty RFA 20 Bde Vol IX August 15		
War Diary	Bois Grenier	01/08/1915	31/08/1915
Heading	27th Division 364th Batty R.F.A. 20 Bde Vol X Sept 15		
War Diary		01/09/1915	14/09/1915
War Diary	Steenwerk	14/09/1915	14/09/1915
War Diary	Sheet 75th Dutersteen	15/09/1915	19/09/1915
War Diary	Sheet C E B I S F	22/09/1915	24/09/1915
War Diary	Sheet 25th 75 Cappy	25/09/1915	25/09/1915
War Diary	Cerisy Sheet 26th 75	26/09/1915	30/09/1915
Heading	27th Division 20th Bde. RFA August Col Vol I 19.12-31.1.15		
War Diary		19/12/1914	30/01/1915
Heading	27th Division August Col 20th Bde R F A Vol II 2-28.2.15		
Miscellaneous	War Diary of The 20th Brigade Amm. Col. R.F.A.	01/03/1915	01/03/1915

WO95/22575

27TH DIVISION
DIVL ARTILLERY

20TH BRIGADE R.F.A.
Nov ~~DEC~~ 1914-DEC 1915

27th Division

20th Brigade R.F.A.

121/3588

Vol I. 16.11 — 23.12.14

Army Form C. 2118.

WAR DIARY
or
INTELLIGENCE SUMMARY.
(Erase heading not required.)

H.Q. 20th Brigade R.F.A. consisting of 98th, 99th & 100th Batteries

Hour, Date, Place	Summary of Events and Information	Remarks and references to Appendices
9 a.m. Nov 16th '14 DEVONPORT	Arrived from INDIA, Brigade consisting of 98th, 99th & 100th Bties. Disembarked ex S.S. Avon.	
7 p.m. Nov 19th WINCHESTER	Arrived by train from DEVONPORT & went into camp on MORN HILL, 4 miles S.E. of WINCHESTER. Mobilization started at once.	
Nov. 26th	New organization came into force. All batteries split into two. 98th split into 98th & 133rd & went to form part of 1st Bde. 20th Brigade then consisted of 99th, 364th & 67th Batteries. The 364th was formed from the left half of the 99th, & the 67th from the left half of the 100th, which left the Brigade each battery armed with 4 guns & 8 wagons. The Battery Commanders were as follows:— 67th Capt. E.C. Hall. 99th Major E.O. Anderson. 364th Major R.W. White. Lieut. E.W.G. Wilson from 99th Bty became Adjutant vice Major R.W. White. Captain J.B. Orde appointed Staff Captain to 27th Divl Art'y. The brigade formed part of the 27th Divisional Artillery commanded by Brig.-Gen A. Stokes. 27th Division, commanded by Maj. Gen. T.D.O. Snow contained the 80th, 81st & 82nd Int'y Brigades. The weather was very bad. The first week there was frost, but after that there was a great deal of rain, & the camp soon became a morass. As the main road was ½ mile from camp, the drawing of stores, equipment, rations, forage etc. was thus rendered very difficult.	
Nov. 30th	Ammunition Column formed from details sent from various places.	

Army Form C. 2118.

WAR DIARY
or
INTELLIGENCE SUMMARY.
(Erase heading not required.)

Hour, Date, Place	Summary of Events and Information	Remarks and references to Appendices
Dec. 16th WINCHESTER.	Officers were attached to H.Q. of the brigade as follows:—	
Dec. 19th	Rev. W.H.L. Miller S.C.F. from Nov 27th; Lieut T.A. McCreath A.V.C. from Nov 21st; Lieut A.O.P. Reynolds R.A.M.C. from Nov 21st to Dec 10th Lieut H.S. Pemberton R.A.M.C. from Dec. 10th.	
2.0 h.	Inspection of 27th Division by H.M The King.	
	67th Bty, left by road for SOUTHAMPTON – 14 miles.	
" 3 p.m.	H.Q., 99th + 364th Batteries + Amm. Col. left by road for SOUTHAMPTON.	
	H.Q. arrived SOUTHAMPTON + embarked on S.S. "City of Edinburgh"	
	Col. P.E. Gray was O.C. Troops on board – 3rd KRR + the H.Q. 1st + 20th Bn RFA	
Dec 21st 1 pm	Arrived HAVRE. Disembarking arrangements very slow compared with those at SOUTHAMPTON.	
7.30 pm	Marched to Laleure des Marchandises – 2 miles + waited at "Pont" till 1 a.m. when horses + vehicles were entrained.	
Dec. 22nd 5.30 a.m.	Left HAVRE – H.Q. + 364th Bty in one train. "ABBEVILLE" was confidentially communicated as the destination.	
7 pm	Arrived ABBEVILLE + sent on to ARQUES, 2 miles E of ST OMER.	
Dec 23rd 3 a.m.	Arrived ARQUES and detrained at once.	
	Billets for the brigade were found in SERCUS + WALLON CAPPEL about 9 miles E. of ARQUES; + reached by H.Q + 364th Bty at 10 a.m. The other units of the brigade arrived at their billets independently as follows:— 67th 22nd Dec.; 99th 9 p.m. 23rd; Amm. Col. 4.30 p.m. 24th. H.Q. + the 99th Bty were in billets at "Le Chateau", 1 mile N.E. of SERCUS. Headquarters of the Brigade billeting Area were at BLARINGHEM 3 miles S.W.	
Dec 26th	27th Div formed part of 2nd Army under Sir Horace Smith Dorrien with 1st + 3rd Corps the 27th Div Artl in ARQUES.	

121/4258

27th Division

20th Brigade R.F.A.

Vol III. 6 — 31.1.15

Nil

WAR DIARY of H.Q. 20th Bde R.F.A.
or INTELLIGENCE SUMMARY. January 1915

Army Form C. 2118.

Hour, Date, Place	Summary of Events and Information	Remarks and references to Appendices
11 a.m. Jan 6th	Left SERCUS for billets in STRAZEELE - 9 miles. H.Q. + 3 batteries in STRAZEELE. Amm. Col. in PRADELLES, 1 mile W.	
11 a.m. Jan 7th	Marched via BAILLEUL and LOCRE to billets in ZEVECOLEN. 67th Bty billeted + Amm. Col. bivouached in ZEVECOLEN. 99th + 364th bivouached near OUDERDOM. Units arrived about 6 p.m. Very wet night. D.C. Brigade + Adjutant met the Commandant of the 2nd Groupe 3rd Regt of Artillery which formed part of the 32nd French Division at his H.Q. (H.35.a.6.3 - Ref. map BELGIUM 40,000). Thorough arrangements were made for taking over the French positions. Battery Commanders came up at 1·30. and made their arrangements for occupying the positions.	
Jan 8th	One section 99th Bty relieved a section of the French left Bty; one section 364th Bty relieved a section of the right Bty. This took place before daylight. The 2 batteries were in line along a thin hedge. Cover from view was all that there was in most gun pits, as the dug outs were full of water. A little brushwood over the guns gave cover from view from aeroplanes. The guns for the brigade extended from this a line running through the middle of BOIS 40 (O.7) to the road running S.E. from ST ELOI. The german trenches ran along the front of BOIS 40 + about 200ˣ roads at ST. ELOI. See sketch D attached.	See sketch D

WAR DIARY
or
INTELLIGENCE SUMMARY.
(Erase heading not required.)

Army Form C. 2118.

Hour, Date, Place	Summary of Events and Information	Remarks and references to Appendices
Jan 8th Cont.	French Artillery were in action on our left, and the 15th Bde R.F.A. (attached to 27th Div) on our right. The 67th Bty remained in reserve at ZEVERCOTEN. Communication between guns + forward art'y observing officers was by artillery telephone to an exchange in VOORMEZEELE; by infantry line from there to battalion H.Q. in ST. ELOI; and from there by artillery line to forward observing officer. Communication between guns + infantry in the trenches was by the same line. This being unsatisfactory of the inf'y line was busy, 2 artillery lines were run out from VOORMEZEELE to ST. ELOI. Amm Col moved into billets near ZEVERCOTEN.	H.Q. established in Restaurant on edge of lake H 35 a 2 9.
Jan 9th	Remaining sections of 99th + 364th Batteries relieved remaining sections of French batteries at 6 a.m. The mud in the gun positions and in the approaches to them was very thick; + 10 horses were necessary in each team. 67th Bty ordered to come into action.	
" 10th	80th Inf'y Bde relieved by 81st in the trenches in the zone of the brigade. Trenches in front of ST. ELOI particularly bad + deep in mud. Infantry relieved every 48 hours, and in some cases every 24 hours.	
" 11th	Lieut R.F. Gore-Browne, 364th Bty, missing from 6.45 a.m. Last seen at the humulus at ST. ELOI, 70 yards behind our trenches, on his way to his observing station. Tumulus which had been used as an artillery observing station for some time became impossible owing to enemy fire, + Lieut Gore-Browne was at the time looking for a new one.	

WAR DIARY
or
INTELLIGENCE SUMMARY.
(Erase heading not required.)

Army Form C. 2118.

Hour, Date, Place	Summary of Events and Information	Remarks and references to Appendices
Jan 12th '15	67th Bty came into action before daylight in some old French gun pits on the left of the other 2 batteries (H 29 c. 8.1.). Cannot small interval in hedge of willow-trees. The zone of the brigade was now divided into 3. No 1 Zone, engaged by right centre battery (99th) extended from the centre of the Northern edge of Bois 40 (O.7) to N.E. corner of wood. No 2 Zone, engaged by left battery (67th) extended from N.E. corner of wood 40 to PICCADILLY FARM (O.8.a.3.8) inclusive. No 3 Zone, engaged by right battery (364th) extended from PICCADILLY FARM exclusive to road running S.E. from ST. ELOI.	WD
Jan 14th VOORMEZEELE.	Telephonic communication between 364 Bty + Bty + thus with infantry in the trenches breaking down, a new line was laid out to by night from Brigade H.Q. to VOORMEZEELE.	WD
Jan 17th 6 a.m.	Brigade relieved by 19th Brigade R.F.A. Guns, wagons or wagon bodies, water carts + everything except instruments (telephones, directors etc.) left for relieving Brigade. 20th Brigade proceeded to billets in farms along road running from M.7a. to M.2.b., formerly occupied by 19th Bde. (about 1 mile N.W. of WESTOUTRE). Bde. H.Q. at M.1.d.2.0. Communications with Div. Art. H.Q. at BOESCHEPE, 3 mile N.W. were by telephone + by motor cyclist orderly twice daily. All billets were very cramped + insanitary + number of men going sick increased daily.	WD
Jan 18th	Bde. H.Q. moved to G.32.d. 3.9. on HEKSKEN - POPERINGHE road	WD

Army Form C. 2118.

WAR DIARY
or
INTELLIGENCE SUMMARY.
(Erase heading not required.)

Hour, Date, Place	Summary of Events and Information	Remarks and references to Appendices
Jan 20th	Instruction in cooperation between aeroplanes and artillery near LOCRE. Too misty for aeroplanes to ascend. Demonstration of Very lights and code of signalling. During this week baths were provided for the Brigade at the brewery at BOESCHEPE.	hds
23rd	67th Bty ordered into action on the bank of the Lake at DICKEBUSCH in pits dug by 19th Bde. (H.28) This position was occupied during the night. Bty came under orders of 19th Bde R.F.A. 99th & 364th Batteries were ordered to be ready to proceed to positions partially prepared by 1st Bde R.F.A. H.33 about 1 mile S.W. of former battery positions. The new positions were improved during 24th & 25th. Several officers went over to 33rd Bde Arty. H.Q. W. of MONT KEMMEL to see observing stations & procedure generally.	hds
26th	Received orders not to relieve 19th Brigade till further orders. Relief was to have been carried out this day. A German attack was apparently thought probable, the 27th being the Kaiser's birthday.	hds
28th	Received orders to take over new zone, on the left of the old one, from a French groupe, in H.29.d.	hds
29th – 31st		hds
30th	Arrangements made for taking over new zone on 1st & 2nd 1st Feb. 2nd Lieut T.P. Lysaght joined Brigade Amm" Column.	hds hds

Sketch ①

176a

ST. ELOI
Fm Piccadilly
Bois Konfluent
Bois 40
Observing Station
Brasserie
Bois Carré
Observing Station
Wuschaetzeek
Holland Cheshuut

Scale 1/10,000

.... = telephone
PC = Poste de Commandant
━━ = Our Trenches
----- = Zone of Brigade

Situation on Jan 15th 15.

121/4612

27th Division

20th Brigade R.F.A.

Vol III 1 - 28.2.15

Feb 10th. formation of 4 gun batteries
" 25th. Periscopes required —

nil

WAR DIARY H.Q. 20th Bde R.F.A.   Army Form C. 2118.
or
INTELLIGENCE SUMMARY.   February 1915.
(Erase heading not required.)

Hour, Date, Place	Summary of Events and Information	Remarks and references to Appendices
Feb. 1st. 8 p.m.	99th Bty came into action in a new position along a ridge at H.35.a.8.8. The French battery, which the 99th relieved, left its position in H.29.d.8.6 the same night.	No 2.
2nd. 8 p.m.	364th Bty put their guns into the emplacements vacated the night before by the French battery H.29.d.8.6, & then took over the guns of 67th Bty in H.29.c.8.2, where they had been since Jan 12th. The 67th Bty came under orders of 20th Bde R.F.A. from their date, & took over the guns of 364th Bty in H.29.d.8.6. This position had been located by German batteries and frequently shelled, so it was decided to keep the battery there as a reserve one with a guard on the guns. Ranges & lines were found to points on the roads running S.E. + S.S.E. of ST ELOI + the men returned to billets close behind ready to man the battery if necessary. The flashes from this position were visible to the Germans, but no alternative position could be found. The Zone of the brigade was from the ST ELOI – OOSTAVERNE Road at O.2.d.4.0. to E. end of wood at O.3.b.5.2. The 99th took the right of this zone and the 364th the left, the dividing line passing just E. of farm O.3.d.3.9. The remaining two French batteries, which the 67th & 364th Batteries relieved did not leave their positions on this night as intended, as an attack was expected on the trenches to the	No 2.

179

WAR DIARY of INTELLIGENCE SUMMARY.

H.Q. 20th Bde R.F.A. Army Form C. 2118.

(Erase heading not required.)

Hour, Date, Place	Summary of Events and Information	Remarks and references to Appendices
8 p.m. Feb. 3rd 1915 8.10 p.m. Feb. 4th.	Remaining French batteries (of 56th Regt) left their position. Orders received to man all the guns & harness up horses. About 20 rounds were fired by batteries at roads S.E. of ST ELOI. Forward observing officer at O2 B 9.1 reported all quiet on his immediate front throughout the night.	hrs.
7 a.m. Feb 5th.	Orders received allowing batteries to resume normal state of readiness. From 9 a.m. zones were altered as follows:— 364th Bty from pond at O.8 a 7.8 to point O 2 C 7.1. 99th Bty from O 2 d 7.1. to bend of road at O 9 a 8.9. Observing Station of 364th Bty was the tumulus at ST ELOI O 2 d 2.7. 99th Bty a ruined farm at O 2 B 9.1. The H.Q. of the infantry battalion on the left were also in this farm, from which there was a telephone line to the 99th Bty guns. The 364th Bty had a telephone line from the tumulus to the guns, passing through the H.Q. of the infantry battalion in the trenches in front of ST ELOI. The H.Q. were in VOORMEZEELE	
8.30 p.m.	Orders received to man the guns and harness up horses. Guns did not fire as observing officer at farm O 2 B 9.1 reported all quiet on his immediate front.	
11 p.m.	67th Bty (in reserve) allowed to return to billets.	hrs.
9.50 a.m. Feb. 6th.	Orders received from 5th Corps H.Q. to be ready to move at 1/2 hour's notice.	
10.30 a.m.	Above order cancelled.	hrs.

WAR DIARY or INTELLIGENCE SUMMARY

Army Form C. 2118.

Hour, Date, Place	Summary of Events and Information	Remarks and references to Appendices
Feb. 6th. Cont.	Zone of brigade shortened on the left to a N. & S. line dividing square O2 from O3. This was also the dividing line between 27th & 28th Divisions. The infantry trenches in the zone of 27th Divn were divided into 2 sections, each held by an infantry brigade. The right section extended from VIERSTRAAT – WYTSCHAETE road exclusive to road leading from H.29.b through KRUISSTRAATHOEK and VOORMEZEELE to N.E. corner of O.7.6. The left section extended from this line to centre of square O.3. H.Q's of 2 Infy battalions in trenches of left section were at farm O.26.9.i. + in VOORMEZEELE. Direct communication was established between both these H.Q.s and the batteries of the brigade. H.Q of right infantry battalion of left section moved from VOORMEZEELE to house in St ELOI at O.2.a.4.7. Direct communication established between this point and guns of 364th Bty, an artillery operator being kept at Inf'y Battn. H.Q. night + day. An officer from 99th Bty was kept at their observing station at O.2.b.7.1. all day; and an officer or telephone operator was left there at night, in direct communication with guns of 99th Bty. Plan of communications attached – lettered (A)	W.D.
Feb. 10th.	New battery formed from 1 section from 11th battery and 1 section from 39th Bty, called 11A, + came under orders of 20th Bde from this date, on reorganization of brigades into 4 batteries of 4 guns each. Captain W.K.Twedie, 2nd Lieuts C.R.Jackson & W. Strahan joined the Brigade with the new battery.	W.D.

WAR DIARY
or
INTELLIGENCE SUMMARY.
(Erase heading not required.)

Army Form C. 2118.

Hour, Date, Place	Summary of Events and Information	Remarks and references to Appendices
Feb. 14th	Lt. Col. P.E. Grant comdg. the brigade admitted to hospital. Major R.W. White, 364th R.F.A. assumed the command of the brigade.	
3.48 p.m.	Fire opened on German trenches on request of Infantry at ST ELOI. Leinster Regt. on the left, driven out of trenches 19–22 by German shell fire. Artillery of the Division supported during the night with battery fire at rates varying from 5 secs to 2 mins. Trenches 21 & 22 enfiladed by 67 & 13 Bty. R.F.A. 82nd Inf.y Bde. H.Q. (Brigade in left section of trenches) moved from DICKEBUSCH to VOORMEZEELE.	
Feb. 15th		
4.45 a.m.	Counter-attack successful and all trenches retaken. Artillery of Division congratulated by Corps Commander on the support given. Casualties in the brigade:- 3 killed & 3 wounded, all in 364th Bty caused by a direct hit on one of their guns. News received that 2/Lieut R.F. Gore Browne, missing since Jan 11th, is a prisoner in Germany.	Full report in Appendix I
16th	364th Bty registered targets by means of observation by aeroplane using coloured lights. Fire opened from 9-9.30 p.m.	/w/2.
18th	Infantry & Lieut Boxand joined the brigade & was posted to 11 A/Bty.	/w/3.
	27th Division took over the extreme right trench of 28th Division during the night. This trench was now numbered 23, & was about 200 yards long. Zone of brigade extended on the left to cover the ground in front of this trench.	/w/2.

182.

Army Form C. 2118.

WAR DIARY
or
INTELLIGENCE SUMMARY.
(Erase heading not required.)

Instructions regarding War Diaries and Intelligence Summaries are contained in F.S. Regs, Part II. and the Staff Manual respectively. Title pages will be prepared in manuscript.

Hour, Date, Place	Summary of Events and Information	Remarks and references to Appendices
Feb. 19th 1915	No 23 trench taken over again by 28th Division. H.Q. of left battn of left section withdrawn from SHELLEY'S FARM, as the farm had been shelled regularly for some days. The second in command of this batt. was left in the cellar of the farm, with our observers and telephone.	W.D.
22nd	99th Bty took over gun position + guns of 364th Bty, which took over guns in reserve position, vacated by 99th Bty.	W.D.
25th	SHELLEY'S FARM given up as an observing station for left of Brigade gone, a new was was very restricted towards the right. Observer for this battery now at tumulus at ST ELOI, which was thus the observing station for both batteries. A telephone from the left battery who still left at H.Q. of left inf'y battn which were now in a house on the YPRES–ST ELOI road. This telephone was in direct communication with the guns.	Revised plan of communications attached, marked (B)
	The observing station is undoubtedly a bad one, in that it is very conspicuous being on top of a mound 20 feet above the surrounding ground, and only 150 yards from the German trenches. But it is the only place from which one can see the German trenches, which at this point are on the reverse slope of the ridge. It is impossible to observe without periscopes, + these get fired at as soon as they are put up + frequently broken. The present issue of periscopes supplemented by many private ones has all been broken, and 3 have been borrowed from other brigades, till more are forthcoming from Ordnance. There seems to be some doubt as to whether artillery are entitled to an issue of periscopes, and it is hoped that this will not delay the	

(73989) W4141–463. 400,000. 9/14. H.&J. Ltd. Forms/C. 2118/10.

Army Form C. 2118.

WAR DIARY
or
INTELLIGENCE SUMMARY.
(Erase heading not required.)

Instructions regarding War Diaries and Intelligence Summaries are contained in F.S. Regs., Part II. and the Staff Manual respectively. Title pages will be prepared in manuscript.

Hour, Date, Place	Summary of Events and Information	Remarks and references to Appendices
25th Feb. (cont)	Supply of a second issue, as they are indispensable in the case of observing stations so near the front. Cheap tin periscopes capable of standing hard wear, and with a large field of view are the best.	hrs.
26th	2nd Lieut E. Wilfred posted to 148th Bty (the new number for 11A since 23rd). 2nd Lieut A. Board transferred from 148th Bty to 39th Bty.	hrs. hrs.
27th – 28th	Nothing to record.	
	General Remarks.	
	The weather has been good, mostly bright & sunny, there has not been much rain. The sides of the main roads are still bad, especially the main DICKEBUSCH – YPRES road, E. of DICKEBUSCH, where carts get stuck & turn over every day. Several drafts have arrived – about 40 men including a Staff Sgt. Fitter for each battery. 148th Battery is about complete in men + horses, but is still a lot of equipment deficient, and will not be ready to take its place in the firing line for some weeks. 3 R.H.A. subalterns were attached to the brigade early in the month, one being attached to 67th, one to 99th, + one to 364th. One subaltern in each of these batteries was attached to R.H.A. in place of the 3 R.H.A. subalterns, for training purposes. Lieut M.W. Smith R.H.A. joined 67th Bty. + Lieut S. Cunningham taking his place in R.H.A. battery; Lieut J.D. Macneece joined 99th Bty, 2nd Lieut A. Wood taking his place. Lieut S.C.M. Archibald joined 364th Bty. 2nd Lieut Bellingham taking his place. This latter officer has since been accidentally wounded + returned to England.	hrs.

APPENDIX I.

WAR DIARY
or
INTELLIGENCE SUMMARY.
(Erase heading not required.)

Army Form C. 2118.

Hour, Date, Place	Summary of Events and Information	Remarks and references to Appendices
	German attack on trenches at ST ELOI Feb. 14-15 1915.	
Feb 14th. 3.41½ p.m.	Message asking for artillery support received from inf[y] at SHELLEYS FARM. Support at once given by 67th & 364th Batteries. 99th moved up to man their guns. Information received that Lincoln Regt. on the left, had been driven out of their trenches by shell fire. These trenches are Nos 19 - 22 on attached sketch. All batteries were switched on to the ground behind these trenches.	
3.55 p.m.	"S.O.S." signal received from 1st battalion of left section). "S.O.S." had been agreed on previously to mean that artillery support was wanted by the infantry in the trenches in front of ST ELOI.	
4.20 p.m.	Message received from H.Q. Royal Irish Fusiliers at ST ELOI. — "Regiment on left has been shelled out of their fire trenches and also out of their support trenches, from which they have retired. R.I.F. are being heavily shelled, but are hanging on.	
7 p.m.	Batteries switched back to normal zones and a slow rate of fire kept up while waiting for the counter attack, the time for which was first fixed for 2.30 a.m.	
Feb 15th 2.34 a.m.	Message received that counter attack was postponed till 3.30 a.m. The time was later altered to 4 a.m. but nothing definite was heard until 4.48 when a message was received that the counter attack had begun. Rate of fire quickened.	

APPENDIX I (Cont.)

Army Form C. 2118.

WAR DIARY
or
INTELLIGENCE SUMMARY.
(Erase heading not required.)

Instructions regarding War Diaries and Intelligence Summaries are contained in F.S. Regs., Part II and the Staff Manual respectively. Title pages will be prepared in manuscript.

Hour, Date, Place	Summary of Events and Information	Remarks and references to Appendices
Feb. 15th. 6.34 a.m. 6.57 a.m.	Message received that 21 + 22 trenches had been retaken. Ceased fire. It was soon after ascertained that 19 + 20 trenches had also been retaken after severe fighting. The Brigade expended 1950 rounds during this attack. Casualties 3 killed and 3 wounded; 2 guns out of action, one with the sights carried away by a shell, and one with a damaged buffer. The following telegram was received by the Division from the Officer Comdg 5th Corps:— "Well done. Congratulations to Gen. Langley (Comdg. 82nd Inf¹ Bde) and his troops, and to Gen. Stokes and his guns. G.O.C. 82nd Inf¹ Bde wired as follows at 7 a.m :— "All trenches were reoccupied. Very grateful to R.A. for tremendous help. Please communicate to all ranks."	

PLAN OF TRENCHES.

LEFT SECTION
S8] S9] ST. ELOI S14 S15
15 16 17 18 19 20 21 22 → 28th DIVⁿ

☐ = British trenches
× = H.Q. of Leinster Reg¹ & Art¹ⁿ Obsⁿ Stⁿ.

Scale 1/10,000

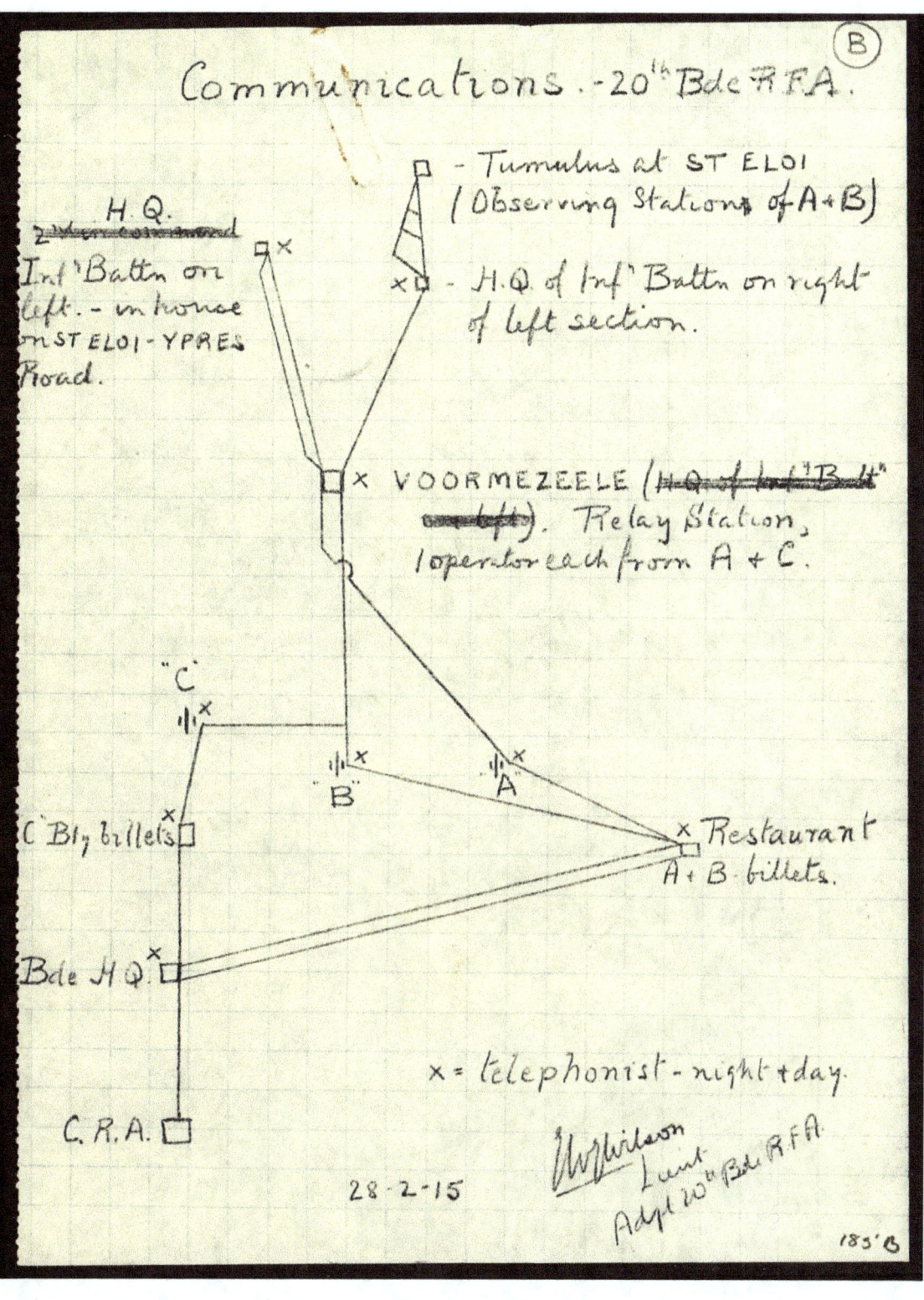

A. 24

Communications - 20th Bde R.F.A.
12-2-15.

O.S. "A" Bty.
(Shelley's Farm
[O 2 b 9.1.]
Inf¹ Batt^n H.Q.

O.S. "B" Bty
Tumulus ST ELOI
[O. 2 d 2.7]

Inf¹ Batt^n H.Q.
1 telephonist from B (night & day).

VOORMEZEELE (Relay Station).
1 telephonist from A and 1 from C.

(Reserve) "C"
H 29 d 8.6.

"B"
H 29 c. 8.2

"A"
H 35 a. 8.8

H.Q. "C" Bty

Restaurant
(H.Q.'s "A" & "B" Bty_s)

Bde H.Q. x

x = telephonist awake.

G.O.C.
R.A. 27th DIV^n

155 a.

151/4893

27th Division

20th Brigade R.F.A.

Vol IV 1 – 31.8.15

187.

Army Form C. 2118.

WAR DIARY
or
INTELLIGENCE SUMMARY.
(Erase heading not required.)

H.Q. 20th Bde R.F.A. 27th Division
March 1915

Hour, Date, Place	Summary of Events and Information	Remarks and references to Appendices

March 1st 1915
 	
10 p.m.
	No 21 trench, occupied by P.P.C.L.I. bombed in the early morning from a German sap. Our guns were unable to fire as the sap was only 25 yards in front of our trench. The parapet of 21 trench was destroyed by bombs, and 50% of the occupants were killed or wounded.
	    German advanced trench was now very close to 21 trench; & it was decided to attack and occupy it.
	    H.Q. 80th Inf. Bde + 19th + 20th F.A. Brigades moved up to VOORMEZEELE. Direct communication was established with the guns of all 3 batteries of the brigade, C.R.A. in DICKEBUSCH and the 2 forward artillery observing officers, one at the tumulus at ST ELOI and the other at SHELLEY'S FARM with the officer commanding the attack.
		62

March 2nd 12.30 a.m.	2 Coys of the 3rd K.R.R. attacked the forward German trench from the direction of SHELLEY'S FARM. The signal for the attack to begin was a round of gun fire from the 6 Yrs Bty. All batteries of 19th + 20th Brigades supported with rates of Bty. Fire varying from 5 secs to 2 mins until 2.57 a.m. when a report was received from the Infantry that artillery support was no longer required. H.Q. were moved back to DICKEBUSCH about 6 a.m. The 364th Bty in the Reserve position was shelled during the night, but no damage was done.	

Army Form C. 2118.

WAR DIARY
or
INTELLIGENCE SUMMARY.
(Erase heading not required.)

H.Q. 20th Brigade R.F.A.

Hour, Date, Place	Summary of Events and Information	Remarks and references to Appendices
March 2nd. (continued)	The following message was received from G.O.C. 27th Div by the C.R.A:- "your artillery's most valuable assistance to Infantry last night. G.O.C. wishes to express his thanks to you and through you to O.C. Brigades and batteries concerned." The infantry had only taken half the German trench, being stopped by a strong barricade. They were bombed out of it during the morning, 21 was also deserted as it was so knocked about, but the Germans could not hold it either as it was enfiladed by a machine gun. A new trench was dug in front of SHELLEYS FARM during the night.	h.2
March 3rd.	Germans now sapping from E. end of advanced trench towards 22 trench. This was a very difficult point to get at with artillery fire, owing to its proximity to own trenches. The infantry however decided to accept the risk & moved out of the W. end of 22. 67th Bty. then fired at the sap. The rounds were observed by an infantry officer in 22 and by the artillery officer on the tumulus. The battery succeeded in stopping all work on the sap throughout the day.	h.2

WAR DIARY
or
INTELLIGENCE SUMMARY.

HQ 20th Bde R.F.A.

Army Form C. 2118.

(Erase heading not required.)

Hour, Date, Place	Summary of Events and Information	Remarks and references to Appendices
March 4th.	Nothing to report.	
" 5th.	Trench 23 taken over by 27th Divn. Bombardment of German trenches in front of ST. ELOI. During the night 5th–6th the C.O. & Adjutant were in ST ELOI fixing up communications. Double lines of wire were laid from the tumulus to BUS HOUSE & WHITE HORSE CELLARS, and also from the breastwork to the E. of the tumulus to WHITE HORSE CELLARS. The brigade left 2 officers in the Breastwork, who were to observe fire only if observation from the tumulus broke down.	ws.
" 6th.	The infantry vacated the trenches in the zone of the brigade at dawn and occupied the breastwork & a trench called "R.B." on the W. of the mound. The batteries of the brigade opened fire about 7 a.m. to keep the Germans from attacking our vacated trenches. The batteries ceased fire at 12 noon, when the 6" + 4.5" Hows + 4.7" guns opened fire. These guns shelled the German trenches till dusk. The effect could not be seen from the breastwork, but is said to have been very good. The German heavy howitzers shelled ST ELOI, the breastwork and other support trenches throughout the morning, but did little damage. Observation continued to be from the Tumulus throughout the day; & at dusk the infantry reoccupied their trenches covered by the fire of 19th & 20th Brigades. Points © 9,18,18 Bty. suffered 5 casualties - 1 killed & 4 wounded, one of whom died during the night.	ws.

WAR DIARY
or
INTELLIGENCE SUMMARY.   H.Q. 20th Bde R.F.A.

(Erase heading not required.)

Army Form C. 2118.

Hour, Date, Place	Summary of Events and Information	Remarks and references to Appendices
March 7th	Nothing to report.	
" 8th	Nothing to report.	
" 9th	Nothing to report.	
" 10th	Nothing to report.	
" 11th	Bombardment of German trenches in front of 23C. trench. Main objective was enemy's redoubt and works at O 3 c. 8.5. References are to attached sketch Ⓐ. Observing was carried out from the tunnels at ST ELOI by the C.O. Additional observers found by 20th Bde & 116th Heavy battery were on the canal bank in I 33 d. 3.6. Fire was not opened till 11 a.m. owing to thick mist. Procedure was as follows :— 2 batteries of 20th Bde opened on lines AC & AD for registering purposes. Heavy batteries of 27th & 28th Divisions registered AC and BC.	
2.30 p.m	One battery of 20th Bde fired 50 rounds on AC for purpose of wire-cutting.	
2.45 p.m	Infantry in 23 trench opened rapid rifle fire for 5 minutes.	
2.50 p.m	99th & 364th batteries opened on DC increasing elevation by 100 yards. 120 rounds were fired. At the same time heavy batteries opened on whole of work ABC. The bombardment was very effective and the German trenches were badly knocked about.	
10 p.m	82nd Inf'y Brigade relieved 80th in left section. By new system, 81st Bde remained permanently in right section, the 80th & 82nd relieving each other every 6 days in left section.	

WAR DIARY or INTELLIGENCE SUMMARY

H.Q. 20th Bde R.F.A.

Army Form C. 2118.

Hour, Date, Place	Summary of Events and Information	Remarks and references to Appendices
March 12th. 1915	Nothing to report.	ws.
" 13th.	Observers report 8.2" German howitzers firing at ST ELOI; the first time for 6 weeks.	ws.
" 14th. 10 a.m.	148th Bty took over position and zone of 99th Bty. 99th Bty took over position and zone of 67th Bty, which went into rest vice 148th Bty.	
5.15 p.m.	German attack on ST ELOI, starting with the springing of a mine under the tumulus. Trenches 14 to 20 both inclusive captured by Germans. Counter attacks during the night made, supported by artillery fire, were unsuccessful. Detailed account in Appendix I.	
	Major E. O. Anderson, 99th Bty R.F.A. was wounded about 6 p.m. by splinters from a shell. Captain the Hon. D. H. Stanley from Bde. Amm. Col. assumed command of 99th Bty.	ws.
	The C.O. went up to VOORMEZEELE about 7 p.m., so as to be with the HQrs Brigadier comdg. He remained there till the morning of the 16th.	
" 15th	A broken down windmill at H36.d.8.2. was used as an observing station until a better could be found.	ws.
" 16th	Nothing to report.	ws.
" 17th	Lt.Col. P. E. Gray, who has been away sick, returned and took over command of the brigade.	ws.

WAR DIARY
INTELLIGENCE SUMMARY. H.Q. 20th Bde R.F.A.

Army Form C. 2118.

Hour, Date, Place	Summary of Events and Information	Remarks and references to Appendices
March 18th – 20th	Nothing to report.	Wd. Weather fine & bright.
21st	2/Lieut R. Dickie joined 20th Brigade R.F.A. & was posted temporarily to 99th Bty. After the trial of many observing stations, including those on the canal bank in I.33.d., the following were chosen:- for right zone, covered by 148th Bty, an observing officer was kept in trench 21. For left zone, covered by 364th Bty a small house in H.35.d.S.2. was used. H.Q. of ht" Battn. on left of left section were in SHELLEY'S FARM and an artillery telephonist was left there at night.	Wd.
22nd	Nothing to report.	Wd.
23rd	Nothing to report. G.O.C. 3rd Div" assumed command of front held by 27th Div" 8 p.m.	
24th	Arrangements made for handing over positions & zone of brigade to 23rd Brigade R.F.A. 3rd Division and for movement of 20th Brigade R.F.A. into billets S.W. of POPERINGHE C.R.A. 3rd Division assumed command of artillery covering front of 27th Division at noon.	
25th	67th Bty. R.F.A. in rest, marched to new billets, 2 miles S.W. of POPERINGHE on ABEELE road. Major H.C.V. Harrison arrived & took over command of Bde. Amm. Col. Major A.K. Main arrived & took over command of 99th Bty from Capt The Hon. O.H. Stanley, appointed to Gen'l S'n Amm Col.	Wd.

19¹

Army Form C. 2118.

WAR DIARY
or
INTELLIGENCE SUMMARY.
(Erase heading not required.)

Instructions regarding War Diaries and Intelligence Summaries are contained in F.S. Regs., Part II and the Staff Manual respectively. Title pages will be prepared in manuscript.

Hour, Date, Place	Summary of Events and Information	Remarks and references to Appendices
March 25th 1915 (continued)	At 7.30 p.m. the following reliefs took place :— One section of 364th Bty was relieved by one section of 108th Bty, 23rd Brigade. One section of 148th Bty was relieved by a second section of 108th Bty. One section of 99th Bty was relieved by one section of 109th Bty.	hrs
26th. 6 a.m.	Orders received cancelling relief of 20th Bde. Section of 23rd Bde in action to be replaced by sections of 20th Bde withdrawn on night of 25th. 67th Bty recalled from billets near POPERINGHE to its former wagon lines.	
27th. 9 a.m.	At 7.30 p.m. sections of 23rd Bde were taken out of gun positions + replaced by those of 20th Bde.	hrs
10 a.m.	67th Bty took over "A" position + left zone from 364th Bty. 364th Bty took over "C" position + right zone from 99th Bty, which proceeded to wagon lines to a state of rest. The German trenches between the 2 roads running S. from ST. ELOI was now added to the zone of the brigade, "C" Bty taking over the new part of the zone, and being responsible for searching the ST ELOI – OOSTAVERNE road as far South as _____	
	By 8 p.m. the last guns in position had been changed over by batteries, leaving each battery shooting with its own guns.	hrs
28th.	Nothing to report.	hrs
29th.	Captain L. Fry left the brigade from sick leave.	hrs
30th.	Nothing to report.	hrs

Hour, Date, Place	Summary of Events and Information	Remarks and references to Appendices
March 31st 9 p.m.	99th Bty and Amm. Col. moved to new billets S.W. of POPERINGHE. One section each of 67th, 148th, and 364th Batteries relieved in action by sections of 23rd Brigade R.F.A. During the month a "wireless" aeroplane worked with the batteries, and many targets were registered. March 18th. The 3 R.H.A. Subalterns attached to batteries rejoined their own units, 2/Lieut St C. U. Cunningham + 2/Lieut A. Wood rejoining 67th & 99th Batteries. 2/Lieut N. W. Haddock joined 364th Bty vice 2/Lieut Bellingham, accidentally wounded while attached to R.H.A. Weather during the month has been very good, with bright sun most days; ground drying up very quickly.	W2.

195

WAR DIARY
or
INTELLIGENCE SUMMARY.
(Erase heading not required.)

Army Form C. 2118.
Appendix I.

Instructions regarding War Diaries and Intelligence Summaries are contained in F.S. Regs., Part II and the Staff Manual respectively. Title pages will be prepared in manuscript.

Hour, Date, Place	Summary of Events and Information	Remarks and references to Appendices

Fighting at ST ELOI March 14th–15th 1915

March 14.9.15
5.15 p.m.

148th & 364th Batteries opened fire on German trenches in their zones, on hearing 19th Bde. R.F.A. firing "gun fire". Communication with forward observing Officer on Mound at ST ELOI was cut owing to the Mound having being blown up, + the telephonist + instrument being buried in it. The springing of mines simultaneously under the Mound and under 17 + 18 trenches was apparently the signal for all German batteries to open fire on our trenches. This was quickly followed by an assault on the Mound.

Communication with White Horse Cellars soon cut by shell fire.

6.8 p.m.
20th Brigade placed under the orders of Gen. Longley. Comdg. 82nd Inf. Bde. Major R.W. White Comdg. 20th Bde. R.F.A. left at once for VOORMEZEELE to join Gen. Longley.

6.57 p.m.
First definite + official information received as to what had happened. C.O. reports trenches 19 to 22 in German hands. Range of batteries covering right zone dropped so as to shoot into trenches 19 + 20.
Major E.O. Anderson, Comdg. 99th Bty. R.F.A. was wounded at gun position of his battery, by splinters of German shell.

Appendix I. (continued).

WAR DIARY
or
INTELLIGENCE SUMMARY.

Army Form C. 2118.

Hour, Date, Place	Summary of Events and Information	Remarks and references to Appendices
March 14th 1915. 7.50 p.m.	Orders from C.O. to 148th Bty. to turn its fire on the mound.	
8.45 p.m.	Message from C.O. saying we held trenches S.9 + S.10 + the Germans were in trenches 14-22 + the mound.	
9.50 p.m.	Rate of fire, which started at Bty. fire 5 secs + which had been slackened to 10 secs, then to 30 secs + then to 1 min, was now brought down to Bty. fire 2 mins.	
10.50 p.m.	News of counter attack arranged for 2 a.m. Also that we held trenches 21 + 22.	
March 15th 1.30 a.m.	Bty. fire 1½ mins.	※ {Gr. Cassin } 364th Bty {Bm. Wells}
2 a.m.	Range raised by all batteries.	※ {Gr. Smythe}
4.35 a.m.	News that Leinster Regt. had retaken trenches 19 + 20, but that other counter attacks had failed.	✕ {Cpl Ratte } 99th Bty {Gr. Potter} {Gr. Blake.}
6.5 a.m.	All batteries ordered to shell the mound. Batteries of brigade were ranged by one from the old windmill at H.36.d.8.2.	
11.15 a.m.	Guns on original lines, firing at Bty fire 2 mins throughout the day.	
7.20 p.m.	Ceased fire. Casualties on 14th. 1 Officer ✕ + 2 men wounded ※.	× Major E.O. Anderson
	" " 15th. 1 Man killed ✗, 2 men died of wounds + 1 wounded §. All the casualties on this day were in the 99th Bty. in the reserve position, which was badly shelled about 1 p.m.	

Army Form C. 2118.

Sketch. Ⓐ

WAR DIARY
or
INTELLIGENCE SUMMARY.
(Erase heading not required.)

Hour, Date, Place	Summary of Events and Information	Remarks and references to Appendices

Canal

Hollebeke Chateau

Eikhof Fm.

Shelley's Fm

Scale 1/10,000

121/5254

29th Division

29th Bde R.F.A.

Vol V 1 — 30.4.15

Army Form C. 2118.

WAR DIARY
INTELLIGENCE SUMMARY.
H.Q. 20th Bde R.F.A.

(Erase heading not required.)

Hour, Date, Place	Summary of Events and Information	Remarks and references to Appendices
April 1st 1915 8 a.m.	Command of zone handed over to O.C. 23rd Bde R.F.A. Batteries moved to new billets on ASEELE - POPERINGHE Road. H.Q. were on the main road 3 miles S.W. of POPERINGHE. Bde Amm. Col. had moved to this area the previous night.	
10 p.m.	Sections of batteries remaining behind in action with 23rd Brigade were relieved and proceeded direct to the new billeting area.	h2
April 2nd.	C.O. and adjutant rode out to E. of YPRES to see new gun positions to be taken over from the French - in I.11.c.6.8., I.17.A.4.5, I.17.D.9.2 and I.16.c.2.2. h2.	
April 4th. 5th.	Battery Commanders visited gun positions. Adjutant and telephone wagon and part of Brigade Staff moved to new area. H.Q. of French Commandant were at BELLEVARDE FM, but this farm was now given to a howitzer battery. 20th Brigade H.Q. were now in a dug-out in the railway embankment at I.11.c.2.8. Lines were laid from here to all batteries and to 62nd Inf. Bde H.Q. at HOOGE. One section of each battery relieved one section of each French battery.	h2 h2

WAR DIARY
INTELLIGENCE SUMMARY.

Place	Date	Hour	Summary of Events and Information	Remarks and references to Appendices
	April 6th	2 a.m.	Brigade Staff arrived at billets at I.10.D.9.5. The C.O. assumed command of the zone at noon. The batteries were disposed as follows :- 67th Bty at I.11.C.6.8. with a billet in farm at I.11.C.0.5. Position called "B" 99th Bty at I.17.A.4.5. - no billets for gunners. Position called "A" 148th Bty at I.17.D.9.2. - no billets. Position called "C" 364th Bty at I.18.C.2.2. - no billets. Position called "D". "B" position was the best. C & D were only 2,500 yards behind the trenches and half a mile off the main road. This made the occupation of these 2 positions very difficult, the ground being very muddy after the rain on 4th and 5th. Wagon lines were divided into two echelons, the first consisting of firing battery teams E. of YPRES and the second consisting of 1st line wagon teams W. of YPRES at H.10.B.3.6. Zones. 99th Bty. from covered the support trenches in front of our Nos 1 to 10.; 67th in front of 11 to 21; 364½ in front of 22 to 27; 148½ in front of 28-36. Owing to the trees round the trenches, & the fact that ours and the German	

WAR DIARY

INTELLIGENCE SUMMARY

Army Form C. 2118.

Instructions regarding War Diaries and Intelligence Summaries are contained in F.S. Regs., Part II. and the Staff Manual respectively. Title pages will be prepared in manuscript.

Place	Date	Hour	Summary of Events and Information	Remarks and references to Appendices
	April			
			were very close together in some places, it was impossible to fire on the German fire trenches. What was aimed at was a "barrage" of fire over the German support trenches.	
		11.45 P.M.	Remaining section of each battery relieved remaining sections of French batteries.	W2.
	7/4.		Batteries finished registering their lines. 50 rounds extra per battery were allowed for this purpose. 3 men wounded, 2 horses killed & 5 wounded in 148th waggon line billet.	I, 11.A.9.8. W2.
	8/4.		Zone of brigade shortened on the left so as to include the right edge of trench 26. 148th Bty detached to 1st Bde from 6 a.m. for tactical purposes only. Brigade zone was divided up among batteries as follows :— German trenches in front of our Nos 1–8 allotted to 99th Bty; in front of 9–16 to 67th Bty; in front of our Nos 17–25 to 364th Bty. The whole of this front was held by 82nd Infantry Brigade, the Divisional front being divided into 3 sections, each held by an Infantry Brigade. Warning stations for 67th & 99th Batteries were in the trenches; for 364th at J 19 D 9.6, as used by the French, but very little could be seen from it.	W2.

WAR DIARY
or
INTELLIGENCE SUMMARY.
(Erase heading not required.)

Army Form C. 2118.

Place	Date	Hour	Summary of Events and Information	Remarks and references to Appendices
April	April 8th (cont)		System of communications was as follows :- Bde H.Q. communicated direct with 82nd Infy Bde H.Q. Each battery communicated direct with infantry trenches by day and with Batten. H.Q. by night. 2nd Lieut J.A. Arkwright joined the brigade and was attached to Bde. Ammn. Col. Lieut. R. Crewdson from Bde Ammn. Col. joined H.Q. Staff of Brigade as Orderly Officer, an orderly officer for this each brigade being sanctioned by Brig. H.Q.	
	9th		One N.C.O. in 364th Bty wounded by piece of H.E. shell	WD
	10th		Nothing to report.	WD
	11th		Nothing to report.	WD
	12th		Major A.K. Mann, comdg. 99th Bty, wounded while observing in the trenches	WD
	13th	11.30 p.m.	Zeppelin dropped 4 bombs near the Ammn. Col. billet. No damage done.	WD
		10 a.m.	G.O.C. 5th Corps visited the C.O. at H.Q. 20th Bde R.F.A.	WD
	14th		Nothing to report. Lieut C.E. Ryan, 67th/15th R.F.A. left for R.F.C. at G.H.Q. for instruction as an artillery observer.	WD
	15th		Nothing to report.	WD

Army Form C. 2118.

WAR DIARY
INTELLIGENCE SUMMARY.
(Erase heading not required.)

H.Q. 2O2 Bde R.F.A.

Place	Date	Hour	Summary of Events and Information	Remarks and references to Appendices
	April 16th		Nothing to report.	
	17th	7.15 p.m.	5th Div. on the right attacked and took hill 60. 364th Bty fired on its zone for 3/4 hour as a demonstration.	W2.
	18th	8.27 am	99th Bty fired at slow rate at wood in I.35 B and D. 67th Bty at edge of wood fired from I.36 C.1.6 I.36 A.9.4 and at Road Junctions at I.36 B.2.1 and I.36 B.3.2. 99th Bty fired at railway from I.36 3.06 I.35 B.5.5 and searched and swept wood in I.35B and D. This was to assist attack of 5th Div. on hill 59 in I.35A. Rate of fire till 6.15 p.m. was Bty. fire 1 min. Then Bty. fire 2 mins till 4 p.m. Reopening again from 8.15 p.m. to 8.45 p.m.	
			One man wounded slightly in 264th Bty, but remains at duty. Ground between 67th and 364th Batteries heavily shelled at 6.15 p.m.	
		6 p.m.	Batteries brought up the following to new billets E. of YPRES:- 8 ammn wagons + 4 teams per battery. 67th + 99th occupied billet at I.9 B.6.9 148th + 364th occupied billet at I.11 A.0.7. One officer per battery was with this first echelon wagon line. The remainder of the men and horses remained in the old billets W. of YPRES.	W2

WAR DIARY or INTELLIGENCE SUMMARY.

Army Form C. 2118.

204

Place	Date	Hour	Summary of Events and Information	Remarks and references to Appendices
	April			
	19th		YPRES heavily shelled all day.	
	20th		1 man wounded in 148th Bty.	W2
	21st		2 Officers, Lieut Ludlam + Lieut Madge, belonging to New Army, arrived for a fortnight's attachment to 99th & 364th Batteries respectively.	W2
	22nd	5 P.M.	Heavy rifle fire to the North where the Germans attacked the French line. Fumes blowing over from the scene of the fighting made the eyes very painful.	W2
		7.30.	Orders from C.R.A. to harness up.	
		9.15.	67th Bty ordered to fire down MENIN ROAD.	
		9.45.	99th Bty and 1 Section 364th Bty, ready to shoot N.	
	23rd	1.32 AM.	"S.O.S." signal received from infantry in normal zone. All guns switched back to normal zone again and opened fire about 1.40 a.m.	
		1.42"	"Stop firing" sent from 82nd Inf¹ Bde. Apparently no attack on our trenches and S.O.S. signal sent in error.	
		4.55	Observing officer starts with telephone line to observe country to N.	
		5.38.	C.R.A. orders guns to face North.	
		12.15.	Zones for batteries to be as follows 67th. C11A0.8 – C5C10.5 99th C10C0.0 – C10C10.10 364th C10B0.0 – C10B10.8.	

Army Form C. 2118.

WAR DIARY
or
INTELLIGENCE SUMMARY.
(Erase heading not required.)

Place	Date	Hour	Summary of Events and Information	Remarks and references to Appendices
Cont.	April 23rd	P.M. 4.50.	Remaining horses of batteries formerly in wagon line near VLAMERTINGHE moved up to forward lines E. of YPRES near POTIJZE. Observing officer for North zone was in farm at time of Bde Amm. Col. missing but believed to be in hospital. Wagon & clear horses now of which the grooms were in charge were found in YPRES.	hd. hd2.
	24th 1 P.M 3.P.M		Teams up close to batteries on order of R.A. 672 + R X 364th Bty fired on N. zone then to S. & S.E. of ST JULIEN. Slow rate of fire	
		3.25.	Guns as above switched on to area in D7A and C12B.	
		4 "	67th switched on to S. edge of ST JULIEN. 364th on to wood W. of ST JULIEN C11	
		5.25 "	" " area in D13A " " area in C12D	
		7.52 "	Batteries stopped firing. Casualties during the day were 2 men of 67, 3 of 99th 1 of 148th + 1 of Amm. Col. – all wounded. The whole of the ground in the neighbourhood of the brigade was swept with hostile shell fire from N. and S. Weather very fine.	4|2
	25th A.M 4.45.		Horses returned to Bty wagon lines near POTIJZE.	
		6.10.	672 Bty opens fire on wood in C10 +11 during counter attack by us.	
		Noon.	Range raised by 672 on to N. edge of wood, later target for this bty were the stream crossing D7 Range raised from D7 to D13 and ridge crossing D7 1740 rounds expended since noon 24th.	

WAR DIARY
or
INTELLIGENCE SUMMARY.
(Erase heading not required.)

Army Form C. 2118.

Place	Date	Hour	Summary of Events and Information	Remarks and references to Appendices
	Oct 25th		67th, 99th & 364th Batteries fired throughout the day at various targets to N. and a few gun targets to S. near KLEIN ZILLEBEKE. One counter attack apparently failed. 67th fired throughout night. Observing officer still out night & day at C 29.d.4.7. (Lieut Thompson 99th Bty). One of his telephonists was killed & one wounded. Casualties for the day - 1 man of 67th wounded, 2 men of 99th wounded & 1 killed. Horses at POTIZE shelled daily, with a few casualties among the horses.	hrs.
	26th		Batteries firing at slow rate at various targets to N. during morning. 2 Lieut Cunningham observing.	
		12.55 am.	Copy of 5th Corps operation orders received for attack on wood in C.10 + 11 at 2.30. Observe report our infantry 600x S. of wood & being held up by machine gun fire from wood in C. 10 + 11.	
		2.15.		
		6.10 pm	All batteries stopped except 67th which continued on D6d throughout night. 67th Bty continued firing all day and throughout the night & the 364th at intervals. Fire directed chiefly on △ of roads east & N.E. of ST JULIEN in C.12. Various points on N. zone registered with help of observing officer. All batteries firing all day at slow rate.	hrs.
	27th			
	28th		Major R.W. White & Lieut Lewis at observing station.	

1577 Wt.W10791/1773 500,000 1/15 D.D. & L. A.D.S.S./Forms/C.2118.

WAR DIARY
or
INTELLIGENCE SUMMARY.

(Erase heading not required.)

Army Form C. 2118.

Place	Date	Hour	Summary of Events and Information	Remarks and references to Appendices
	April 28th cont.	7 p.m.	Adjutant proceeded to R.A.H.Q. to receive orders as to retirement to take over positions of LAHORE Divnl. Art'y near BRIELEN.	h2.
	29th	8.30 p.m.	364th + 99th stopped firing on wood. 67th firing all day. 99th Bty lost 25 horses in wagon line near POTIJZE and moved inside ramparts of YPRES.	
		5.30 p.m.	Zones allotted to batteries as follows in case fire required, as attack on our lines reported probable 99th Bty C17A2.7 – C17A6.5, 364th Bty C17A6.5 – C17B2.5. 67th Bty C17B2.5 – C17C2.1. No attack was made + 67th Bty fired at triangle of roads E. + N.E. of ST JULIEN.	h2.
	30th	10.50 A.M.	364th Bty took over the firing on S. of roads as above, from 67th Bty. Quiet day. Casualties 67th Bty 5 men wounded in wagon line in.der.ramparts in YPRES, whither 67th horses had moved on 29th inst from POTIJZE. 99th 3 men wounded in wagon line. 148th Bty 4 men wounded in gun position	h2.
			Casualties among horses in wagon lines E. of YPRES since 22nd inst. amount to 67. Horses were ordered to be kept E. of YPRES and it is ~~almost~~ impossible to keep them under cover from view from aeroplanes. The whole of the YPRES Salient has been shelled daily since the 22nd, and it has been difficult	

Army Form C. 2118.

WAR DIARY
or
INTELLIGENCE SUMMARY.
(Erase heading not required.)

Instructions regarding War Diaries and Intelligence Summaries are contained in F. S. Regs., Part II. and the Staff Manual respectively. Title pages will be prepared in manuscript.

Hour, Date, Place	Summary of Events and Information	Remarks and references to Appendices
	to find a safe place for the horses. Half the Amm. Col. came up to POTIJZE about the 23rd, and besides their horses and those of batteries, there were those of other brigades and R.E. Nearly all the inhabitants of the farms in the neighbourhood had left by the end of the month. Rev. Miller, chaplain for Div¹ Troops and attached to 20th Bde H.Q. left for No 4 General Hospital at VERSAILLES on 21st. On April 3rd, G.O.C. 5th Corps inspected the men of all batteries + the horses in billets W. of POPERINGHE, telling each battery in turn what good work had been done by the whole of 27th Div⁴ Art⁴	WS.

27th Division

20th Bde R.F.A.

Vol VI   1 — 31.5.15

121/554

WAR DIARY
INTELLIGENCE SUMMARY

HQ. 20th Bde. R.F.A.

Army Form C. 2118.

Place	Date	Hour	Summary of Events and Information	Remarks and references to Appendices
	May 1st		In the morning various targets S of the wood in C.10.d.11 were registered by the 364th and 67th batteries. In the afternoon a large French counter attack took place; our fire being mainly directed on area in front of wood. Casualties:- 2 slightly wounded.	T/C
	2nd	5 pm	Northern observing officer reported that yellow gas fumes were being spread toward our trenches. 364th & 67th batteries ordered to fire on edge of wood.	T/C
		5.10	67th Bty very heavily shelled. In the evening Lt Lucas AVC joined the Bde and took up quarters at the column. At 11 pm the Bde commenced to move west of YPRES. Casualties:- 1 killed and 10 wounded.	
	3rd	4 am	The Bde arrived billets at H.16, leaving the telephonists to reel in all wire possible. Casualties 1 killed 1 wounded.	T/C
	4th		No incident of importance.	
	5th		No incident of importance.	
	6th		The C.O. reconnoitred gun positions S of YPRES. In the evening, batteries commenced work on their new positions which were as follows:- 67th at H.24.b.9.8. 99th at H.18.d.3.4. 364th at H.18.d.10.5. 148th at H.18.d.3.4. One section at H.18.d.7.1. The other at H.18.d.10.5. Major Harrison left the Bde on account of illness.	T/C
	7th		In the morning, batteries continued their work on new positions.	T/C

Army Form C. 2118.

WAR DIARY
or
INTELLIGENCE SUMMARY.
(Erase heading not required.)

Instructions regarding War Diaries and Intelligence Summaries are contained in F.S. Regs., Part II. and the Staff Manual respectively. Title pages will be prepared in manuscript.

Place	Date	Hour	Summary of Events and Information	Remarks and references to Appendices
	May 8th	11 am	Orders received from C.R.A. to harness up and be ready to move. 11:30 am Lt Col T. E. Gray left the Bde owing to illness. Major T.W. White assumed Command of the Bde which had been prepared in case the infantry fell back to GHQ line.	see 6th T.C.
		12 pm	The Bde moved HQ billeting at H 24 a 4.8.	T.C.
	9th		The Bde moved into the new positions. An officer went up in the morning to hill 40 to observe for the Bde. Lt E. Chalker 67th Bty wounded and sent to hospital. Other Casualties :— 1 man wounded	T.C.
	10th	5 pm	The 99th Bty fired on hill 50 and the 67th on ridge 41. The 99th Bty moved up after dark to relieve the 98th Bty in the avenue. The HQ billets E of YPRES. At 12 midnight the Adjt had out telephone Communications to the new bty positions as follows :— 67th H24 b 9.8. 148 K 1.20 & c 5.10. 364 K 113 d 3.4.	T.C.
	11th	1 am	The 99th Bty came under the Command of the C.O. 1st Bde.	
		6 am	The 364th Bty fired a few rounds along line from J13 a 5.9 to J13 a 6.3. The 148th fired from J13 a 6.3 to J13 c 7.8. 3 pm HQ shifted to H24 a 9.9.	T.C.
	12th	2:30 pm	148th Bty opened fire on a Minenwerfer at STIRLING CASTLE in J13 d 5.5 and the observing officer reported that it had been hit. 3 pm Permission to use TROTYL received. 3:40 pm The 148th Bty shot at a working party at J13 c 10.10.	T.C.
	13th	9 am	Lt Captain ARKWRIGHT attached to 67th Bty from Bde Amm Col	

Army Form C. 2118.

WAR DIARY
or
INTELLIGENCE SUMMARY.
(Erase heading not required.)

Place	Date	Hour	Summary of Events and Information	Remarks and references to Appendices
	May 13th		The Telephonic Communications of the Bde. with the infantry during this time were as follows:- Direct wire to the 80th and 82nd Inf Bdes. Communication to the 81st Bde via the 148th Bty. Each Bty sent out an observing officer each morning who returned at night. The Bty observation posts were in direct communication by wire with their respective Btys, the telephones and an operator being left at each post every night. These posts were as follows - 67th I.21.b.3.5 at bend of Zillebeke lake. 148th at Santuary Wood in J.13.d.4.3. 364th at I.16.b.5.3. HQ Conds Huis reach the three Inf Bdes and the three Observation posts direct.	
		10.05am	The 364th Bty opened fire on wood in S.E. Corner of I.12.b in Consequence of a report that the Germans were massing there. The Bty ceased firing at 11.30	VC
		2.12pm	Counter attack by Cavalry began. 364th and 148th open fire on b, c, and d. Bty fire 30 secs. Casualties 4 wounded - 364th one, 148th one, 99th two.	VC
	14th		Throughout the morning the 364th and 148th btys searched I.12.b. On report being received that the Germans were advancing. 364th & 148th searched I.6.a + I.6.b at Bty fire 30 secs	
	15th		In the afternoon the 148th + 364th registered their new zones which were - 364th left of line joining centres of sqp I.30.b and I.19.c. 148th right of line. During the day the 364th & 148th Btys find on the trenches in their zones.	VC

1577 Wt.W10791/1773 500,000 1/15 D.D.& L. A.D.S.S./Forms/C. 2118.

WAR DIARY
or
INTELLIGENCE SUMMARY.
(Erase heading not required.)

Army Form C. 2118.

Place	Date	Hour	Summary of Events and Information	Remarks and references to Appendices
	15th	5.30 pm	Lt Col W H Kay R.F.A. assumed command of the Bde.	VC
	16th		No important incident	VC
	17th		A report received that the Germans had poisoned the water around St Eloi Rivos affecting the Ypres Canal and Moat. 2/Lt H E Pitt left the Bde to take up the position of Adjutant in the new army. 2/Lt Benesk joined the Bde and was posted to the Column.	VC
	18th	12.30pm	News was received from the Royal Irish Regiment that Major T W WHITE TFA commanding the 364th Battery had been killed whilst observing fire from the trenches. Brig-Gen A Stokes DSO commanding 27th Div Arty sent a message to convey his regret.	VC
		12.35	364th Bty opened fire on Clonmel Copse in J.19 at request of infantry. Capt MORGAN joined the Bde and assumed command of the Ammunition Column.	VC
	19th	8.30am	Col Kay went out to look for new positions round Zillebeke Lake, but found all the ground very much under observation from Hill 60.	VC
		6.10pm	Report received from BMTFA that Col EMERY has assumed command of 275 Div Arty	
	20th	11.00am	Capt G F Strickland TFA(T) joined the Bde and was attached to the 148th Bty. The Bde seeing the 67th Bty commenced to dig positions for our advanced sections at I.15.d.9.6. Casualties. 1 man of the 67th Bty wounded	VC

WAR DIARY
or
INTELLIGENCE SUMMARY.
(Erase heading not required.)

Army Form C. 2118.

Place	Date	Hour	Summary of Events and Information	Remarks and references to Appendices
	21st			T.C.
	22nd	6:00	Brig. Gen. A Stokes K- assumed command of 27th Div Arty. Orders were received that commencing from 6 am on the 23rd instant the new bde would take over the new zone which was allotted to batteries as follows :- $$\begin{cases} 67^{th} & J\,25a\,2.10 - I\,30b\,7.7 \\ 148^{th} & J\,25a\,2.10 - J\,19c\,5.5 \\ 364^{th} & I\,30b\,7.7 - I\,30b\,2.0 \end{cases}$$ During the afternoon Lt H.Q. Vincent found the bde for 14 days instruction and was attached to the 67th Battery. In the evening the 67th bty moved on orders into its new position.	T.C.
	23rd	7:50am	The 67th Bty registered its new zone. In the afternoon an attempt was made to communicate by helio from bde HQ to western edge of SANCTUARY WOOD in I 24 b 25. This was partially successful, lights being easily seen, but actual communication failing owing to inexperience of operators.	T.C.
	24th	3 am	The Germans attacked the 28th Div front N of MENIN RD with heavy shell fire and use of gas which penetrated so far back as to affect the bde wagon lines. The Bde	T.C.

WAR DIARY
or
INTELLIGENCE SUMMARY.
(Erase heading not required.)

Army Form C. 2118.

Place	Date	Hour	Summary of Events and Information	Remarks and references to Appendices
	May 24th (Continued)		opened fire on its zone at a slow rate. Although heavy firing could be heard in that direction, at 4:50am and again at 5:50 am, the 148th observing officer (2/Lt Tackson) reported all quiet. At 5:57, in consequence of these reports, the bde ceased firing. At 11:30 the Brigade Major reported that the infantry were falling back N of the Menin Road, the 364th and 148th Btys therefor opened fire on their zones with 30 rounds each. Later, the 148th fired an additional 60 rounds on its zone.	
		2:00	Report received from 15th Inf bde that the line held except the 3rd brigade from right in the 28th divisional area. This bde had been gassed out of trenches on the MENIN ROAD. Also further north, the 25th bde had lost one or two trenches. 2:30 Message received from Bde Major re Counter-attack. 148th and 364th ordered to open fire on their zone when counter-attack was heard to begin. The 364th opened fire at 3:40, an a heavy bombardment was heard and ceased fire at 6:20. The 148th observing officer reported all quiet at 8 pm on our zone, the Counter-attack having failed owing to lack of cooperation between the two infantry bdes engaged. Casualties - 2/Lt Bowick of 364th Bty, wounded.	VC
	25th	8:00pm	After a very quiet day, orders were received that the bde would be relieved by the 3rd Northumbrian bde of Territorial Artillery. Orders were at once sent out to all units to harness up and be ready to move at 1/2 midnight. At 11 pm the Col and	

Army Form C. 2118.

WAR DIARY
or
INTELLIGENCE SUMMARY.
(Erase heading not required.)

Instructions regarding War Diaries and Intelligence Summaries are contained in F. S. Regs., Part II. and the Staff Manual respectively. Title pages will be prepared in manuscript.

Place	Date	Hour	Summary of Events and Information	Remarks and references to Appendices
	26th	8 am	Orderly Officer arrived and held a consultation. An hour later orders were received that the bde would move off at 8 am. The batteries changed during darkness and waited till morning at their wagon lines.	TC
			The bde left YPRES at 8 am and proceeded via BAILLEUL and NIEPPE to ARMENTIERES were it relieved the 2nd bde T.F.A. and came into action at 9 pm. The 67th and 364th were attached for tactical purpose to the 24th and 53rd bdes, and the 43rd Howitzer battery was attached for the same reason to the 26th bde. On the road from YPRES, the bde arrived at temporary billets at 1.15 pm. Reference sheet 36 squared map, these billets were as follows:— Bde H.Q. – B14c00, 67th bty – B19b 7.3, 99th bty – B20a 3.5, 148th bty – B19a 24, 364th – B26a 7.6. Amm Col – B19a 2.5. At 5 pm the Col accompanied by the battery commanders visited the H.Q. of the 2nd Bde of ARMENTIERES at C 26 b 71. At 7 pm the bde moved up to its new positions, except the 364th bty and the Amm Col which remained at their billets for the night. The gun positions were:— 67th bty – 12a/3, 99th bty – C27d 1.6, 148th bty C27b 2.2. Wagon lines were allotted as follows:— 67th – C25b 10.2, 99th – C26d 0.9, 148th – C26d 77. The positions of the 43rd Howitzer bde was at C27a 7.7.	TC

1577 Wt. W10791/1773 500,000 1/15 D. D. & L.   A.D.S.S./Forms/C. 2118.

WAR DIARY
of
INTELLIGENCE SUMMARY.
(Erase heading not required.)

Army Form C. 2118.

Place	Date	Hour	Summary of Events and Information	Remarks and references to Appendices
	27th		In the morning the 99th and 148th batteries registered the new guns which lay from FRIELINGHEIN on the extreme left to BRUNE RUE on extreme right. During the day the Amm Col moved into new billets at H24c5.5, passing for tactical purposes under the command of the O C 53rd bde. By evening stations were as follows:- 99th I.4.a.58. 148th C.27.b.6.69 and the howitzer bty at C.21.b. The 6th Divisional T.A. was at g.12.b.0.6 and the 12th Inf bde at C.25.d.6.5. The Communications of the bde at this time were as follows:- Direct wires to T.A.H.Q, the 12th Inf bde the T.A. bdes on either side which were the 52nd and 24th bdes — the latter of which was relieved two days later by the 1st bde. Direct wires also to the three batteries and to the 43rd bty also to the 9th Hussars. The OP's of the 99th 148th and 43rd btys were connected up to their respective units, and thus to battalion H.Q's	T.C.
	28th		No incident of importance	R.C.
	29th		2nd E.N.KENT LEMON posted to 67th bty. Lt Clarke and Lt Gage, both of the New Army were attached to the 148th and 99th btys for instruction. The 148th bty at 7.30 am fired 15 rounds on enemy's trenches in retaliation for enemy's fire on our trenches	R.C.
	30th		No important incident to report	R.C.

Army Form C. 2118.

WAR DIARY
or
INTELLIGENCE SUMMARY.
(Erase heading not required.)

Place	Date	Hour	Summary of Events and Information	Remarks and references to Appendices
	31st	6 am	G.O.C. The 27th Div. Arty assumed command in relief of G.O.C. 6th Div. Arty. The 82nd Inf bde relieved 18th Inf bde. The 364th and 67th btys passed from the command for tactical purposes of O.C. 24th 53rd & 24th bdes to O.C. 20th 26th bde RFA. No further incident of importance.	
			With reference to the fighting round YPRES, the following was received by the O.C. 20th Bde RFA, from the GOC RA 27th Division, accompanied by a copy of a letter received by GOC RA from GOC 27th Division.	
			To GOC RA 27th Division	
		"	The Major General Commanding the Division directs me to express to you his admiration at the way the R.A of the division has fought and endured day and night during the last five weeks.	
		"	The devotion to duty which they have shown when batteries have been under appalling and concentrated shell fire in never failing to succour the Infantry	

when called upon, in unfailing supply of ammunition, in bringing up teams by approaches rendered well nigh impossible by the enemy's guns, is worthy of the great records of the Royal Artillery.

The Major General Congratulates you and all ranks on their gallant behaviour and humself on having had the honour of including such troops in his Command."

(Sgd) H. L. Reed
Lt. Col. g.s.
27th Division

27th May 1915.

To O.C. 20th Bde. R.F.A

" The g.o.c R.A wishes to endorse all that the g.o.c of the Division has been pleased to say about all ranks of the R.A of the 27th division and to convey his very best thanks to all for the splendid work they have done, more especially during the fighting since April 22nd, work which has been carried through under the most arduous and trying conditions, and which has called forth the highest appreciation of the Commander-in-Chief, The Army Commander, the Corps Commander, and the

G.O.C. the division

(sgd) J B Orde Capt R A
Staff Captain 27th Div Arty

On May 16th, the 99th battery, which had been in actions in 1/10 D10C East of YPRES but which was now at rest under the Command of O.C. 20th Bde RFA, was reviewed by General Sir H.C.O Plumer as representing the Bde brigade who congratulated the Battery upon the magnificent work which they had performed under the most trying conditions.

Total Casualties for the Month of May 1915

Officers - 1 killed; 2 wounded.
NCO's and Men 2 killed; 27 wounded. Suffering from effects of gas - 2 men

121/6023

27th Division

20th Bde: R.F.A.
Vol VIII 1 — 30.6.15.

WAR DIARY
or
INTELLIGENCE SUMMARY.
(Erase heading not required)

HQ 20th Bde RFA

Army Form C. 2118.

Place	Date	Hour	Summary of Events and Information	Remarks and references to Appendices
	JUNE			
	1st		Capt. J.F. STRICKLAND RFA(T) wounded whilst observing for the 148th Bty to which he was attached. Casualties:- 1 man wounded. No further incident to report.	RC
	2nd	11 am	Major General T. D'O SNOW. C.B. commanding the 27th Division visited Bde H.Q. and discussed with Col Kay the communications between the Inf Bde and the 20th Bde. The Col explained to the G.O.C. the system whereby batteries were in communication with battalion HQ, and the Bde with the 20th Inf bde.	Vide May 27th RC.
	3rd		The following zones were allotted to batteries. 364th Theor to centre of sq 17. 148th Sq 17 to centre of sq 23 67th Sq 23 to C.29.b.07. 99th C.29.b.07 to BTune RUE 43rd Old Zone During the day, the batteries registered various points in their new zone.	RC
	4th	12.30	Brg- Gen J.J.S. CAREY, assumed command of the 27th Divisional Artillery at 6 am noted Bde HQ, in succession to Brig-Gen A Stokes, DSO appointed Artillery adviser to the 3rd Corps. The following special order of the day, dated 4th June 1915 was received "On relinquishing the Command of the 27th Divisional Artillery — which he does	

WAR DIARY
INTELLIGENCE SUMMARY

Army Form C. 2118.

Place	Date	Hour	Summary of Events and Information	Remarks and references to Appendices
			"with the greatest regret - Brig- Genl Stokes desires to thank all ranks for the cordial support they have given him at all times, and for the prompt and willing way in which they have carried out all duties however arduous the conditions. Genl Stokes is proud to have commanded batteries which have won such envinted praise from the Divnl Commander as well as from other commanders on more than one occasion. General Stokes wishes all ranks "Good bye" and the best of luck.	
			(Sd) V. Aoon. Major R.A. Brigade Major 27th Divisional Artillery.	
	4th June 1915			
		5.30 pm	2nd Lt. P.B. JOHNSON RFA and 2nd Lt. J. VEREKER RFA joined the bde and were posted to the 99th Bty and Amm Col respectively. Casualties- Nil.	R.C.
5-16		9 am	The Inf bde reported that there were German snipers in "THREE DECKER FARM" at C 23 d 90. Accordingly during the day the 43rd & 148th btys fired 20 rounds into the farm obtaining several direct hits.	R.C.
		11 am	Capt MORGAN, RGA, left the bde to join a MOUNTAIN BTY. At 1pm the CRA visited	

WAR DIARY
INTELLIGENCE SUMMARY

Army Form C. 2118.

Place	Date	Hour	Summary of Events and Information	Remarks and references to Appendices
	6th	9.30 pm	Bde HQ and informed the CO that at the wish of the GOC 27th Division he would have to move his HQrs to a house nearer the 80th Inf Bde HQ. He also said that one section of the 364th Bty would relieve one section of the 131st Bty at H24c15 after 3pm that evening – this section passing for tactical purposes under the command of OC 12th Bde. The 20th Bde in future to support the 80th Inf Bde. The Zones allotted were as follows:- 67th Bty to cover front of our trenches running from C29c27-I5c87. 99th Bty from I5A73-I11A05. 148th Bty from I11A05to I16B57. C65th How Bty covered the front of 82nd & 80th Inf Bde from C16B84-I16B57.	T.C. Ins.
	7th	3 pm	Bde HQ changed to I1A77 so as to be nearer the 80th Inf Bde at I1d66. The [struck through] The 62nd Bty bds of the 12th div of the 1st New Army was attached to the 20th Bde duty for instructions and "C" battery 62nd Bde. was attached to the 26th Bde.	T.C.
	8th	noon	The 67th and 99th btys fired several rounds for the purpose of registering their zones. In the evening the C 62nd Bty entered its new position at C200b68 its wagon lines remaining at B29b108. At 3.45 pm the GOC 20th Bde and the CO visited the trenches in their zone.	T.C.
	9th 10th		All btys including C 62nd Bty fired several rounds for registration purposes. Numbers were received from 80th Inf Bde for each of the trenches in their line and	T.C.

WAR DIARY
or
INTELLIGENCE SUMMARY

Army Form C. 2118.

Place	Date	Hour	Summary of Events and Information	Remarks and references to Appendices
			Orders were received from 27th T.A. that all battery Commanders must be able to understand reports from battalions in which a number of a trench is given and no sq. map reference. "B" 65th howitzer battery was attached to the bde for instruction, and commenced to build a position at C.21.C.2.2. Orders were received however, a day later, for their work to cease. The Communications of the bde at this time were as follows:—	
			A. One main line along the river used to which all batteries tapped on and which was used as line to "C"62 Bty, "B" 65 and 148th. The other batteries labelled this were "duplicate" and hung it up on a nail off the instrument.	
			B. A second main line by the asylum to which all batteries tapped on, but which the 67th and 99th used. The other batteries keeping it as described above. Direct communication also with T.A.HQ. 80th Inf Bde. 1st Bde RFA and 19th Bde RFA. All batteries were in communication with their battalion HQ and with all their observing stations.	RC
	11th		No important incident	
	12th		Our observation stations of the bde at this time were as follows:— 67th Bty:— The distillery at I.40.59 from which a good general view could be obtained	RC

WAR DIARY
or
INTELLIGENCE SUMMARY.
(Erase heading not required.)

Army Form C. 2118.

Place	Date	Hour	Summary of Events and Information	Remarks and references to Appendices
			from C29A7.3 to form GRANDE PORTE EBAL. Also cottage at C28 B7.4 and The Asylum Church Spire at T2a 5.4 99th Bty :- Distillery. Also attic of HOSPICE des ALIENS in T2, 148th Bty :- House at C27 b6.9 from PONT BALLOT, but not the trenches in front of it. Trenches from 3 Dicken team to ½ Khatab cottage. From L'AVENTURE. Also house at PONT BALLOT from which trenches can be seen.	RC
	13th	8	In the morning the linesmen of the HQ staff commenced to lay the buried wire. This was intended for use in case the town was shelled. It was buried down the street from HQ to the railway embankment, then along the railway line — the batteries tapping on to the main line by means of buried wires. The wires along the railway was pushed up under the bevelling by small pegs. Divs Bde HQ had a (private?) wire in case of Emergency. In the evening "D" 65 battery belonging to the 65th howitzer bde of the 12th division of the 1st New Army was attached to the bde for tactical reasons. One section of this battery relieved one section of the 43rd Bty during the evening. Orders were received from RA that in future the artillery would be arranged	RC
	14th			

WAR DIARY
or
INTELLIGENCE SUMMARY
(Erase heading not required.)

Army Form C. 2118.

Place	Date	Hour	Summary of Events and Information	Remarks and references to Appendices
			in groups for tactical purposes:— each group to consist of 3 18pr QF batteries and one howitzer battery. The 20th Bde became C group and consisted of the 67th, 99th and 148th bty and the "B" 65th howitzer battery. The C 62nd bty remained in C group for instruction whilst the 364th paraded under the Command Off "A" group for tactical purposes. Instruction were received from RA also that "TEST" messages would be sent from RA which meant that targets would be given to batteries and batteries would lay on them and report when ready to fire. These times were to be forwarded to RA.	
	15th		In the morning the second section of the "B" 65th battery relieved the last section of the 43rd bty, and the 99th bty dug a new position at C20d 2.4	VC
	16th		No important incident to report	VC
	17th		In the morning one section of the 99th bty moved to its new position. The remaining section moved into its new position. It was decided that the old position should remain intact and be used as a dummy position	VC
	18th		During the day the C O issued an order instructing battery observing officers to render to this office at 6 pm each evening a report of important events such as hostile shell, movements of enemy's aircraft etc. At 5. pm. two mines were exploded	VC

WAR DIARY
or
INTELLIGENCE SUMMARY.
(Erase heading not required.)

Army Form C. 2118.

Place	Date	Hour	Summary of Events and Information	Remarks and references to Appendices
	19th		by us in the neighborhood of FRIELINGHEIN. In order to guard against a sudden gas attack by the enemy, it was directed that in future all men should carry smoke helmets with them as well as respirators whenever they left the billet	RC
	20th		No important incident to report.	RC
	21st		No important incident to report	RC
			In the morning a secret document was received from R.A. giving the 27th Divisional plans for retirement. At 5 pm "B" 65th battery fired 20 rounds on a sap which the Germans had constructed towards trench 75, obtaining 7 rounds which damaged the sap. The Germans retaliated on our trenches, whereas our batteries which had been saving ammunition for two days, put 60 rounds into the enemy's trenches.	
	22nd		No important incident to report	RC
	23rd		No important incident to report	RC
	24th		"C" Bty left the group on the previous evening. The "DISTILLERY" was again shelled by guns from the direction of LA FRESNELLE. Snipers having been reported to be very active from LES 4 HALLOTS FARM, B/65th Bty fired 7 rounds lyddite on it and considerably	

1577 Wt. W10791/1773 500,000 1/15 D. D. & L. A.D.S.S./Forms/C. 2118.

Army Form C. 2118.

WAR DIARY
or
INTELLIGENCE SUMMARY.
(Erase heading not required.)

Place	Date	Hour	Summary of Events and Information	Remarks and references to Appendices
	25th		damaged at "B" 65th Bty fired on PERENCHIES BRIDGE in retaliation to the enemy's fire on our trenches at L'EPINETTE. It was noticeable that their fire ceased at once. Two (evening) suppard observation stations were engaged. The 67th Bty fired on the cross roads at LA FRESNELLE obtaining some direct hits on the houses and B/65th Bty on 3 decker farm hitting the walls.	P.C.
	26th	8.30 pm	One gun of the No 2 MOUNTAIN BTY shelled the Sap head also the left of No 5 house at L'EPINETTE. the whole Sap was practically demolished. The batteries held themselves in readiness in case of German retaliation to above, but no action was necessary. Later in the evening B/65th was relieved by C/65, our sections	P.C.
	27th	6 pm	C/65th fired on the Sap taken at FRIELINGHEIN obtaining 9 direct hits. This was at the request of the infantry who reported the town to be used by the enemy for Snipers. The second section of C/65th came under command of "C" group.	P.C.
	28th		No important incident to report	P.C.
	29th		The town of ARMENTIÈRES was shelled by the enemy, our Howitzers retaliated on PERENCHIES	P.C.

Army Form C. 2118.

WAR DIARY
or
INTELLIGENCE SUMMARY.
(Erase heading not required.)

Instructions regarding War Diaries and Intelligence Summaries are contained in F. S. Regs., Part II. and the Staff Manual respectively. Title pages will be prepared in manuscript.

Place	Date	Hour	Summary of Events and Information	Remarks and references to Appendices
	30th		No important incident to report	FC

T2134. Wt. W708—776. 500000. 4/15. Sir J. C. & S.

Army Form C. 2118.

WAR DIARY
or
INTELLIGENCE SUMMARY.
(Erase heading not required.)

Summary of Events and Information

APPENDIX I.

The following officers of the brigade were mentioned in Despatches in London Gazette dated June 22nd, for period up to April 5th 1915:-

Major D.K. Tweedie, Major E.O. Anderson (since wounded), Captain E.C. Hall, Captain E.W.G. Wilson, Lieut. O.W. Sherwell, E. Chalker and Lieut H.S. Pemberton R.A.M.C. (attached)

In the London Gazette dated June 23rd the following honours and rewards were given to officers of the brigade:-

D.S.O. - Major D.K. Tweedie

Military Cross - Captain E.W.G. Wilson & Lieut O.W. Sherwell.

27th Division

121/6356

20th Bde R.F.A.

1-31-7-15

Army Form C. 2118.

WAR DIARY
or
INTELLIGENCE SUMMARY.
(Erase heading not required.)

H.Q. 20th Bde R.F.A.   July 1915

Place	Date	Hour	Summary of Events and Information	Remarks and references to Appendices
ARMENTIÈRES	1st	8.30 P.M.	Distillery at I5A4.9, used as an O.P. by 67th Bty shelled by German field guns. Trench 96 at I5A8.0, shelled by field guns and trench howitzer. 99 Bty fired on German trenches opposite 96 in retaliation.	
	2nd		NIL.	
	3rd		Distillery again shelled.	
	4th	3.30 A.M.	C 65th fired on a trench mortar on request of D.C.L.I. (82nd Bde).	
		4 A.M.	Heavy howitzer dropped several shell into HOUPLINES. On this and on preceding days occasional shell fell into the town of ARMENTIÈRES.	
	5th	3 P.M.	67th Bty fired at machine gun emplacements located in farm y C. German artillery more active. Several shell fell in the town and many of the civilians are leaving. Capt C. HODKINSON-SMITH from 39th Bty took over command of Ammn Col.	
	6th		C 65th obtained direct hits on enemy works N. 4 HALOTS FARM and FRELINGHEIN water tower.	
	7th		148th Bty registered enemy trenches in C 24 B + C 23 c. These were in zone of D group, but were enfiladed from 148th Bty position. Arrangements were made so that this Bty could turn one gun on to their trenches on request of D group.	

Army Form C. 2118.

WAR DIARY
or
INTELLIGENCE SUMMARY.
(Erase heading not required.)

Instructions regarding War Diaries and Intelligence Summaries are contained in F. S. Regs., Part II. and the Staff Manual respectively. Title pages will be prepared in manuscript.

Place	Date	Hour	Summary of Events and Information	Remarks and references to Appendices
	8th		Enemy put 60 shell into the town, the majority falling near HOSPICE DES ALIÉNÉS. A kind shell which fell near H.Q. of the brigade was from a captured 4.7" gun, probably at I.30.A.32 from bearing taken to flashes.	hq.
	9th		Nil	hq.
	10th		Lt Col Hay proceeded on leave to England. Major D.K. Tweedie, 148th Bty took over command of the brigade.	
	11th		Nil	hq.
	12th		Nil	hq.
	13th		Nil	hq.
	14th		The towns of ARMENTIÈRES and HOUPLINES were heavily shelled throughout the day, more than 200 shell falling into the town. Gun batteries retaliated on PÉRENCHIES.	FC
	15th		The applications of Major D.K.Tweedie and A.G. Slawsley for a transfer to England were granted and Major Slawsley left at once. On the evening the naval Howitzers gun fired 28 rounds on NOELLE DE LA BLANCHE, obtaining a large proportions of huts.	FC

WAR DIARY
or
INTELLIGENCE SUMMARY.
(Erase heading not required.)

Army Form C. 2118.

Place	Date	Hour	Summary of Events and Information	Remarks and references to Appendices
	16th		A strong working party of 50 men was observed at G.2.d.3.7 and along the road at G.2.d.5.6. This party has been observed on several occasions, but its object has not yet been discovered. The DISTILLERY at I.4.b.5.9, formerly used as an observing station, still continues to effectively draw the enemy's fire in that direction. Some 50 shell including two incendiary shell falling during the day on it the incendiary shell set fire to a haystack at true de la BUTERNE	
	17th		The large working party was again observed at T.31. The GKA visited HQ, and captured to Major Tweedie the new plan. The NORTHUMBRIAN DIVISION was taken over from the 27th Division, and the latter division was moving to the right so as to cover the BOIS GRENIER area the area for the division was to be from NEW MACQUART on the left to H.8.d.0.7 on the right. Only two infantry brigades at a time were to be in the trenches and consequently only two groups of artillery were needed "A" group was therefore disolved, and the 99th & 364th and "C"/65th Bys were attached to the first brigade and the 67th & 148th to the 19th Bde. The CO only held the administrative department of the 20th Bde. The New Bde HQ were to be H.17.d.3.3; 1st Bde HQ as before, and HQ of 19th Bde at HQ "A group"	

T2134. Wt. W708-776. 500000. 4/15. Sir J. C. & S.

236

Army Form C. 2118.

WAR DIARY
or
INTELLIGENCE SUMMARY.
(Erase heading not required.)

Instructions regarding War Diaries and Intelligence Summaries are contained in F. S. Regs., Part II. and the Staff Manual respectively. Title pages will be prepared in manuscript.

Place	Date	Hour	Summary of Events and Information	Remarks and references to Appendices
	17th		In the evening the HQ staffs of the 1st & 2nd Northumbrian Brigades arrived, and the 2nd Northumbrian the took over from us the old 99th & 148th positions on the stream and also the 67th position by the railway.	RC
	18th		Command of the zone having been handed over to OC 2nd Northumbrian Bde. HQ moved into new billet and "A group" being abolished, Major O.M. HARRIS DSO took over command of the bde pending the arrival of Lt Col KAY	RC
	19th		Lt Col KAY returned from leave. Major General G.T. MILNE having around Command of the division vice General Snow promoted.	RC
	20th		Nil	RC
	21st		The positions of the batteries were as follows:- 67 - H29687. 99th - H1267.5 1 Za5.2 364th - H24c 52	RC
	22nd		Nil	RC
	23rd		The communications of the bde at this time consisted of direct wires to all btys. to VA and to the HQ 1st & 15th bdes.	RC
	24th		Major F.H.S. GILES and Capt. O.S. CAMERON CAMPBELL joined the bde and were posted to the 99th bty.	RC

T2134. Wt. W708—776. 500000. 4/15. Sir J.C. & S.

WAR DIARY
or
INTELLIGENCE SUMMARY.
(Erase heading not required.)

Army Form C. 2118.

Place	Date	Hour	Summary of Events and Information	Remarks and references to Appendices
	25th		Major R.G. KEYWORTH joined the bde from "X" Battery T.H.A and on the evening of the next day assumed command of the bde vice Lt Col W.H. KAY who left to join the 3rd Cavalry Division)	R.C.
	26th		2/Lt A BOARD left the 148th bty and proceeded to England to join the new army.	R.C.
	27th		2/Lt W DICKIE was posted to the 148th bty from the Ammn Col.	R.C.
	28th		nil	R.C.
	29th		2/Lt E.D HOLBACK and D.J. CARY ELWES joined the bde and were attached to the 148th and 67th batteries.	R.C.
	30th		Lt W STRACHAN left the bde and proceeded to England to join the new army	R.C.
	31st		2/Lt A DRAKE BROCKMAN joined the brigade and was attached to the Ammn Col. In the morning a demonstration against the enemy took place along the divisional front, in which about 500 rounds were fired by the batteries of the division. There was no infantry attack. As a result the enemy's parapets were damaged, and several of their batteries located by the flash of their guns during their retaliation.	R.C.

239

121/6874

27th Biraun

20th Bde. R.F.A.
Vol IX
August 15

WAR DIARY
-or-
INTELLIGENCE SUMMARY.
(Erase heading not required.)

20th Bde R.F.A. H.Q.
August 1915.

Army Form C. 2118.

Place	Date	Hour	Summary of Events and Information	Remarks and references to Appendices
August	1st		As in the last days of July, the Brigade had no tactical position. The 6yt and 148th Btys remained with the 19th Bde and the 99th & 368 Btys with the first Brigade.	ed
	2nd		Nil	ed
	3rd		Nil	ed
	4th		Lieut Perrins resumed his commission as RAINY joined the Bde and was posted to the 148th Bty.	ed ed ed
	5th		Nil	ed
	6th		Nil	ed
	7th		The Amm. Col. were inspected by the corps Commander Lieut General Sir W.P. PULTENEY.	ed
	8th		Nil	ed
	9th		The Amm Col. was inspected by Brigadier General A. STOKES. the corps artillery adviser.	ed
	10th		Nil	ed
	11th		Nil	ed

War Diary or Intelligence Summary

Army Form C. 2118.

Place	Date	Hour	Summary of Events and Information	Remarks and references to Appendices
	12th		Orders were received from T.A. that the 20th Bde would become Aeroplane Bde, ie that all targets on the divisional gun that were not visible from OPs in trenches should be registered by one of the btys of this brigade. The wireless apparatus was established at LA ROLANDERIE FARM at the Bde HQ staff wagon line. The wireless telephonic arrangements were all to be carried out by the operators from the Royal Flying Corps, whilst the passing of the signals to btys and to the aeroplane by means of strips of white cloth laid on the ground was under the charge of an Officer of this brigade. The battery zones were as follows roughly:—	
			67th bty I 31 d 0.8 ---- I 26 c 5.3	
			99th " I 15 d 3.2 ---- I 16 a 8.0	
			148th " I 26 c 5.3 I 21 c 6.0	
			364th " I 21 c 6.0 I 15 d 3.2	R.C.
			Lines were laid by T.A. signals to all btys from the Wireless Station	
			In the afternoon the Corps Adviser inspected the battery wagon lines	9th instant

Army Form C. 2118.

WAR DIARY
or
INTELLIGENCE SUMMARY.
(Erase heading not required.)

Place	Date	Hour	Summary of Events and Information	Remarks and references to Appendices
	13th		nil	T.C.
	14th		The Aeroplane commenced registration of Corringham 57th Bty. was appointed Aeroplane Officer for the week. Communications between the Aeroplane Observer and the Wireless Station worked well and four targets were registered viz:- I 34 c 3.2 I 34 c 8.8 I 34 d 6.1, I 34 d 6.1, O 4 c 1.1. The observer sent down his observations by means of the clock code which consisted of the face of a clock with concentric circles starting at 50 yards and increasing by 25 yards and named A, B, C and D E F G H etc. A smaller ring of radius 25 yds was used for greater accuracy when necessary. XII represents North.	T.C.

243

Army Form C. 2118.

WAR DIARY
or
INTELLIGENCE SUMMARY.
(Erase heading not required.)

Place	Date	Hour	Summary of Events and Information	Remarks and references to Appendices
	15th / 16th		The weather was too bad for the Aeroplane to start with a view to a possible retirement to the BOIS GRENIER line of defence it was decided that the 67th & 364th batteries would have to move father back. Positions were allotted to them as follows:- 67th 264th Continual rain prevented the Aeroplane from observing	T/C
	17th		The 67th Bty Zone was changed by the 19th Bde to the two new trenches No 49 & 48 taken over by the 27th division from the 8th Division. For purpose of Aeroplane registration the 67th Bty added these two trenches to their original zone. Aeroplane did not ascend.	T/C
	18th		In the morning Communication between the Aeroplane Observer and the wireless stations failed for some unexplained reason, but in the afternoon two targets were registered viz:- I 29 d 0.1 and I 35 a 9.1. Orders were received that only 16 rounds HE per gun were to be kept this side of railhead.	T/C
	19th		Major DRESSER, T.F.A Special reserve joined the brigade to relieve Major D.K.TWEEDIE R.F.A DSO (who proceeded to England) after having	T/C

WAR DIARY
or
INTELLIGENCE SUMMARY.

Army Form C. 2118.

247

Place	Date	Hour	Summary of Events and Information	Remarks and references to Appendices
			Commanded the 148th Bty since its formation in February.	
			Ato Capt E.C. HALL RFA Commanding 67th Bty RFA to be Hon. Major.	T.C.
	20th		Altogether six targets were registered by the aeroplane during the day viz:- Aero Trench at I35b54, I34b32. LE BAS CHAMPS in O9b8·7. Houses in C16b96, I29a94. HALTE Railway Crossing I34a09. Lt. SHERWELL became Aeroplane Officer for the week. The following targets were registered during the day. Cross Roads at I29b10 q I29a13 I30a74. LA VALLEE Cross Roads at I34d91 and Houses at I36a18.	T.C.
	21st		Bty Commanders received orders to reconnoitre positions to three to four hundred yards away from their present positions and to a flank.	T.C.
	22nd		Bty observing stations at this time were:- 67th H30A2·3. 99th I9c53. 148th I19B63. 364 H24D2·1.	T.C.
	23rd		Work continued during this time with the aeroplane. General communication trenches being registered. Many of these communication trenches were not shown on the map, but were drawn from the aeroplane Photographs on which they were very clearly marked.	T.C.

WAR DIARY
or
INTELLIGENCE SUMMARY.
(Erase heading not required.)

Army Form C. 2118.

Instructions regarding War Diaries and Intelligence Summaries are contained in F. S. Regs., Part II. and the Staff Manual respectively. Title pages will be prepared in manuscript.

Place	Date	Hour	Summary of Events and Information	Remarks and references to Appendices
	24th		NIL	N.C.
	25th		NIL	N.C.
	26th		NIL	N.C.
	27th		NIL	N.C.
	28th		The Aeroplane continued to report bivouac fires which were not to be observed from O.P.s. On several occasions he gave two targets or more to one bty, but this was found impracticable	N.C.
	29th		2nd Lt W. Parsons proceeded to the Base on being Commissioned. The first line of gathering Operations was issued.	N.C.
	30th		Preparation for above. The following batteries were grouped with a group known as KEYWORTH'S GROUP and was placed under the G.O.C. 8th Division for tactical Command — 19th Bde 39th, 95th, 96th, 131st bty. 20th " 148th " 364 bty. 1st " 11th bty. 3rd Bde 8th Div 33rd bty.	N.C.
	31st		Continued Preparation	N.C.

246

121/7140

27th Division

10th Bde R.F.A.
Oct &
Sep 15

Army Form C. 2118.

WAR DIARY
or
INTELLIGENCE SUMMARY. 20th Bde TFA
(Erase heading not required.)

Place	Date	Hour	Summary of Events and Information	Remarks and references to Appendices
	September		The Bde was still under the tactical command of the 8th DIVISIONAL ARTY and was known as "K" group.	
	1st		It was understood that the offensive at BOIS GRENIER was to be more of a different demonstration than a part of the main attack, but on the other hand, a definite object was arranged, and a forward push, if possible, contemplated. The plan was to capture the German front line along a front of about 1000 yards and is best shown by following diagram:-	
			[diagram showing German front line, marsh land, our front line]	
			It had been found impossible during the winter months to hold the marshy land and our line had been taken up as shown on the diagram. Now, however, it was proposed to capture the German line Afrist Rin	

Army Form C. 2118.

WAR DIARY
or
INTELLIGENCE SUMMARY.
(Erase heading not required.)

Summary of Events and Information

wards. In the diagram the red dotted line shows the method by which it was hoped to link up on line and the German front line. "K" group which was on the left of the attack had a zone allotted from the RADINGHAM road to line GAUTIER, and they were to cover the country behind the trenches and not the trenches themselves. Bty positions were to be as follows. The 33rd 39th 95th and 131st Btys were to remain in their original positions whilst the 148th 364th Btys moved to positions in the left & right of GRIG POT, the 11th Bty moved forward to the left and the 96th moved down to H.Q. The It was arranged that four batteries should make a barrage of fire along the RADINGHAM — Fm GAUTIER road and the other three should enfilade the RADINGHAM — LE BAS KAO road and an Hty, the 33rd, should be a Counter-battery to engage any enemy targets that might appear during the battle.

Communications.

Every Bty had a direct wire to "K" group H.Q, and every Bty was connected with another Bty, thus enabling every Bty to have a duplicate means

WAR DIARY
or
INTELLIGENCE SUMMARY.
(Erase heading not required.)

Army Form C. 2118.

Place	Date	Hour	Summary of Events and Information	Remarks and references to Appendices
			of communication. As a third means, "R" group could communicate with the Brigade to which the attached battery belonged. In view however of the possibility of all wires being cut, helio communication was arranged. For communicating with the infantry, it was arranged to have a Brigade Observer who was to be in touch by wire with Group HQ and with the Inf Bde, and who, in the event of the attack being successful, was to push forward with the Inf', and stay at a line after him to stem a dug-out which was prepared for him, where his Operator could stay and keep touch with Gunf HQ. This wire was of D5 cable and buried the whole way to Gunf HQ. All the wires to Infantry and to Observation stations were duplicated and either buried or slain in ditches. So far as was possible D5 cable was buried 8in to 2 ft deep at all [crossed out] points where the wire was considered likely to be cut. A line was also laid from the 8th Div Arty to Group HQ.	
	2nd		Bdys spent the day registering and digging & improving their positions. Night firing. For night firing the 95th & 131st Htys were to be under their Bde Commander	R.C.

WAR DIARY
or
INTELLIGENCE SUMMARY.
(Erase heading not required.)

Army Form C. 2118.

Place	Date	Hour	Summary of Events and Information	Remarks and references to Appendices
			on him worked guns, and throughout the day, whilst preparation for the demonstration were in progress, an action of all the armies under their group commanders in their original positions.	
	3rd–5th		Btys continued registering. The aeroplane was of aid registered those points to btys which could not be seen from OP's. As many btys as possible registered the LA MOTTE HOUSSAIN which was considered a point of particular importance as it was expected to harbour reserves of men & ammunition. In addition to the zones already allotted, the group arranged to establish reserves of important communication trenches, and to cover certain portions of the German front line trench.	PL
	6th		Continued preparation.	PL
	7th		This was the day on which the battle was supposed to commence, for four days air preliminary bombardment was to take place, afterwards another	PL
	8th		three days for consolidating the position gained. The fourth day was to be the day for the infantry attack. No news of the commencement	PL

WAR DIARY or INTELLIGENCE SUMMARY

Army Form C. 2118

Place	Date	Hour	Summary of Events and Information	Remarks and references to Appendices
	8th 9th		reached the group. The weather which up to this time has been brilliant, became bad.	P.C.
			News was received that some of the HE shell provided was faulty. Previous to this, it had been arranged that each Hty was to keep 200 rounds per gun at the Hty steps of which a certain portion was to be HE. The real amount was never decided upon. The Army G² moved up to an advanced position near ERQUINGHEM and brought an wagon per Hty, and the 1st line Hty wagons (empty) with them. It was arranged that the 364th & 99th Htys should test HE firing about 300 rounds each with a lanyard.	P.C.
	10th		An order was received from the WAR OFFICE to strike 41.IV.S. KBDS, 67 lb from our strength owing to sickness. Continued preparations	P.C.
	11th 12th		" " The HE experiment was carried out. The 99th fired their rounds without casualty	P.C. P.C.

WAR DIARY
or
INTELLIGENCE SUMMARY.
(Erase heading not required.)

Army Form C. 2118.

Place	Date	Hour	Summary of Events and Information	Remarks and references to Appendices
	13th		except that the enemy, in retaliating, burnt down the farm just behind their batteries. After the 364th Bty gun has fired 200 rounds, however, the gun was damaged by a faulty shell. News received that the 104th Bde was coming to relieve the 26th Bde RFA. General K.D. WHITE-THOMSON C.B. D.S.O. assumed Command of the 27th Div Arty	Re
	14th		The 104th Bde arrived and assumed command of the group. Col. KENWORTHY left to join Everything was handed over to them. Complete watching the 13 miles of wire and all maps.	Re
	15th		The Bde left for OUDERSTEEN, one section and the ammunition column having preceded the brigade two days earlier to allow the incoming battery to settle down comfortably in their new Position.	Re
	16th		The Bde at rest at OUDERSTEEN	Re
	17th		A parade of Bde in marching order which was inspected by the new C.R.A	Re

WAR DIARY
or
INTELLIGENCE SUMMARY.
(Erase heading not required.)

Army Form C. 2118.

Place	Date	Hour	Summary of Events and Information	Remarks and references to Appendices
	18th		The C.O. left for his destination	R.C.
	19th		Bde entrained at STEEN BECQUE at 11.0 in the morning and arrived at LONGEAU outside AMIENS at 9 p.m. heading up to CERISY arriving 2 pm. There billets were found for the night	
	20th		The Bde billeted at CERISY. 2/Lt J STEVENS joined the Bde and was posted to the Bde Amm Col. 2/Lt E.N. KENT LEMON struck off strength by orders of WAR OFFICE owing to sickness.	R.C.
	21st		NIL	R.C.
	22nd		Orders received re wire-cutting. A demonstration was to take place on the 27th DIV ARTY front with a view to obtaining part of the attention of the enemy from the main attack elsewhere. The 148th Hy was attached to another group but the 364th and 67th Hys were to cut wire on our front. The 99th and Amm Col and HQ remained at CERISY. The Hys passed under the tactical command of OC 1st Bde.	R.C.
	23 and 24th		Preparations for wire-cutting.	R.C.
	25th		At 2 p.m. the 364th 67th cut wire. There was little retaliation from the	

WAR DIARY
or
INTELLIGENCE SUMMARY.
(Erase heading not required.)

Army Form C. 2118.

Instructions regarding War Diaries and Intelligence Summaries are contained in F. S. Regs., Part II. and the Staff Manual respectively. Title pages will be prepared in manuscript.

Place	Date	Hour	Summary of Events and Information	Remarks and references to Appendices
	26th		Germans except Trench Mortars. Previous to this the two batteries reported. In all 200 rounds each were allotted. In the evening the two batteries returned	R.C.
	27th		NIL	R.C.
	28th		NIL	R.C.
			CAPT E.W.G. WILSON R.F.A. Adjutant, left the Bde to be Staff Captain to the 12th Corps Artillery. He had been in the Bde since 1909, and had been Adj. since 2nd November 1914. Lt D.J. STEEVENS 99th Bty, were appointed in his place. 2Lt J. VENERER posted to 99th Bty from Amm Col.	R.C.
	29th		NIL	R.C.
	30th		NIL	R.C.
	31st		NIL	
			The following have officers joined the brigade and were posted as follows: 2Lt M.L.Q. BOLGER to 67th Bty. 2Lt W.P. DRAPER to 364th Bty. 2Lt J.H. MILNES to 148th Bty.	

12/
7449

27th Burmum
20th Bne. R.E.A.

Dec-15

Vol XI

HQ 20th Bde R.F.A.

WAR DIARY
or
INTELLIGENCE SUMMARY.

Ref AMIENS & CAMBRAI scale 1/80,000. Army Form C. 2118.

OCTOBER 1915.

Place	Date	Hour	Summary of Events and Information	Remarks and references to Appendices
CERISY	1st to 5th		Batteries practised field drill, coming into action etc with one or two days allotted to Bde practice. This was in view of the contemplated advance of this line forward when an advance on our side would have necessitated batteries being moved forward over the ground won.	R.S.
	6th		Orders arrived for our Bde to relieve the 19th Bde R.F.A., & take over "B" group. One subaltern and 2 signallers per battery were sent for attaching to the corresponding batteries of the 19th Bde, to learn the country & have the telephone lines were laid.	R.S.
	N/24 6th/7th	7pm	Reliefs as follows took place. 1 sec 67th Battery relieved 1 sec 39th Battery " 99 " " 95 " " 148 " " 131 " " 368 " " 96 " } For positions see sketch "A"	R.S.
	7th	3pm	Major R. Keyworth took command of "B" group consisting of the following units besides the Bde:— "C" 129 Bty 4.5" Hows. 1 sec 6" Hows 27th siege Bty	R.S.

Army Form C. 2118

WAR DIARY
or
INTELLIGENCE SUMMARY.
(Erase heading not required.)

Instructions regarding War Diaries and Intelligence Summaries are contained in F. S. Regs., Part II. and the Staff Manual respectively. Title pages will be prepared in manuscript.

Place	Date	Hour	Summary of Events and Information	Remarks and references to Appendices
CHUIGNOLLES	7th		and 11th BRs. N/5 belonging to 1st Bde RFA – Group head quarters were in CHUIGNOLLES and the group covered the 81st Inf. Bde. "Iyeling" HQ of both the 2/ Bde. Hqs at FONTAINE-LES-CAPPY.	B.G.
	7th	7pm	Remaining sections of 29th Bde. relieved those of 19th Bde. The front of the howitzers covered extended from F1 trench to H2 trench, about 3000', i.e. 150' per field gun. Each battery could switch so as to cover any part of the group front. The 67th N/5 was used mainly to enfilade the German trenches to the North.	
	8th		6) DOMPIERRE. Batteries checked the registration of the batteries they relieved. The front front is normally very quiet except for the fact F1 + F2 when owing to the close proximity of the enemy trenches, running in the great feature of operations. Main lines of the Bde were for the most part in the valley, 1/2 mile S. 6) CHUIGNES and in the village itself.	N.I.
	9th to 14th		Very quiet.	

Sketch "A"

Army Form C.2118

WAR DIARY
or
INTELLIGENCE SUMMARY.
(Erase heading not required.)

Place	Date	Hour	Summary of Events and Information	Remarks and references to Appendices

Dompierre

364 — 67
II
99 — Zone
148 — 7

H2 H1 G3 G2 G1 F2 F1

Fontaine-lès-Cappy

Chuignes

French Map. Plan Directeur
Scale 1/20000

WAR DIARY
or
INTELLIGENCE SUMMARY
(Erase heading not required.)

Army Form C. 2118

Place	Date	Hour	Summary of Events and Information	Remarks and references to Appendices
SUIGNOLLES	15th		6" Hows. shot at 4 trench mortars in DOMPIERRE; after 14 rds they stopped.	
	16th-19th		Comms through Advanced Bde HQ. back to batteries being established.	
		To HQ Rt.	Bde HQ Chuignolles ▪	
		To Bt 3-8 Nov	(sketch map showing Bde HQ Chuignolles, Chuignes, and batteries 11A, E59, F C129, 364, E148, 67, with Adv Bde HQ (Foucaucourt-Cappy))	
			3 telephonists + linesmen were kept at both places HQ. + fighting HQ.	
	20th		Nil	
	21st		Orders came that the 27th Div was to be relieved by troops of the French 6th Army. Relief to begin on 23rd + completed by 25th	
		8pm	364 Battery (Major K.J.) Battery moved out of action back to their Wgn Line	
	22nd	11am	The above two batteries moved back to billets in CERISY.	
	23rd	6pm	C129 Hows. Battery left the group + moved back to its Wgn line.	
			Informed that the French did not propose making use of any of our positions.	

Army Form C. 2.

WAR DIARY
or
INTELLIGENCE SUMMARY.
(Erase heading not required.)

Instructions regarding War Diaries and Intelligence Summaries are contained in F.S. Regs., Part II. and the Staff Manual respectively. Title pages will be prepared in manuscript.

Place	Date	Hour	Summary of Events and Information	Remarks and references to Appendices
CHOIGNOLLES	24		The 81st Inf Bde were relieved by French troops. Received orders that our Bde was to come under command of 81st Inf Bde for marching billetting purposes. We had orders that the 27th Division was to be relieved by French troops of the 6th Army.	
"	25	4 am	9th Bde went over command + 9th, 148th Bys moved out + marched back to join the rest of the Bde in billets in CERISY.	
CERISY	26th	11 am	Bde marched as a unit to billets in BOVES, 12 miles march, getting in at 3 pm. Fine weather.	
BOVES	27th	Noon	Marched with 81st Inf Bde to BRICQUES MESNIL, arriving at 2 pm. Orders attached, + billeting area diagram.	
BRICQUES MESNIL	28th–31st		Batteries employed their time cleaning horses, kit, orders, marching, order parades, riding drill, inspection of clothes etc.	[signature]

T134. Wt. W708—776. 500000. 4/15. Sir J. C. & S.

SECRET.   Copy No. 5

81st Infantry Brigade Group Operation Order No.62

1. Units will march tomorrow to their new area as per march table attached.

2. Intervals for the Infantry units will be as under-
    between each Company 50 - 100 yards.
    "   Platoon not more than 10 yards.

3. Halts.   The usual hourly halt will be made. O.C. Units must ensure that this takes place at the right moment. Brigade time must be obtained.
    The cookers must be with the First Line transport and not sent on ahead. The duration of the halt for dinners is at discretion of Battalion Commanders. The road must be cleared.

4. Blankets - Lorries for blankets will be at Hd.Qrs. of Infantry units at 7 a.m.

5. Advanced Billetting parties. These should be sent forward under regimental arrangements.

6. Ambulances. - Horse ambulances will report at Hd.Qrs. of units as under.
    Hd.Qrs. 1st A. & S. Hrs. at 7.40am for 9th R.Scots, 2nd Camerons, & 1st A. & S. Highrs.

    Hd.Qrs. 1st R.Scots at 9-15am for 1st R.Scots.
    Hd.Qrs. 2nd Gloucesters at 10-25a for 2nd Gloucester Regt.

    They will remain with these units for night of 27th/28th and rejoin 81st Field Ambulance at MONTENOY on 28th. They should have rations with them.

7. Brigade Head Quarters will close at BOVES at 9am and reopen at SEUX at 2pm.

8. Reports.   Units will report numbers falling out by 10am 28th.

                                        [signature] Captain,
Issued at 6 pm.   Brigade Major, 81st Infantry Brigade.

        Copy No. 1 to File.
          "   2 to War Diary
          "   3 to 27th Divn.
          "   4 to 81st Fd. Ambce.
          "   5 to 20th Bde. R.F.A.
          "   6 to 2nd Wessex Coy. R.E.
          "   7 to 1st R.Scots
          "   8 to 9th R.Scots.
          "   9 to 2nd Gloucesters.
          "   10 to 2nd Camerons.
          "   11 to 1st A. & S. Hrs.
          "   12 to 97 Coy. A.S.C.

MARCH TABLE.

Unit	Starting Point	Time	Route	Destination	Halt for dinner should be made
9th F. Scots	Road Junction of Boves–St Fuscien & Bois–Cagny roads. (1 mile North of E. of Boves)	7 am	St. Fuscien–Dury–Vers–Clairy–Pissy–Fluy	Bourgainville	Any place after Pissy
2nd Camerons		7.20 am			
1st A. & S. Hrs.		7.40 am			
81st Fd. Amble		8.10 am	St. Fuscien–Dury–Vers–Clairy–Revelles–Fresnoy	Montenoy	If desired any place after Clairy
20th Bde RFA.		8.30 am	St. Fuscien–Dury–Saleux–Guignemicourt–Bovelles	Briquemesnil	If desired any place after Bovelles
1st R. Scots.		9.15 am	St. Fuscien–Dury–Saleux–Guignemicourt–Bovelles	Saisseval	Between Guignemicourt & Bovelles
9 Coy ASC		6 am	St. Fuscien–Dury–Saleux–Bovelles	Floxicourt	
2nd Wessex RE.		10 am	St Fuscien–Dury–Saleux–Guignemicourt–Bovelles	Saissemont	If desired between Guignemicourt & Bovelles
Hqrs 81 I.B.		10.15 am	— do —	Seux	
2nd Gloster		10.25 am	— do —	Seux	Between Guignemicourt & Bovelles

BILLET AREA.

- Brenly
- R.A. Group
- Div. A.C.
- 120 Bde.
- Ferrières
- Bovelles
- Div. H.Q.
- Div. M.T.
- Guignemicourt
- 80th Group
- Saisseval
- Briquemesnil
- Seux
- Pissy
- Revelles
- Clairy
- Fluy
- Flixecourt
- Bougainville
- 81st Group
- Montenoy
- Fresnoy
- Bussy
- Courcelles
- Movencourt
- Fricamps
- 82nd Group
- Theolly

Scale = 1:80000

A R E A S.

80th. Infantry Brigade Area.

80th. Infantry Brigade.
1st. Brigade R.F.A.
17th. Field Company R.E.
83rd. Field Ambulance.
96 Company A.S.C.

81st. Infantry Brigade Area.

81st. Infantry Brigade.
20th. Brigade R.F.A.
2nd. Wessex Fd.Co.R.E.
81st. Field Ambulance.
97 Coy. A.S.C.

82nd. Infantry Brigade Area.

82nd. Infantry Brigade.
19th. Brigade R.F.A.
1st. Wessex Fd.Co.R.E.
82nd. Field Ambulance.
98 Coy. A.S.C.

H.Q. Area.

Divisional Headquarters.
Divisional Yeomanry.
Cyclist Company.
Mobile Vety. Section.

R.A. Area.

129th. Brigade R.F.A.
Divisional Ammn. Column.

20ù. Bsa R.I.A.

Notes Dec.

Vol XII

Army Form C. 2118.

WAR DIARY
HQ 20th Bde RFA
or
INTELLIGENCE SUMMARY.
NOVEMBER
(Erase heading not required.)

Instructions regarding War Diaries and Intelligence Summaries are contained in F. S. Regs., Part II. and the Staff Manual respectively. Title pages will be prepared in manuscript.

Place	Date	Hour	Summary of Events and Information	Remarks and references to Appendices
BRICQUEMESNIL	1st			
	2nd		Orders arrived for all life pattern enemy helmets to be packed in cases for transport	
	3rd		M.O. started lectures in the village for the R.As, one battery could be billeted daily. A large Bde incinerator was also built worked very successfully	B.J.S.
	4th-30th		Bde practising rifle orders, riding drill & harness instruction for young drivers recently joined from the Base. Gun drill for young gunners.	
	5th-20th		The new S.A.A. section Ammn Col. was started to be formed. It consisted of the S.A.A. section of the Bde A.C. & also many Indians G.S. wagons additional drivers & gunners etc to complete. It was so organized that it could accompany an Inf Bde if the latter pushed forward without the artillery Bde. Attached are the orders received. X	B.J.S.
			2 LIEUT CASBOLT. H. R.F.A. joined the Bde.	B.J.S.
	18-30 2		Consistently cold weather with snow at first. Thawing during the last week of the month to hard frosts at night. X They will be and later as they are required.	B.J.S.

WAR DIARY or INTELLIGENCE SUMMARY

Army Form C. 2118.

20th Bn RFA

DECEMBER 1915

Place	Date	Hour	Summary of Events and Information	Remarks and references to Appendices
	1st - 5th		Nil.	
	6th	9am	Bde marched from BRICQUESMESNIL via FERRIERES - LONGPRES to billet HQ 99 67 36d in RAINNEVILLE and 148 AC in COISY. About 7 hours were taken to march to the former place.	N.S.
	7th		Owing to the prevalence of diphtheria in COISY the 148 Bty RAC moved its billets in RAINNEVILLE	N.S.
	8 - 22nd		Bde practised route marches, drill in the field, call the mens clothing were minutely inspected.	N.S.
	?	20th	Captain C.H. SMITH evacuated sick	
		22nd	2nd Lieut L. ARKWRIGHT " "	
		28th	Captain M. VOYSEY from 4th Bsn joined Bde	N.S.
		"	2nd Lieut W. THOMPSON " "	
	23rd	9am	The Bde marched to billets in CONDE-FOLIE PICQUINY - HANGEST about 23 miles took 7 hours. Watered tps for 1½ hours at RIVER SOMME.	
	25th		Lieut R.H. LUCAS AVC Veterinary Officer to 20th Bde died through meningitis. He had been with the Bde since May	S.J.

Army Form C. 2118.

WAR DIARY
or
INTELLIGENCE SUMMARY
(Erase heading not required.)

December

Instructions regarding War Diaries and Intelligence Summaries are contained in F. S. Regs., Part II. and the Staff Manual respectively. Title pages will be prepared in manuscript.

Place	Date	Hour	Summary of Events and Information	Remarks and references to Appendices
CONDE FOLIE	30		Information received that the Bde would entrain for MARSEILLES on Jan 1st at following hours	D.S.

27ᵉ division

67ᵗʰ Batt͡y R.F.A.

Vol I. 26.11 —— 31.12.14

121/3944

CONFIDENTIAL

War Diary
of
67th Battery, Royal Field Artillery.

From 26-11-14 To 31-12-14

(Volume I)

Army Form C. 2118.

WAR DIARY
or
INTELLIGENCE SUMMARY.
(Erase heading not required.)

Instructions regarding War Diaries and Intelligence Summaries are contained in F. S. Regs., Part II. and the Staff Manual respectively. Title pages will be prepared in manuscript.

Hour, Date, Place	Summary of Events and Information	Remarks and references to Appendices
Sep 29 1916 WINCHESTER	for training recruits chiefly. Strength of Brigade 40 officers attached to the 82nd & 3rd Bns for issue & supply of ammunition.	

WAR DIARY
or
INTELLIGENCE SUMMARY.
(Erase heading not required.)

Army Form C. 2118.

Hour, Date, Place	Summary of Events and Information	Remarks and references to Appendices
26th Nov 1914 WINCHESTER	Battery formed as a four-gun battery from left half of original 100th Battery. Brigaded with 99th & 364th Batteries as XX Brigade R.F.A.	Officers Captain E C HALL Lieut C E RYAN Lieut E CHALKER (S.R.) 2nd Lieut. J/C U CUNNINGHAM (S.R.)
26th Nov – 13th Dec 1914 WINCHESTER	Mobilization and training of the battery carried on with difficulty owing to ill-fed weather and excessive amount of mud. Friction among the non-commissioned ranks very rapid consequently many of the non-commissioned officers young and inexperienced in their duties. A large proportion of the personnel (about 65 per cent) consist of reservists, re-enlisted and specially enlisted men, drawn from various training Centres. The men as a whole are willing and keen but require a considerable amount of training before they can be considered thoroughly proficient in their duties. All the horses were drawn from the Remount Depot at WINCHESTER, they were of a good stamp and with few exceptions sufficiently trained to the work required of them. The lendency of the horses and men was, under the circumstances good. About 5 men were struck off the strength as medically unfit and 28 horses were cast for various reasons. Chiefly strangles and catarrh. The Brigade was affiliated to the 8th Infantry Brigade for normal supply of ammunition	

Army Form C. 2118.

WAR DIARY
or
INTELLIGENCE-SUMMARY. SCB

(Erase heading not required.)

Instructions regarding War Diaries and Intelligence Summaries are contained in F.S. Regs., Part II. and the Staff Manual respectively. Title pages will be prepared in manuscript.

Hour, Date, Place	Summary of Events and Information	Remarks and references to Appendices
Dec 19th 1914 11am WINCHESTER SOUTHAMPTON 7pm	The battery marched to SOUTHAMPTON and entrained on the Transport "CITY OF DUNKIRK", which sailed at about 9.7pm	SCB
Dec 20th 1914 12 noon HAVRE 10.30pm	The ship arrived at the docks and after considerable delay, due to a large consignment of meat having to be unloaded, the disembarkation was effected at about 9.10.30pm. The night was spent in a shed in the docks.	SCB
Dec 21st 1914 3.45pm 4pm HAVRE	The battery entrained at GARE DE MARITIME (Point 6) destination unknown. The train left the station at 345pm	SCB
Dec 22nd 1914 12 noon ARQUES 7pm 11pm	The battery detrained at ARQUES and marched to WALLON CAPELLE to billet. On arrival at WALLON CAPELLE at about 7pm it was found that no billets had been arranged, after considerable difficulties got finally settled down at about 11pm. Men in two billet-rooms and horses and vehicles in an adjoining field.	SCB
Dec 23rd 1914 WALLON CAPELLE	Remainder of the Brigade arrived in their billets 364th Battery at SERCUS, 99th Battery and Brigade Headquarters between this place and WALLON CAPELLE. Brigade comes under Orders Commander of 80th Infantry Brigade, held quarters at BLARINGHEM	SCB

Army Form C. 2118.

WAR DIARY
or
INTELLIGENCE SUMMARY.

(Erase heading not required.)

Instructions regarding War Diaries and Intelligence Summaries are contained in F.S. Regs., Part II. and the Staff Manual respectively. Title pages will be prepared in manuscript.

Hour, Date, Place	Summary of Events and Information	Remarks and references to Appendices
Dec. 26th 1914 WALLON CAPELLE	Battery (as part of 27th Div.) became a unit of 2nd Army under Gen H. SMITH DORIEN (2nd, 3rd Corps and 27th Division)	
Dec. 23rd - Dec 31st 1914. WALLON CAPELLE	Training and completing of the battery in stores continues.	

121/4193

27th Division

67th Bde: RFA.

Vol II. 1 — 31.1.15.

Jan 15 — Orders for guns to be laid by day for night firing —

CONFIDENTIAL

War Diary
of
67th Battery Royal Field Artillery

From 1-1-15
To 31-1-15

(Volume II)

Army Form C. 2118.

WAR DIARY
or
INTELLIGENCE SUMMARY.
(Erase heading not required.)

Instructions regarding War Diaries and Intelligence Summaries are contained in F.S. Regs., Part II. and the Staff Manual respectively. Title pages will be prepared in manuscript.

Hour, Date, Place	Summary of Events and Information	Remarks and references to Appendices

(73989) W4141—463. 400,000. 9/14. H.&J.Ltd. Forms/C. 2118/10.

268

WAR DIARY
or
INTELLIGENCE SUMMARY.

(Erase heading not required.)

Army Form C. 2118.

Instructions regarding War Diaries and Intelligence Summaries are contained in F.S. Regs., Part II. and the Staff Manual respectively. Title pages will be prepared in manuscript.

Hour, Date, Place	Summary of Events and Information	Remarks and references to Appendices
Jan 5th 1915 WALLON CAPELLE	Training of battery continued	Sgt.
Jan 6th 1915 10.30am 3.0pm WALLON CAPELLE	Battery left at 10.30 a.m, arrived STRAZEELE at 3 p.m and went into billets, men in barns, horses and vehicles in a field	Ref Map BELGIUM (OSTEND I) Scale 1/100,000 Sgt
Jan 7th 1915 11:10am STRAZEELE	Left at 11.10 a.m and marched to ZEVECOTON via BAILLEUL, LOCRE, WESTOUTRE & RENINGHELST went into bivouack at about 8 p.m with Brigade Headquarters and Ammunition Column. 99th and 364th Batteries in bivouack near OUDERDOM.	Sgt
Jan 8th 1915 ZEVECOTON	99th and 364th Batteries take over and occupy gun positions from 2nd Groupe of 9th Regiment of French Artillery. 67th Battery remain in reserve in bivy night's bivouack. Headquarters Rebt annexy at N.E corner of ETANG DE DICKIEBUSCH	Sgt

(73989) W4141—463. 400,000. 9/14. H.&J.Ltd. Forms/C. 2118/10.

Army Form C. 2118.

WAR DIARY
or
INTELLIGENCE SUMMARY. ECH

(Erase heading not required.)

Instructions regarding War Diaries and Intelligence Summaries are contained in F.S. Regs., Part II. and the Staff Manual respectively. Title pages will be prepared in manuscript.

Hour, Date, Place	Summary of Events and Information	Remarks and references to Appendices
Jan 9th 1915 3 p.m. ZEVECOTEN	Orders received to bring battery into action in the vicinity of the other two batteries of the Brigade. Position chosen 200ᵗ N.N.E of the left flank of the 99ᵗʰ Battery, which is in action in line with & 50ᵗ to the left of the 364ᵗʰ Battery.	ECH
Jan 10 1915 5 a.m. DICKEBUSCH	Gun position prepared during darkness in the early hours of the morning by planting boughs trunkward etc along the front and above the gun positions to obtain concealment from view from aeroplanes.	
10 a.m.	Proposed position of the battery altered. New position 150ᵗ further north, in some emplacements prepared and vacated by the French artillery. Concealment from view obtained by willow trees growing along front/edge of position and a few bushy planted in the ground. These solidly built shelters in the spaces between the gun positions afford good protection against shrapnel and splinters. Shelters are in good state of preservation and are entirely above ground. ECH	

(73959) W4141—463. 400,000. 9/14. H.&J.Ltd. Forms/C. 2118/10.

270

Army Form C. 2118.

WAR DIARY
or
INTELLIGENCE SUMMARY. ECA

(Erase heading not required.)

Hour, Date, Place	Summary of Events and Information	Remarks and references to Appendices
Jan 11th 1915 3 a.m. DICKEBUSCH	Gun platforms of and approved to the new position were improved during the hours of darkness	ECA
Jan 12th 1915 5 a.m. DICKEBUSCH	Guns brought into action with firing battery wagon bodies under cover of darkness. 3 officers and 54 men accompany the guns, 1 officer, the remainder of the men the horses (except officer chargers) the limbers and the 1st line wagons remain in billet at ZEVECOTEN. Gun positions and approach very muddy, rendering handling of the guns difficult and laborious. Battery position O 29 C 8.1. Zone allotted to the battery from PICCADILLY FARM (O 8 a 2.8) (inclusive) to N.E edge of wood (BOIS CARRÉ) O 7 6 5. entering about 4°. Great difficulty experienced in finding suitable observing station owing to the high nature of the ground and the number of trees between the battery and the enemy's position. Observing station chosen behind hay stack about 1400 x from enemy's trenches, situated at O 8 d 1, 6. A train line of one is obtainable but is mounted attached by ridges. 2 Guns 1 Sea trolley and 3 men per extraction between remainder of the gun position. The officers and the remainder of the men are billeted in a brewery about 700 x in rear of the battery	Ref map BELGIUM "B" Series Sheet 28 NW Scale 1/20,000 Ref map BELGIUM & FRANCE "B" Series Sheet 28 SW Scale 1/20,000 ECA

(73969) W 4141—463. 400,000. 9/14. H.&J.Ltd. Forms/C. 2118/10.

WAR DIARY
or
INTELLIGENCE SUMMARY.

Army Form C. 2118.

Hour, Date, Place	Summary of Events and Information	Remarks and references to Appendices
Jan 13th 1915 DICKEBUSCH 12.35 p.m.	Battery opened fire at 12.35 p.m. Target enemy's trenches. Owing to the mist observation was difficult & the rate of fire consequently slow. Range was found to be about 3500x. Effect appeared to be fairly good. Orders received for a fresh officer to come to billets at DICKEBUSCH and for no officer to remain at gun position during daylight hours. The Battery is ordered to headquarters, falling back in & clearing station of Kattepie.	E.C.H
Jan 14th 1915 DICKEBUSCH 12.45 p.m.	Orders received that not more than 5 rounds of ammunition per gun are to be fired in a day, except in case of real necessity. Battery opened fire at 12.45 p.m. Target PICCADILLY FARM. Effect did not appear good as the shards of the guns had not yet buried themselves in the ground and consequently the guns were jumping	
10.15 p.m.	the lines were rather erratic. Orders received at 10.15 p.m. for guns to be prepared to open fire & to report when ready. Battery reported "Ready to open fire" at 10.15 p.m. This excessive delay was caused by guns not having been layed & graded before night fell. No rounds were fired.	E.C.H

WAR DIARY
INTELLIGENCE SUMMARY.

Army Form C. 2118.

Hour, Date, Place	Summary of Events and Information	Remarks and references to Appendices
Jan 15th 1915 11.55 a.m. DICKEBUSCH	Battery opened fire at 11.55 a.m. Target PICCADILLY FARM and the trenches. The Dials have now a good grip in the ground and the shooting was consequently very much steadier. The effect did not appear very good as many of the rounds fell over. This was probably due, in one to avoid any chance of shelling on our own trenches, which are very close to those of the enemy a great difficulty is experienced in clearly distinguishing between the two lines. Orders given to keep the guns layed & loaded when not actually being fired. Want so that fire can be brought to bear on the Zone of the battery, either by night a day with the least possible delay. G¹ SEABOURNE died at ZEVECOTEN. He was buried at Farm. G 35 b 0.3.	Ext. Ref ᵐ of BELGIUM "B" Series Sheet 28 N.W. Scale 1/20,000
Jan 16th 1915 11.33 a.m. DICKEBUSCH	Battery opened fire at 11.33 a.m. at trenches and ground beyond. Range was increased by 200 x. Owing to the state of the ground, the effect was impossible	

275

WAR DIARY
or
INTELLIGENCE SUMMARY. Ec/B.
(Erase heading not required.)

Army Form C. 2118.

Hour, Date, Place	Summary of Events and Information	Remarks and references to Appendices
Jan 17th 1915 DICKEBUSCH.	to judge. Only 15 rounds were fired. Another artillery officer reported ready in 5½ minutes a great improvement on previous first No which were fired.	Ec/B
7.45 am 1.30 pm	Battery was relieved by 95th Battery, commanded by Major BRODRICK. Guns, wagon-bodies & 76 rounds a gun were left and taken over by incoming Battery. 6⅔ Battery left the billets at DICKEBUSCH at 7.45 a.m. & reached the new billets at 1.30 pm Position of new billets 1 mile NNE of WESTOUTRE M2c1.9.	Ref. map BELGIUM - FRANCE "B" Edn Sheet 28 S.W Scale 1/20,000 Ec/B
Jan 18th 1915 WESTOUTRE (HERKEN)	During the night and morning about 4 inches of snow fell. This is the first snow that has fallen since the battery left ENGLAND.	Ec/B
Jan 20th & 21st 1915 WESTOUTRE (HERKEN) BOESCHEPE	Officers & men of the battery had hot baths at	Ec/B

274

WAR DIARY
or
INTELLIGENCE SUMMARY. ECB

(Erase heading not required.)

Army Form C. 2118.

Hour, Date, Place	Summary of Events and Information	Remarks and references to Appendices
Jan 23rd 1915 8.30 a.m. WESTOUTRE (HEKSKEN)	Battery left WESTOUTRE to come into action on embankment at N.E. corner of ETANG DE DICKEBUSCH, spent entire night getting guns into action.	ECB
Jan 24th 1915 6.15 a.m. DICKEBUSCH	Battery tried in action at 6.15 a.m. Rest of day spent in improving position. 1 Gun Waggon and Party of Battery remained in rear billets at WESTOUTRE (HEKSKEN), remainder of men in DICKEBUSCH. Firing Battery.	ECB
Jan 25th 1915 11 a.m. DICKEBUSCH 4.20 p.m.	Commenced firing at 11 a.m. Ceased firing at 4.20 p.m. 20 rounds fired 18. Position of Battery at (Camera al) O 2d 33, O 2d 104, O 8 b 108, O 3 b 67. Range about 4800-4900. "13 Lines" chay 28 S.W Scale 1/5000	Ref map BELGIUM and FRANCE ECB
Jan 26th 1915 11.4 p.m. DICKEBUSCH 2.15 p.m.	Fire commenced at 11.14 p.m. Ceased firing at 2.15 p.m. 20 rounds fired 25. Target German trench invisible from Observing Station position about O 8 a 10.9 to O 2d 22. Range about 4400–4450.	Ref map as above ECB
Jan 27th 1915 11.30 a.m. DICKEBUSCH 4 p.m.	Fire commenced at 11.30 a.m. Ceased at 4 p.m. No. of rounds fired 20. Target same as on 26th Jan.	Map ECB

Army Form C. 2118.

WAR DIARY
or
INTELLIGENCE SUMMARY. Sc/H

(Erase heading not required.)

Instructions regarding War Diaries and Intelligence Summaries are contained in F. S. Regs., Part II. and the Staff Manual respectively. Title pages will be prepared in manuscript.

Hour, Date, Place	Summary of Events and Information	Remarks and references to Appendices
Jan. 28ᵗʰ 1915 11.45 a.m. DICKEBUSCH 7.45 p.m.	Fire commenced at 11.45 a.m. & ceased at 7.45 p.m. Rds. of amn fired 20. Target same as on 26ᵗʰ Jan.	Scott
Jan. 29ᵗʰ 1915 11.30 a.m. DICKEBUSCH 1.30 p.m. 5.30 p.m.	Fire commenced at 11.30 a.m. & ceased at 1.30 p.m. Rds of amn fired 20. Target same as on 28ᵗʰ Jan. Exchanged gun positions & fours with 91ˢᵗ Battery R.F.A. 67ᵗʰ Battery thus regain their original position, which are in the same position as they were when taken over by the 91ˢᵗ Battery on the morning of the 17ᵗʰ Jan.	Scott
Jan. 30ᵗʰ 1915 11 a.m. DICKEBUSCH 11.45 a.m.	Fire commenced at 11 a.m. & ceased at 11.45 a.m. Rds. of amn fired 12. Target track from 0.8.a.2.8 to 0.7.8.b.5. Ref. R. of BELGIUM & FRANCE 1:B "Ieren Sheet 28 S.W. Calc/90,000 good light	Scott
Jan. 31ˢᵗ 1915 12.40 p.m. DICKEBUSCH 12.30 p.m.	Fire commenced at 12.40 p.m. & ceased at 12.30 p.m. Rds of amn fired 12. Target same as on the 30ᵗʰ Jan.	Scott

121/4468

CONFIDENTIAL

War Diary
of
67th Battery Royal Field Artillery
27th Division
From 1.2.15   To 28.2.15

(Volume III)

Army Form C. 2118.

WAR DIARY
or
INTELLIGENCE SUMMARY.
(Erase heading not required.)

Instructions regarding War Diaries and Intelligence Summaries are contained in F. S. Regs., Part II. and the Staff Manual respectively. Title pages will be prepared in manuscript.

Hour, Date, Place	Summary of Events and Information	Remarks and references to Appendices

(73989) W4141—463. 400,000. 9/14. H.&J.Ltd. Forms/C. 2118/10.

Army Form C. 2118.

WAR DIARY
or
INTELLIGENCE SUMMARY.

(Erase heading not required.)

Instructions regarding War Diaries and Intelligence Summaries are contained in F.S. Regs., Part II. and the Staff Manual respectively. Title pages will be prepared in manuscript.

Hour, Date, Place	Summary of Events and Information	Remarks and references to Appendices
Feb 1st 1915 DICKEBUSCH — 10.30 am	Commenced firing at 10.30 a.m. & ceased at 10.45 a.m.	Ref map BELGIUM & FRANCE
10.45 am	No. of rounds fired 14. Target battery under cover at 08 a. 9.4.	1" & Centre Sheet 28 SW Scale 1/20,000 Ect
Feb 2nd 1915 DICKEBUSCH — 11.40 am	Commenced firing at 11.40 a.m. & ceased at 11.45 a.m.	Ect
11.45 am	No. of rounds fired 5. Target same as at 1.2.15. Ways of horse thins near to MILLEKRUISSE	Ref map BELGIUM Sheet 28 South Ypres
Feb 3rd 1915 DICKEBUSCH — 8.30 am	Took over 364° Battery guns in position occupied by a Groupe of 75th Regiment of French Artillery. Some French guns still in position.	Ect
9.0 pm	French guns withdrawn from position. A gun & crew consisting of 1 N.C.O. & 3 men remain at position, remainder of detachments in billets.	Ect
Feb 4th 1915 DICKEBUSCH — 9.45 am	Commenced firing at 9.45 a.m. & ceased at 10.30 a.m. No. of rounds fired 17. Target roads at Q.3.d.4.1. × 0.8.6.9.3.	Ref map as above.
10.30 am	Observing station at F.33 c.5.9. Observation difficult.	
3.30 pm	3 Rounds fired at 3.30 pm to shoot lines. LIEUT. M.W. HOISH attached from "C" Battery R.H.A.	

WAR DIARY
or
INTELLIGENCE SUMMARY.

(Erase heading not required.)

Army Form C. 2118.

Hour, Date, Place	Summary of Events and Information	Remarks and references to Appendices
5:15 p.m.	Ordered to man guns. Guns remained manned	ECH
7.10 a.m.	till 7.10 a.m. (6.2.15). 4 rounds fired during night.	
5 Feb 1915 8 p.m.	Ordered to man guns. Guns manned till 12.45 a.m.	ECH
DICKEBUSCH	(6.2.15). No rounds fired.	
11 Feb 1915 10 a.m.	Changed gun position and billets with 99th Battery	
	R.F.A. Commenced firing at 11.15 a.m. Ceased at	Ref map BELGIUM & FRANCE
DICKEBUSCH 11.15 a.m. 11.30 a.m.	11.30 a.m. No rounds fired. 12. Target daytime	sheet 28 S.W Scale 1/20,000
	from 02d72 to 09a89. At dusk guns layed on	"B" Series
	night zone from 08b5.6 to 09a89.	ECH
12 Feb 1915 1.30 p.m.	Commenced firing at 1.30 p.m. & ceased at 2.0 p.m. 20 of	Ref map same as above.
DICKEBUSCH 2.0 p.m.	rounds fired 20. Target wood 09a77.	ECH
13 Feb 1915 10.15 a.m.	Commenced firing at 10.15 a.m. & ceased at 10.20 a.m. only	
10.20 a.m.	3 rounds fired owing to difficulty of observation due	
DICKEBUSCH 2.0 p.m.	to rain and mist. Opened fire again at 2.0 p.m. &	
2.30 p.m.	ceased at 2.30 p.m. 17 rounds fired. Target same as	
	on the 11th Feb.	ECH

WAR DIARY or INTELLIGENCE SUMMARY. Ect.

Army Form C. 2118.

Hour, Date, Place	Summary of Events and Information	Remarks and references to Appendices
14 Feb 1915 DICKEBUSCH	3.0 p.m. Fire commenced at 3.0 p.m. and ceased at 3.30 p.m. 6 rounds shrapnel fired at Battery under cover of O,9,&,9,1 as key. 3.30 p.m. Infantry called for immediate support at 4 p.m. as they 4 p.m. were being attacked. Fire was opened on Eng. Zone and	Ref. map BELGIUM & FRANCE 1 series scale 1/40,000
15 Feb 1915 DICKEBUSCH	7 a.m. a continuous fire was maintained till 7 a.m. (15.2.15) 11 p.m. except for about 11 to 11.30 p.m. as rates varying from 11.30 p.m. Battery fire 2 minutes to 30 lengths of seconds. At 11.30 a.m. 1.30 a.m. fire was all turned on the guns of Verbranden, which had been 4 a.m. occupied by the Germans and fire kept on them till 4 a.m. (at which time Counter attack was to have been launched) when rapid was increased by our guns and guns entered 1° to the right after 2 or 3 intervals. It was impossible to maintain a continued rate of rapid fire owing to the cap't & merely state of the platform, which accounted running the guns of from 2 to 4 feet after each round. Replenishing of ammunition difficult owing to the mud and distance and to the great extent of East 300 yards led to do done by hand. Number of rounds fired 640 shrapnel and 8 wrought. Morning of the 15th Feb spent in repairing the gun platforms, which had suffered badly from the continuous fire during the night. 10.30 p.m. Fired 8 rounds shrapnel at 10.30 p.m. at enemy Support trenches. As everything was very quiet, infantry attacks we do stop firing.	Ect.

WAR DIARY
or
~~INTELLIGENCE SUMMARY.~~ Ect.

(Erase heading not required.)

Army Form C. 2118.

Hour, Date, Place	Summary of Events and Information	Remarks and references to Appendices
16th Feb 1915 DICKEBUSCH	9.15 pm Infantry asked for immediate support at 9.15 pm. 16 rounds shrapnel fired. Infantry then reported that all was quiet in front and firing was stopped	Ect
21 Feb 1915 DICKEBUSCH	3.15 pm Commenced firing at 3.15 pm & ceased at 3.30 pm. 17 rounds of shrapnel fired at ingstack near EIKOFF FARM 3.30 pm and trenches in zone.	Ref map BELGIUM & FRANCE Trench Sheet 2 DSW Scale 1/20000 Ect
22nd Feb 1915 DICKEBUSCH	3.15 pm Commenced firing at 3.15 pm & ceased at 3.45 pm. 7 rounds of shrapnel & 9 rounds of trotyl fired at igstack 2.45 pm near EIKOFF FARM. 4 rounds of shrapnel at trenches in battery zone.	Ref map as above Ect
23rd Feb 1915 DICKEBUSCH	2.45 pm Commenced firing at 2.45 pm & ceased at 3.25 pm. 12 3.25 pm rounds of ectshrapnel and 8 rounds of trotyl fired at trenches near EIKOFF FARM.	Ref map as above Ect

Army Form C. 2118.

WAR DIARY
or
INTELLIGENCE SUMMARY.
(Erase heading not required.)

Instructions regarding War Diaries and Intelligence Summaries are contained in F. S. Regs., Part II. and the Staff Manual respectively. Title pages will be prepared in manuscript.

Hour, Date, Place	Summary of Events and Information	Remarks and references to Appendices
24 Feb 1915 DICKEBUSCH	1.00 pm Commenced firing at 1.0 pm & ceased at 4.30 pm. 4.30 pm 14 Rounds of Shrapnel fired at trenches in Battery zone.	
26th Feb 1915 DICKEBUSCH	3.10 pm Commenced firing at 3.10 pm & ceased at 3.45 pm. 3.45 pm 20 Rounds fired at trenches in Battery zone. Opened fire again at 4.15 pm a third for 5 minutes. 6 Shrapnel and 4 Trotyl fired at front edge of wood O.7.c.6.9.	Ref map BELGIUM & FRANCE "B" area sheet 28 S.W Scale 1/20,000 EC/H
27th Feb 1915 DICKEBUSCH	1.25 pm Commenced firing at 1.25 pm & ceased at 4.10 pm. 4.10 pm 10 rounds Shrapnel were fired at trenches in Battery zone, 10 rounds Shrapnel were also fired to register enemy's communication trench running from O.13.a.4.8 to O.7.c.4.3) with a view to firing at it at night time. The registration was observed by observing officer of the 39th Battery R.F.A.	Ref map as above EC/H

(73969) W4141—463. 400,000. 9/14. H.&J.Ltd. Forms/C. 2118/10.

67th Batty: R+A.

Vol IV 1 - 31.3.15

29th Division

CONFIDENTIAL

WAR DIARY
OF
67th. BATTERY ROYAL FIELD ARTILLERY

FROM 1-3-15   TO 31-3-15

(VOLUME IV)

Army Form C. 2118.

WAR DIARY
or
INTELLIGENCE SUMMARY.
(Erase heading not required.)

Instructions regarding War Diaries and Intelligence Summaries are contained in F. S. Regs., Part II and the Staff Manual respectively. Title pages will be prepared in manuscript.

Hour, Date, Place	Summary of Events and Information	Remarks and references to Appendices

(73989) W4141—463. 400,000. 9/14. H.&J.Ltd. Forms/C. 2118/10.

WAR DIARY or INTELLIGENCE SUMMARY.

Army Form C. 2118.

67th Bn.

Hour, Date, Place	Summary of Events and Information	Remarks and references to Appendices
1st March 1915 DICKEBUSCH 10.40 a.m. 11.10 a.m.	Commenced firing at 10.40 A.M. & ceased firing at 11.10 a.m. Fuze Trails shrapnel were fired at supports & trenches at 12.30 p.m. 8 rounds of shrapnel were fired at German Sap in front of Trench 21. Observation by artillery officer on the mound south of E.10.1 and infantry officer in trench 22L after 4 rounds communication with trench 22 failed.	Refer to BELGIUM & FRANCE 1/B Series sheet 28 S.W. Scale 1/20,000. ECH
2nd March 1915 DICKEBUSCH 12.30 a.m. 2.17 a.m.	On the night of 1st/2nd an infantry attack was arranged with a view to taking a portion of the forward German trenches. The attack was opened at 12.30 a.m. by the 67th Battery firing 16 rounds gun fire. Battery fire was thereafter maintained at rates varying from 5 seconds to 1 minute till 2.17 a.m. when rapid firing was ordered. Number of rounds fired 12.12.1 gun fired by the supports of shrapnel & 6 Trotyl were fired by the supports of shrapnel & Trotyl at the sap in front of trench 21.	ECH

Army Form C. 2118.

WAR DIARY
or
INTELLIGENCE SUMMARY.
(Erase heading not required.)

Hour, Date, Place	Summary of Events and Information	Remarks and references to Appendices
3rd March 1915 DICKEBUSCH 1.30 p.m	6 Rounds of Shrapnel were fired at Support Trenches at 1.30 p.m and 19 Rounds of Shrapnel and 3 Trotyl were fired at Sap at irregular intervals during the day.	SCH
4th March 1915 9.20 a.m DICKEBUSCH 10 a.m	at 9.20 a.m 3 rounds of Shrapnel & 1 Trotyl were fired at Sap. at 10 a.m battery changed positions with 364th Battery	SCH
6th March 1915 DICKEBUSCH 12 a.m 11 a.m 6.30 p.m	Bombardment of German Trenches. Battery opened pyramidical a rapid volley of Battery fire at 11.45 a.m till 12 a.m, so that to cover the withdrawal of our infantry from their fire trenches. at 12 non Howitzers & heavy guns opened fire and for that time still at 6.30 p.m 67th Battery fired at Battery in 10 minutes. Total number of rounds fired 69 Shrapnel	SCH

WAR DIARY
or
INTELLIGENCE SUMMARY.

Army Form C. 2118.

Hour, Date, Place	Summary of Events and Information	Remarks and references to Appendices
9 March 1915 DICKEBUSCH	2/Lieut. C. N. V. CUNNINGHAM rejoined from "C" Battery R.H.A.	ECB
10 March 1915 DICKEBUSCH	Lieut. M.W. HOISH returned to his own unit, "C" Battery R.H.A.	ECB
14 March 1915 DICKEBUSCH	Battery went back to rest. Took over part of 148th Battery billets at G.36.d.10.7 one mile S.W. of OUDERDOM. Germans attacked our front line trenches abreast 4.30 p.m. Received orders at 5.30 p.m. to harness up and be ready to move. Sent three guns up during night to replace casualties, 2 to 364th Battery and 1 to 148th Battery.	Ref map BELGIUM "B" Series Sheet 28 N.W. Scale 1/20.000 ECB
15 March 1915 OUDERDOM 7 a.m.	Ordered to un harness at 7 a.m.	ECB

Army Form C. 2118.

WAR DIARY
or
INTELLIGENCE SUMMARY.

(Erase heading not required.)

Hour, Date, Place	Summary of Events and Information	Remarks and references to Appendices
17 March 1918 OUDERDOM	Ordered to prepare position for battery, to support Subsidiary line of defence at H 27 D 5.6.	Ref map BELGIUM "B" Series Sheet 28 NW Scale 1/20,000 ect.
18th – 20th March 1918 OUDERDOM	Prepared position for battery.	ect
23rd March 1918 OUDERDOM	Moved guns and firing battery wagons from position where they were in action with 148th Battery at DICKEBUSCH, to field beside battery billets. 2nd Lieut R. DICKIE attached to battery.	ect
25th March 1918 OUDERDOM	7 am Battery left billets at OUDERDOM and marched via RENINGHELST and POPERINGHE to billets in a farm on the POPERINGHE-CASSEL Road, 3 miles from POPERINGHE	Ref map BELGIUM HAZEBROUCK 5A Scale 1/20,000 ect.
26 March 1918 POPERINGHE	2.30 pm at 2.15 pm received orders to return to billets 3.30 pm vacated the previous day at 3 pm. Battery started to march back to billets at OUDERDOM from POPERINGHE and RENINGHELST. 7.30 pm at 7.30 pm Right section went into action, relieving

WAR DIARY
or
INTELLIGENCE SUMMARY.

Army Form C. 2118.

Hour, Date, Place	Summary of Events and Information	Remarks and references to Appendices
27 March 1915 OUDERDOM	Two guns of the 108th Battery (3rd Division) which were in action under the O.C. 364th Battery. 9 a.m. Battery relieved the personnel of the 364th Battery. Two guns were taken over (Q) the Ammunition. Our German gun Trail fired from 0300 a.y to 0 sec 77 (n) Special. Second hostile gun. German returned 12.10 p.m. trenches S.E. of Avant. at 12.15 p.m. 24 rounds to shrapnel were fired to enfilade the trench. 3 m.s. 3.45 p.m. at 3.45 p.m. 10 rounds of gun fire (8 rounds) were fired by action (rapidly) Brigade Comm. Co. 7.30 p.m. at 7.30 p.m. the Left section of the 67th (H) Battery came into action & blazed 2 guns open to 77 F. Battery until arrival in the petition.	BEGIUM Refer to FRANCE "B" Series Map 28 S.W. Scale 1/20,000 Ect Ect
28 March 1915 DICKEBUSCH	2.15 p.m. 12 Rounds were fired at German trenches at 2.15 p.m. 6 at each gun.	Ect

259

Army Form C. 2118.

WAR DIARY
or
INTELLIGENCE=SUMMARY.
(Erase heading not required.)

Instructions regarding War Diaries and Intelligence Summaries are contained in F.S. Regs., Part II and the Staff Manual respectively. Title pages will be prepared in manuscript.

Hour, Date, Place	Summary of Events and Information	Remarks and references to Appendices
29 March 1915. DICKIEBUSCH.	12.30 p.m 7 rounds fired at german trenches in ordinary fire at 12.30 p.m	ECB
30 March 1915. DICKEBUSCH.	3.45 p.m at 3.45 p.m 8 rounds were fired in 4.5 p.m ordinary fire. at 4.5 p.m 12 rounds were fired at gun position at O.15.c.2.3. 2ieut N.S. KYDD attached to Battery in place of 2ieut R. DICKIE transferred to ammunition Column.	Ref. map "BELGIUM & FRANCE" B Series sheet 28 S.W. Scale 1/20,000 ECB
31st March 1915. DICKEBUSCH.	11.45 a.m fired 12 rounds at 11.45 a.m at trenches S.E. of 8.45 p.m opposite at ST ELOI. at 8.45 p.m D/Y Left Section was withdrawn from action and attack to wagon lines. the section of 108th Battery came in to action in position occupied by Left Section.	Ref. map as above. ECB

27th Division.

67th Battery: R.F.A.

Vol V. 1 — 30.4.15.

CONFIDENTIAL.

War Diary
of
67th. Battery Royal Field Artillery

From 1-4-15   To 30.4.15

(Volume V)

Army Form C. 2118.

WAR DIARY
or
INTELLIGENCE SUMMARY.
(Erase heading not required.)

Instructions regarding War Diaries and Intelligence Summaries are contained in F.S. Regs., Part II and the Staff Manual respectively. Title pages will be prepared in manuscript.

Hour, Date, Place	Summary of Events and Information	Remarks and references to Appendices

Army Form C. 2118.

WAR DIARY
or
INTELLIGENCE SUMMARY.

(Erase heading not required.)

Instructions regarding War Diaries and Intelligence Summaries are contained in F.S. Regs., Part II and the Staff Manual respectively. Title pages will be prepared in manuscript.

Hour, Date, Place	Summary of Events and Information	Remarks and references to Appendices
1st April 1915 DICKEBUSCH	8 a.m. At 8 a.m. Major CAREY Commanding 108th Battery, took over command of position & ord. Left section & Battery Staff went back to billets on POPERINGHE-CASSEL Road, 3 miles from POPERINGHE. 10 p.m. at 10 p.m. Right Section came out of action & joined remainder of the Battery, arriving at billets at 4 a.m. on 2nd April	Ref. map BELGIUM HAZEBROUCK 5a Scale 1/40,000
2nd April 1915 POPERINGHE	4 a.m.	Ect
3rd April 1915 POPERINGHE	3 p.m. Battery was inspected by D.O.C. 5th Corps who expressed his satisfaction at the state of the battery.	Ect
4th April 1915 POPERINGHE	6.15 p.m. At 6.15 p.m. Left Section marched via POPERINGHE & YPRES and relieved a Section of the 3rd Battery of the 49th Regiment of French Artillery, in action at I.n.C.8.8. 3/4 mile N.W. of HOOGE. Detachments & line in dug-outs beside guns, Officers & Battery Staff in farm at I.n.C.14. Stinkenhoek known as farm I.n.C.2.10.	Ref. map BELGIUM Sheet 28 Scale 1/40,000 Ect

Army Form C. 2118.

WAR DIARY
or
INTELLIGENCE SUMMARY. 8cB

(Erase heading not required.)

Instructions regarding War Diaries and Intelligence Summaries are contained in F.S. Regs., Part II and the Staff Manual respectively. Title pages will be prepared in manuscript.

Hour, Date, Place	Summary of Events and Information	Remarks and references to Appendices
6 April 1915 HOOGE 12 noon	a{ midday Battery took over charge of position and gun from French Battery. Round 3rd German Support trenches in front of our trenches 9-21. J 31 a 77 to J 31 b 8.10. a{ 11 p.m. Report L.Edn. C. on intersection returning + it remained there later. 1 Lin. Wagon with Ammon in Column at billets a{ A 1064.6.	Ref. map BELGIUM Sheet 28 Scale 1/40,000 8cB
7 April 1915 HOOGE	No rounds were fired as direct Telephone line was in bad state of repair + was the had to be laid to observing station in front of trenches.	8cB
8 April 1915 HOOGE 11.30 a.m. and 1.30 p.m.	Fired 49 rounds between 11.30 a.m. + 1.30 p.m. in an air aplate gun. Owing to woods apparently an obs of same very difficult.	8cB
9 April 1915 HOOGE 12.40 p.m. 2.30 p.m.	12.40 p.m. Registered 3rd{ between 12.40 p.m. + 2.33 p.m. 32 rounds fired 3rd in the evening limbers + Firing Wagon + horses moved to Wilders a{ H 14 B 6.9	Ref. map same as above H 14 B 6.9 8cB

WAR DIARY
or
INTELLIGENCE SUMMARY. Scott

(Erase heading not required.)

Army Form C. 2118.

Hour, Date, Place	Summary of Events and Information	Remarks and references to Appendices
10th April 1915 HOOGE	11.40am 16 Rounds fired at zero between 11.40 a.m and 12.35 p.m 12 35.a.m	Scott
11th April 1915 HOOGE	11.10 a.m At 11.10 a.m fired 8 rounds at guns at J 31 6 1.5. 11.40 a.m Fired 6 rounds at Railway at J 31 C 27	Ref map J 31=16 ch. Heavy 2.8" each 40 am Scott
12th April 1915 HOOGE	12 rounds fired during the day at enemy trenches at J 32 C 29 & J 26 C 32.	Ref map as above Scott
13th April 1915 HOOGE	9.33 a.m At 9.33 a.m 6 Scott 18 rounds fired at guns at J 32 C 27	Ref map as above Scott
14th April 1915 HOOGE	5.10 p.m at 5-10 p.m fired 6 rounds at guns at P 1 a 0 10 & J 32 d 48. Lieut C.E. RYAN proceeded to R.F.C. GHQ for a course of aeroplane observation.	Ref map as above Scott

Army Form C. 2118.

WAR DIARY
or
INTELLIGENCE SUMMARY. Scott

(Erase heading not required.)

Hour, Date, Place	Summary of Events and Information	Remarks and references to Appendices
15th April 1915 HOOGE	3.20 p.m. At 3.20 p.m. started to register 2 targets with aeroplane observation. Registration not completed as it was too misty for observer to identify. 3.50 p.m. At 3.50 p.m. fired 4 rounds at support trenches in Battery zone.	Scott
16th April 1915 HOOGE	6.25 a.m. At 6.25 am registered three gun target at P12.0.10 with aeroplane observation. 14 rounds. Ref map BELGIUM Sheet 28 Scale 1/40,000 3.15 p.m. fired at J.31.0.1.6 and J.31.0.1.6 Also fired 12 rounds at 3 gun targets at J.33.a.0.0 & J.33.c.2.5.	Scott
17th April 1915 HOOGE	11.30 a.m. At 11.30 am 5 rounds were fired at Enfiladed trenches in left of battery zone. At 7 p.m. V Division attacked at Hill 60 and German trenches. Battery stood by ready to open but did not open fire.	Scott

Army Form C. 2118.

WAR DIARY
or
INTELLIGENCE SUMMARY.
(Erase heading not required.)

Instructions regarding War Diaries and Intelligence Summaries are contained in F. S. Regs., Part II and the Staff Manual respectively. Title pages will be prepared in manuscript.

Hour, Date, Place	Summary of Events and Information	Remarks and references to Appendices
18th April 1915 4.00 G.E.	Fired at various times during 1st & 2nd day of the gun at P.1.a.8.10, T.7.c.4.8, T.31.c.16, T.31.d.47, also at wood running N.E. from Railway to point 1.36.a.8.4 and at barn roads at T.36.3.2. & road junction at T.16.0.21. Fired at H guns at T.31.C.97 wide aeroplane observation but stopped was not registered. Total rounds fired during day 87.	Ref. map BELGIUM Sheet 28 Scale /40,000 E.A.
19 April 1915 4.00 G.E.	Fired at various times throughout the day at guns at T.22.d.6.1, T.26.C.4.2, T.31.d.47, also at wood running NE from Railway to point 1.36.a.8.4 and at cross roads at 12.35 pm 1.36.B.3.2. & road junction at 1.36.B.2.1. at 12.55 pm to wooks fired at enemy's stationary station at 1.36.B.8.9. Gun at T.31.d.47 registered by aeroplane. Total rounds fired during day 46. Lieut L. ARKWRIGHT attached from 20th 13rd Cumbr.n Bn. Col.	Ref. map as above E.A.

WAR DIARY or INTELLIGENCE SUMMARY.

Army Form C. 2118.

296

Hour, Date, Place	Summary of Events and Information	Remarks and references to Appendices
20th April 1915 HOOGE 4.00 GE	Fired during the day at guns at T 32 d 4.8, T 31 d 47, 1 36 d 28, ? G 9.5, 1.36 d 32, T 32 d 5.1. Total number of rounds fired during the day 104.	Ref. map BELGIUM Sheet 28 Scale 1/40,000 SB
21st April 1915 HOOGE 10.15 a.m 5.30 p.m	Fired continuously from 10.15 a.m till 5.30 p.m at guns at T 26 d 78, T 36 A 38 × T 36 d 32. 8 rounds of free shrapnel fired from 6 rounds to 10 at intervals at each target. Registered two targets viz T 21 d 52 × T 36 d 32 with aeroplane. At 7.10 p.m fired 4 rounds of enfilading shrapnel — two of 7 of trench R 15. Total number of rounds fired during the day 256.	Ref. map as above SB
22nd April 1915 HOOGE N.00 E 1.15 p.m	Fired at working party in front of trench R.15. 10 rounds at 1.15 p.m × 6 rounds at 4.36 p.m. 9 in the evening was ordered to turn gun round to face N × taken to cover the YPRES-MENIN Rd from the bend in J 13 B to the East. Did not fire in either of these directions.	SB

297

WAR DIARY or **INTELLIGENCE SUMMARY.** Est

Army Form C. 2118.

Hour, Date, Place	Summary of Events and Information	Remarks and references to Appendices
23rd April 1915. HOOGE	1.15 a.m at 1.15 a.m received S.O.S.R signal & fired 9 rounds 3.30 a.m. 3.30 a.m Battery Sane. opened fire again & fired 9 rounds and fired 20 rounds by Rd. same target	Est
24 April 1915. HOOGE	11.50 a.m Between 11.50 a.m & 12.22 p.m fired 12 rounds at each 12.22 p.m of the targets at I.36.d.3.2, I.36.d.2.8, I.36.d.7.8 1.31 p.m from 1.31 p.m to 1.40 p.m fired 19 rounds at Battery 1.40 p.m Sane. 2.37 p.m. At 2.37 p.m received guns and opened fire 3.30 p.m at ST JULIEN. At 3.30 p.m Swept a ranked Square C12D. 3.55 p.m C12D & D7A At 3.55 p.m swept & ranked same C12D. Two Germans wounded — One evening while ploughing remainder	Ref map BELGIUM Sheet 28 Scale 1/40,000 Est
25th April 1915. HOOGE	4.40 a.m At 4.40 a.m opened fire on Wood in C.1 x 11 at 5.21 a.m 5.21 a.m turned to N edge of wood at 8.28 a.m turned on to 6.28 a.m run edge At 8.41 turned on to far edge at 9.15 a.m 8.41 a.m turned on to near edge Stopped firing at 9.58 a.m 9.15 a.m At 10.15 a.m opened fire on village from D7 C.10 9.58 a.m to D7D.10.9 10.15 a.m Stopped firing at 1.18 p.m 1.18 p.m (continued over)	Ref map as above

Army Form C. 2118.

WAR DIARY
or
INTELLIGENCE SUMMARY.

(Erase heading not required.)

Hour, Date, Place	Summary of Events and Information	Remarks and references to Appendices
25th April 1915 HOOGE (continued). 2.4 p.m 5.0 p.m 6.03 p.m 7.0 p.m	At 2.4 p.m shelled line on line C12 a 6.2 to C12 B 10.2. At 5.0 p.m switched to line C12 c 6.8 to C12 d 10.8. Stopped firing at 6.03 p.m. At 7.0 p.m opened fire on line C12 c and fired S of 2 in C12 to S.W. of 1 in C12. Ceased firing at a slow rate during the night. One gun was wounded by hostile shrapnel whilst in action over the battery. Ammun. expended between the hours of 2.3 – 24 and 12 noon 25 – 107 rounds.	Ref. map BELGIUM. Sheet 28 Scale 1/40,000. Self
26th April 1915 HOOGE 7.33 a.m 10 a.m 11 a.m 4.20 p.m 5.30 p.m 7.30 p.m	At 7.33 a.m stopped firing. At 10 a.m searched & swept the ground in front of Battery from line D7 c 0.8 to D7 d 4.8. At 11 a.m switched range down to Chateau along 400x further South. At 4.20 p.m turned on the rear running S.S.W to N.N.E. through C 6 c. At 5.30 p.m turned to North of target to C 10.11. At 7.30 p.m turned to South edge of Square D 8 d. Continued firing at a slow rate until dusk. Target Germany's in the area. Ammunition expended in 12 hours in the day 24 hours 315.	Ref. map as above Self

Army Form C. 2118.

WAR DIARY
or
INTELLIGENCE SUMMARY.
(Erase heading not required.)

Instructions regarding War Diaries and Intelligence Summaries are contained in F.S. Regs., Part II and the Staff Manual respectively. Title pages will be prepared in manuscript.

Hour, Date, Place	Summary of Events and Information	Remarks and references to Appendices
27 April 1915 HOOGE	1.30 am at 12.30 am turned on to triangle of roads in Noon C12, at 11.0 am turned on to line D7 C10.0 to 1.30 pm D7a 10.2. at 12.30 pm turned on to roads from C12 C4.4 to C6 C 9.5 & from C12 d 10.5 to C6 c 9.5. 4.30 pm at 4.30 pm turned on to North edge of wood 10.45 pm at C10 c 11. at 10.45 pm turned on to road from C12 c 4.4 to C6 c 9.5. Continued firing on the targets at a slow rate during the night. at 12 noon ammunition expended with end of 24 hours 226.	Ref. map BELGIUM. Sheet 28 Scale 1/40,000 SC/
28 April 1915 HOOGE	1.0 pm at 1.0 pm turned one gun onto farm at C16 a 6.7 4.0 pm at 4.0 pm turned on to farm in C12. 4.30 pm at 4.30 pm Lieut C.E. RYAN returned from leave. Aeroplane observation of G.H.Q. Battery continued to fire at a slow rate throughout the night. At 12 noon ammunition expended with end day 24 hours 237.	Ref. map as above SC/

(73989) W4141—463. 400,000. 9/14. H.&J.Ltd. Forms/C. 2118/10.

WAR DIARY
or
INTELLIGENCE SUMMARY.

(Erase heading not required.)

Army Form C. 2118.

Hour, Date, Place	Summary of Events and Information	Remarks and references to Appendices
29 April 1915 12 noon HOOGE 12.55 p.m. 4.0 p.m. 4.25 p.m. 6.5 p.m. 7.0 p.m. 7.40 p.m. 11.45 p.m.	A9 12 noon ammunition expended with A9 E.9 Rof mg 380. A9 12.55 p.m. stopped firing. A9 4.0 p.m. opened fire on battery A9 C11c 2.5". Stopped firing A9 4.25 p.m. A9 6.35 p.m. fired 12 rounds A9 round in C11d. A9 7.0 p.m. cancelled & except 2 rounds in Square C11d. A9 7.40 p.m. fired A9 the rate of 5 rounds an hour a wagon in C12 and also at the rate of 10 rounds an hour a Square C11d. A9 11.45 p.m. Stopped firing on square C11d & continued a round in C12 at the rate of 10 rounds an hour.	Ref map BELGIUM Sheet 28 Scale 1/40,000 Sgd
30 April 1915 9.30 a.m. HOOGE 11.0 p.m.	A9 9.30 a.m. A9 9 m ran stopped firing. A9 12 noon ammunition Ref map as above expenditure in the last 24 hours 196. Wagon lines moved from 1.9.0.39 to Ind. Lines 28 YPRES A.15.b.1.5. A9 11.0 p.m. 1 Officer and 3 gunners and 1 driver wounded by shell fire in Wagon lines.	Ref map as above Sgd

121/5706

27th Division.

67th Battery R.F.A.

Journal 1 — 31.5.15.

a 2
a 56

CONFIDENTIAL

WAR DIARY

of

67ᵗʰ BATTERY ROYAL FIELD ARTILLERY

From 1-5-15   To 31-5-15

(VOLUME VI)

Army Form C. 2118.

WAR DIARY
or
INTELLIGENCE SUMMARY.
(Erase heading not required.)

Instructions regarding War Diaries and Intelligence Summaries are contained in F. S. Regs., Part II. and the Staff Manual respectively. Title pages will be prepared in manuscript.

Hour, Date, Place	Summary of Events and Information	Remarks and references to Appendices

(73989) W4141—463. 400,000. 9/14. H.&J.Ltd. Forms/C. 2118/10.

302

Army Form C. 2118.

WAR DIARY
or
INTELLIGENCE SUMMARY.

(Erase heading not required.)

Hour, Date, Place	Summary of Events and Information	Remarks and references to Appendices
1st May 1915 HOOGE	7am at 7am opened fire on woods in front of C12. 7.11am stopped firing. At 9.45 am registered target Sheet 28 Scale 1/40,000 Ref map BELGIUM 9.45am at C10d.17 & C16a.17 & C16a.7.8. At 2.30 pm opened fire 2.30pm at a rapid rate on the C16a.0.8 & C16a.2.8, C4 3.30pm turned to H1cc.27 & C18.8.9. At 3.30pm 3.45pm turned on the Battery at C11c.2.8 at a rate of 12 4.5pm rounds on lines at 4.5pm. Fire C16a.0.8 to C16a.2.8 and continued rapid fire at 12 at Battn trying fire to the wood on line. At 12 noon ammunition exhausted. At 12 noon 29 to June 17. At 7pm stopped firing. The Battery was heavily shelled with high explosive shell from 7 p.m till 8.30 p.m. Total casualties 1 Bombardier slightly wounded.	

WAR DIARY
or
INTELLIGENCE SUMMARY.

(Erase heading not required.)

Army Form C. 2118.

Hour, Date, Place	Summary of Events and Information	Remarks and references to Appendices
2nd May 1915 HOOGE 5.15 p.m. 6.45 p.m.	At noon ammunition expended in last 24 hours 182. At 5.15 p.m. opened fire on wood in C10.a.11 at battery fire 20 seconds. At 6.45 p.m. stopped firing. During this time a few shell were fired by the battery. There were no casualties. In the ways line 2 drivers were wounded and at the forward observing Station 2 gunners were partially asphyxiated by poisonous gases from hostile shells & bombs and admitted to hospital.	Ref. map of BELGIUM Sheet 28 Scale 1/40,000 EW
3rd May 1915 HOOGE 1.30 a.m. 4. a.m.	1.30 a.m. At 1.30 a.m. Battery evacuated its position and marched via YPRES to point H.16.a.4.6 about ¾ mile S.W of VLAMERTINGHE. Arrived at 4 a.m. Horses & vehicles along hedges in field, men some in a barn remainder in bivouacs. There were no casualties on the march. At noon ammunition expended in last 24 hours 136 rounds.	Ref map as above EW

Army Form C. 2118.

WAR DIARY
or
INTELLIGENCE SUMMARY. Scott

(Erase heading not required.)

Instructions regarding War Diaries and Intelligence Summaries are contained in F.S. Regs., Part II and the Staff Manual respectively. Title pages will be prepared in manuscript.

Hour, Date, Place	Summary of Events and Information	Remarks and references to Appendices
4 May 1915 VLAMERTINGHE	2/T. L. ARKWRIGHT rejoined Brigade Ammunition Column	Scott
5 May 1915 VLAMERTINGHE	Battery rested.	Scott
6 May 1915 VLAMERTINGHE	During hours of darkness prepared gun position at H 24 B 9.8	Ref map BELGIUM Sheet 28 Scale 1/40,000 Scott
7 May 1915 VLAMERTINGHE	Continued preparing gun position during hours of darkness.	Scott
8 May 1915 VLAMERTINGHE	12 MM In the evening started to prepare gun position at I 20 A 5.0. At 12 midnight Battery was ordered to come into action in position prepared at H 24 B 9.8	Ref map as above Scott

305

Army Form C. 2118.

WAR DIARY
or
INTELLIGENCE SUMMARY. Sect

(Erase heading not required.)

Instructions regarding War Diaries and Intelligence Summaries are contained in F.S. Regs., Part II and the Staff Manual respectively. Title pages will be prepared in manuscript.

Hour, Date, Place	Summary of Events and Information	Remarks and references to Appendices
9th May 1915 KRUISSTRAAT	3 a.m. Battery in action at 3 a.m. A few high explosive 11.30 a.m. shell fell near battery between 11.30 a.m. & 12 noon. 12 noon 2nd Lieut E CHALKER wounded in the head and admitted to hospital. 1 gunner wounded at forward observing station. Battery did not fire during the day.	Sect
10 May 1915 KRUISSTRAAT	5 p.m. Battery fired from 5 p.m. till 8.10 p.m. at enemy at 8.10 p.m. J7D2.2. Extreme range, rate of fire Battery fire 2 minutes.	Ref map BELGIUM Sheet 28 scale 1/40,000 Sect
11 May 1915 KRUISSTRAAT	3 a.m. Commenced firing at 3 a.m. at edge of wood from J7CJ·3 3.45 a.m. to J7B a·7·8. Stopped firing at 3.45 a.m. Fired at same 10.10 a.m. target from 10.10 a.m. till 12.40 p.m. At 12 noon rounds 12.40 p.m. expended in last 24 hours 182. Received orders not to fire unless ordered to so as not to draw fire on the batteries of the 1st Division which were in the vicinity of the battery.	Ref map as above Sect
12 May 1915 KRUISSTRAAT	Battery did not fire. At 12 noon ammunition expenditure for the last 24 hours 22	Sect

WAR DIARY
or
INTELLIGENCE SUMMARY.

(Erase heading not required.)

Army Form C. 2118.

Hour, Date, Place	Summary of Events and Information	Remarks and references to Appendices
13 May 1915 KRUISSTRAAT	2Lieut L. ARKWRIGHT attached to battery from IX Brigade ammunition Column. Battery did not fire.	Sd/-
14 – 19 May 1915 KRUISSTRAAT	Battery in action, but did not fire	Sd/-
20 May 1915 KRUISSTRAAT	Lieut C.E. RYAN posted to No 1 Squadron R.F.C. as artillery aeroplane observer. Lieut N.S. KIDD (SR) posted to Battery. In the evening commenced preparing a position for a section at I.15.D.8.8. One gunner wounded by rifle bullet. Battery did not fire.	Ref map "BELGIUM" Sheet 28 Scale 1/40,000 Sd/-
21 May 1915 KRUISSTRAAT	LIEUT H.J. VINCENT (21st Division) attached to the battery for instruction. In the evening continued preparing position for advanced section. Battery did not fire.	Sd/-

Army Form C. 2118.

WAR DIARY
or
INTELLIGENCE SUMMARY. ECH/

(Erase heading not required.)

Hour, Date, Place	Summary of Events and Information	Remarks and references to Appendices
22 May 1915 KRUISTRAAT 8.30 p.m.	Battery did not fire. at 8.30 p.m Left Section advanced and took up new position at I.15.D.8.6.	Ref. map BELGIUM Sheet 28 Scale 1/40,000. ECH/
23 May 1915 ZILLEBEKE 7.30 a.m. 8.30 a.m. 4.15 p.m.	Advanced Section registered gun between 7.30 a.m & 11. 30 a.m. No rounds fired 11. 30 to 4 p.m at 4.15 p.m 2 rounds were fired by order of the Brigade Major at the zone. An observing Station in the first line of trenches at I.24.D.8.3.1	Ref map as above. ECH/
24 May 1915 ZILLEBEKE 3.10 a.m. 6.30 a.m.	By use of poisonous gases, enemy drove back our front line for a long way between the Railway and MENIN ROAD. at 3.10 a.m opened fire on zone; communication between Battery and observing Station was broken & Shell fire. Firing was stopped at 6.30 a.m when it was ascertained that all had been quiet in front of our zone. No. of rounds fired 79	Ref map as above. ECH/

Army Form C. 2118.

WAR DIARY
or
INTELLIGENCE SUMMARY.
(Erase heading not required.)

Instructions regarding War Diaries and Intelligence Summaries are contained in F.S. Regs., Part II and the Staff Manual respectively. Title pages will be prepared in manuscript.

Hour, Date, Place		Summary of Events and Information	Remarks and references to Appendices
25th May 1915 ZILLEBEKE	10 p.m.	Battery did not fire. At 10 p.m. received orders to be ready to move as we were to be relieved next night.	
26th May 1915 ZILLEBEKE	3 a.m.	Returned Battery vacated its position at 3 a.m. and joined rest of Battery at Wagon lines. Advanced Section was relieved by a Section of 3rd NORTHUMBRIAN Brigade. The position of the other Section was left unoccupied.	Ref map BELGIUM HAZEBROUCK 5a Scale 1/100,000
	8 a.m.	At 8 a.m. Brigade moved off and marched to bivouac near NIEPPE via OUDERDOM - LOCRE - BAILLEUL.	
	7.15 p.m. 9.0 p.m.	At 7.15 p.m. the Battery moved off and at 9 p.m. took new position from 21st Battery R.F.A. at I.2.A.7.3. Wagon lines situated at C.20.B.9.2. Battery 3rd Gun from LES 4 HALLOTS "B" Series Sheet 36 N.W. FME (C.23.D.3.7) to X Roads at BROWE RUE (I.5.B.6.8) Battery under orders of O.C. 24th Brigade R.F.A. for tactical purposes.	Ref map BELGIUM & FRANCE Scale 1/20,000
27th May 1915 ARMENTIÈRES	11.30 a.m.	At 11.30 a.m. Battery fired 12 rounds for registration purposes.	

WAR DIARY or INTELLIGENCE SUMMARY.

Army Form C. 2118.

Hour, Date, Place	Summary of Events and Information	Remarks and references to Appendices
28th May 1915 ARMENTIERES. 8.45 a.m. 11.45 a.m.	At 8.45 a.m 8 rounds were fired at the trenches by order of O.C. 24th Brigade as retaliation to fire by German Batteries. At 11.45 a.m 4 more rounds were fired at trenches for registration purposes	Sgd
29th May 1915 ARMENTIERES 11.30 a.m 12.5 p.m	Fired 8 rounds at the trenches and farm C30A5&2 between 11.30 a.m and 12.5 p.m	Sgd
30th May 1915 ARMENTIERES 11.30 a.m 12.5 p.m	Fired 6 rounds at trenches between 11.45 & 12.5 p.m	Sgd
31st May 1915 ARMENTIERES	Battery did not fire	Sgd

2nd Division

67th Battery: R+H.

Vol VII 1 — 30.6.15.

CONFIDENTIAL.

War Diary

of

67th Battery Royal Field Artillery

From 1-6-15.

To 30.6.15

(Volume VII.)

Army Form C. 2118.

WAR DIARY
or
INTELLIGENCE SUMMARY.
(Erase heading not required.)

Instructions regarding War Diaries and Intelligence Summaries are contained in F.S. Regs., Part II and the Staff Manual respectively. Title pages will be prepared in manuscript.

Hour, Date, Place	Summary of Events and Information	Remarks and references to Appendices

WAR DIARY
or
INTELLIGENCE SUMMARY.

Army Form C. 2118.

Instructions regarding War Diaries and Intelligence Summaries are contained in F.S. Regs., Part II and the Staff Manual respectively. Title pages will be prepared in manuscript.

(Erase heading not required.)

Hour, Date, Place	Summary of Events and Information	Remarks and references to Appendices
1st June 1915 ARMENTIERES. 9.45 p.m	2Lieut E.N. KENT-LEMON R.F.A. joined Battery. 29 wgn battery moved position, which was occupied by 11th Battery. Right section went into action in prepared position at C.27.D.1.5. Left section guns and vehicles also went into detachments common dugouts & shelters one gun at I.2.B.79 and the other at C.26.D.5.1.	1/ map BELGIUM & FRANCE "B" area. Sheet 36 N.W. Scale 1/20,000 EC.H
2nd June 1915 ARMENTIERES. 9 p.m	Lieut M.T. VINCENT left for ENGLAND to rejoin 21st Division as I.O. n Left Section came into action in position prepared last night. Battery Head quarters established with Left Section. Wgn Lines remain in original position at C.2.B.9.2.	R/ map as above EC.H
3rd June 1915 ARMENTIERES	Battery Zero from derivity line between C.25.B and D. At 11 s.m A was sent to C.29.B.O.7. Battery registered zero between 4.50 p.m & 5.15 p.m, 12 u 2 p.m, and 12.25 p.m & 1.5 p.m. Between 4.50 p.m & 5.15 p.m. Number of rounds fired 26.	EC.H

312

Army Form C. 2118.

WAR DIARY
or
INTELLIGENCE SUMMARY. Ec/s

(Erase heading not required.)

Instructions regarding War Diaries and Intelligence Summaries are contained in F.S. Regs., Part II and the Staff Manual respectively. Title pages will be prepared in manuscript.

Hour, Date, Place	Summary of Events and Information	Remarks and references to Appendices
4th June 1915 ARMENTIERES	Battery did not fire	Ec/s
5th June 1915 ARMENTIERES	9am Fired 4 rounds at farm at C.23.D.81. at 9 a.m. as 8pm fired 4 rounds of shrapnel on Battery fire retaliation to hostile shelling. Send L. ARKWRIGHT attached to Brigade Ammn from Clivedon.	Ref map of BELGIUM & FRANCE 1/8 One sheet 36NW Scale 1/2cm. Ec/s Ec/s
6th June 1915 ARMENTIERES	Noon Registered 6th N 3c at a 3.30 pm repeated same at 3.30pm C.29.C.79 and J.5.B.48 and Vincler ranges which were taken from C.29.C.+J.5.B.20. Ranks of rents 8pm enfiladed 16. at 8pm took our positions from observing station, Dutchy at IN4C-9 4.15pm at 4.15pm fired 8 rounds at farm at J.5.B.48 and 4.10pm registering trenches to be coming school playing 7 observations from Right Bastion at J.2.B.68.	Ref. map as above Ec/s Ec/s Ref. map as above Ec/s
8th June 1915 ARMENTIERES	N.30.A at 11.30am & at 11.30pm regis. tried houses & wood at Ref. J.5.B. x C.30.D.9.1 in the evening ranks of registering observations for Right Bastion.	Ref. map as above Ec/s

WAR DIARY
or
INTELLIGENCE SUMMARY.

Army Form C. 2118.

Hour, Date, Place	Summary of Events and Information	Remarks and references to Appendices
9 June 1915 ARMENTIERES	11.15pm At 12.15 fired 12 rounds to register German trench at trench at C.29.d.4.2. At 9.20 p.m Right Section 9.20pm came into action in new position	Ref. map BELGIUM-FRANCE 1:10,000 sheet 26 NW Edit. Sals 5/20,000 ECW
10 June 1915 ARMENTIERES	9.10 pm At 9.10 p.m registered German front line trenches NE of L'EPINETTE. Battery of 3 guns found 12	Ref. map as above ECW
11 June 1915 ARMENTIERES	2.15 AM At 2.15 am 1 round was fired at 2am at C.10.d.9.6. Owing to mist observation was very difficult so no more were fired. At 6 p.m German battery observed firing with full gun, it was not found by Observer.	Ref. map as above ECW
12 June 1915 ARMENTIERES	9.30 am Fired 4 rounds at trenches NE of L'EPINETTE in retaliation to hostile shelling. At 5.20 p.m re-registered trenches near L'EPINETTE. Number of shells fired 7.	Ref. map as above ECW

314

Army Form C. 2118.

WAR DIARY
or
INTELLIGENCE SUMMARY. Sect

(Erase heading not required.)

Instructions regarding War Diaries and Intelligence Summaries are contained in F. S. Regs., Part II. and the Staff Manual respectively. Title pages will be prepared in manuscript.

Hour, Date, Place	Summary of Events and Information	Remarks and references to Appendices
13th June 1915 ARMENTIERES.	Battery did not fire.	Sect
14 June 1915 ARMENTIERES. 10.15 a.m.	at 10.15 a.m. fired 12 rounds at trenches N.E. of LEPINETTE in retaliation to hostile shelling.	Ref. map BELGIUM & FRANCE Sect
15 June 1915 ARMENTIERES. 5.48 p.m.	Fired 4 rounds at trenches N.E. of LEPINETTE at 5.48 p.m.	Ref. map as above. Sect.
16 June 1915 ARMENTIERES 11.10 a.m.	Registered farm at I.6.A.5.2 & I.6.A.5.2 at 11.10 a.m. Fired 4 rounds & got 3 direct hits. At 7.30 p.m. fired 2 rounds at BRUNE RUE = farm I.6.A.4.5.	Ref. map as above. Sect
17 June 1915 ARMENTIERES. 11.10 a.m.	Fired 7 & 4 rounds at BRUNE RUE = farm I.6.A.4.5 & I.6.A.5.2. at 11.10 a.m. in retaliation to hostile shelling.	Ref. map as above. Sect

(73989) W4141—463. 400,000. 9/14. H.&J.,Ltd. Forms/C. 2118/10.

315

Army Form C. 2118.

WAR DIARY
or
INTELLIGENCE SUMMARY. ECA

(Erase heading not required.)

Instructions regarding War Diaries and Intelligence Summaries are contained in F.S. Regs., Part II and the Staff Manual respectively. Title pages will be prepared in manuscript.

Hour, Date, Place	Summary of Events and Information	Remarks and references to Appendices
18th June 1915 ARMENTIERES	8 a.m. A9 8 a.m. fired 12 rounds at BRUNE RUE, farms at I6A1's × I6A'v's and trenches N.E. of L'EPINETTE, in retaliation to hostile shelling. At 9.20 a.m. Germans fired 8 a.m. field gun shell at observing station. 1 Gunner wounded.	Ref. map BELGIUM & FRANCE "B" series Sheet 36 N.W. Scale 1/20,000. ECA
19th June 1915 ARMENTIERES	9.45 a.m. A9 9.45 a.m. fired 4 rounds at trenches N.E. of L'EPINETTE, BRUNE RUE & farm at I6A1's.	Ref. map as above. ECA
20th June 1915 ARMENTIERES	Battery did not fire.	ECA
21st June 1915 ARMENTIERES	9.30 a.m. A9 9.30 a.m. Germans fired about 30 shells at Observing Station. No particular damage done. A9 5.30 p.m. till 6.30 p.m. fired 20 rounds at trenches at L'EPINETTE and BRUNE RUE and at farm I6A1's: in retaliation to hostile shelli. 2.30 p.m. A9 2.30 p.m. 2/Lieut CUNNINGHAM departed for ENGLAND on 6 days leave.	Ref. map as above. ECA

(73989) W+4141—463. 400,000. 9/14. H.&J. Ltd. Forms/C. 2118/10.

WAR DIARY
or
INTELLIGENCE SUMMARY. ECA

(Erase heading not required.)

Army Form C. 2118.

Hour, Date, Place	Summary of Events and Information	Remarks and references to Appendices
22nd June 1915 ARMENTIERES	10.15 a.m. At 10.15 a.m. 4 rounds were fired at trenches at LEPINETTE & BRUNE RUE and at farm I6A1.5. 4.10 p.m. At 4.10 p.m. registered from at C23D9.0, 6 rounds fired. At 6.30 p.m. 2 rounds were fired at farm I6A1.5.	Ref. map BELGIUM & FRANCE NW "B" Series Sheet 36 NW Scale 1/20,000. ECA
23rd June 1915 ARMENTIERES.	2.45 p.m. 4 rounds were fired at 2.45 p.m. 4 more at 4.40 p.m. 4.40 p.m. at trenches N.E. of LEPINETTE and farm I6A1.5.	Ref map as above. ECA
24th June 1915 ARMENTIERES.	5.30 p.m. At 5.30 p.m. registered Cross Roads at J1C88. 4 6.30 p.m. rounds fired. At 6.30 p.m. fired 6 rounds at Cross Roads at J1cB10.9.	Ref. map as above ECA
25th June 1915 ARMENTIERES.	Battery did not fire.	ECA
26th June 1915 ARMENTIERES	11.30 a.m. Bt at 11.30 a.m. fired 8 rounds to register Cross Roads 5.40 p.m. at LA FRESNELLE (I12B10.9). At 5.40 p.m. registered German front line trenches at J1-C8.2, I 11A7.7 8 rounds fired.	Ref. map as above. ECA

317

Army Form C. 2118.

WAR DIARY
or
INTELLIGENCE SUMMARY.

(Erase heading not required.)

Hour, Date, Place		Summary of Events and Information	Remarks and references to Appendices
27th June 1915 ARMENTIERES	4.30 p.m. 6.10 p.m.	At 4.30 p.m. fired 8 rounds to register L'AVENTURE from (C.30.A.v.2). At 6.10 p.m. fired 4 rounds at Cross roads of LA FRESNELLE and trenches East of LEPINETTE	Ref. map. BELGIUM & FRANCE "B" Series Sheet 36 N.W. ECB
28th June 1915 ARMENTIERES	5.30 p.m.	Lieut. CUNNINGHAM returned from leave. At 5.30 p.m. fired 6 rounds at Cross Roads at LA FRESNELLE and J.1.D.4.4.	Ref. map as above ECB
29th June 1915 ARMENTIERES	11.57 a.m. 1.5 p.m.	At 11.57 a.m. fired 6 rounds at Cross Roads at LA FRESNELLE and J.1.D.4.4. At 1.5 p.m. fired 3 rounds at trenches East of LEPINETTE	Ref. map as above ECB
30th June 1915 ARMENTIERES		Battery did not fire.	ECB

(73959) W4141—463. 400,000. 9/14. H.&J.Ltd. Forms/C. 2118/10.

29th Division.

67th Battery. R.F.A.

Vol VIII

1 - 31.7.15

CONFIDENTIAL.

WAR DIARY

OF

67TH BATTERY ROYAL FIELD ARTILLERY

FROM 1-7-15 TO

(VOL: VIII)

Army Form C. 2118.

WAR DIARY
or
INTELLIGENCE SUMMARY.
(Erase heading not required.)

Instructions regarding War Diaries and Intelligence Summaries are contained in F. S. Regs., Part II. and the Staff Manual respectively. Title pages will be prepared in manuscript.

Hour, Date, Place	Summary of Events and Information	Remarks and references to Appendices

(9 29 6)   W 4141—463   100,000   9/14   H W V   Forms/C. 2118/10

Army Form C. 2118.

WAR DIARY
or
INTELLIGENCE SUMMARY.

(Erase heading not required.)

Instructions regarding War Diaries and Intelligence Summaries are contained in F.S. Regs., Part II. and the Staff Manual respectively. Title pages will be prepared in manuscript.

Hour, Date, Place	Summary of Events and Information	Remarks and references to Appendices
1st July 1915 ARMENTIERES	Battery did not fire.	Ect
2nd July 1915 ARMENTIERES 4.40 p.m.	Wagon lines moved to point C.5.B.0.4. At 4.40 p.m. 8 rounds fired at Farms C.29.C.9.5 and C.29.C.7.8	Ref. map. BELGIUM & FRANCE 1" Series Sheet 36 NW. Ect
3rd July 1915 ARMENTIERES 4.45 p.m.	Fired 12 rounds at Farms C.29.C.9.5 x C.29.C.7.8 at 4.45 p.m.	Ref. map as above. Ect
4th July 1915 ARMENTIERES 3.0 p.m.	Fired 12 rounds at Farm C.29.C.7.8 at 3.0 p.m.	Ref. map as above. Ect
5th July 1915 ARMENTIERES 3.30 p.m.	Observing Station changed to corner house at I.2.B.7.9. Old observing Station at Distillery I.4.A.4.9 being untenable owing to frequent shelling. At 3.30 p.m. fired 12 rounds at Farm C.29.C.7.8.	Ref. map as above. Ect

Army Form C. 2118.

WAR DIARY
or
INTELLIGENCE SUMMARY. ECB

(Erase heading not required.)

Instructions regarding War Diaries and Intelligence Summaries are contained in F.S. Regs., Part II. and the Staff Manual respectively. Title pages will be prepared in manuscript.

Hour, Date, Place	Summary of Events and Information	Remarks and references to Appendices
6th July 1915 ARMENTIERES	4.10 pm reported fired at I.N.C.6.S. 7 Rounds fired. Observation by officer of 148th Battery. 8.15 pm fired 13 Rounds at Minenwerfer at BRUNE RUE Farm, which had been firing at our trenches at LEPINETTE.	Ref of BELGIUM & FRANCE B. Series Sheet 36 N.W. ECB
7th July 1915 ARMENTIERES	Battery did not fire.	ECB
8th July 1915 ARMENTIERES	2/Lieut KYDD left for ENGLAND for 8 days leave. Battery did not fire.	ECB
9 to 12 July 1915 ARMENTIERES	Battery did not fire.	ECB
13 July 1915 ARMENTIERES	At 1.15 pm fired 2 rounds at PERENCHIES in retaliation to hostile shelling. At 3.30 pm registered from T.6.A.6.0, 8 rounds fired.	ECB

Army Form C. 2118.

WAR DIARY
or
INTELLIGENCE SUMMARY. Ech

(Erase heading not required.)

Instructions regarding War Diaries and Intelligence Summaries are contained in F.S. Regs., Part II. and the Staff Manual respectively. Title pages will be prepared in manuscript.

Hour, Date, Place		Summary of Events and Information	Remarks and references to Appendices
14 July 1915 ARMENTIERES	11.10 a.m	at 11.10 a.m 2 rounds were fired at PERENCHIES in retaliation.	Ref. map BELGIUM & FRANCE 1" series. Sheet 36 N.W
			Ech
			Ech
15 July 1915 ARMENTIERES		Battery did not fire	Ech
16 July 1915 ARMENTIERES		Battery did not fire	Ech
17 July 1915 ARMENTIERES	2.30 a.m	at 2.30 a.m Left Ech Right Section withdrew from action and retired to Wagon Lines. Position occupied by a Battery of 2nd Northumbrian Brigade. at 9.30 p.m Left Ech Right Section went into action in new position at H.29.b.6	Ref. map as above. Ech
	9.30 p.m		
18 July 1915 ARMENTIERES	2.30 a.m	at 2.30 a.m Right Section relieved and retired to Wagon Lines. at 2 p.m Wagon Lines were moved to H.8.c.9.4. at 9.30 p.m Right Section went into action in new position. Capt HALL. Lieut. turn ENGLAND for 9 days leave. Lieut. ARKWRIGHT attached to Battery.	Ref. map as above Ech
	2 p.m		

Army Form C. 2118.

WAR DIARY
or
INTELLIGENCE SUMMARY. E.W.
(Erase heading not required.)

Instructions regarding War Diaries and Intelligence Summaries are contained in F.S. Regs., Part II. and the Staff Manual respectively. Title pages will be prepared in manuscript.

Hour, Date, Place		Summary of Events and Information	Remarks and references to Appendices
19ᵗʰ July 1915 BOIS GRENIER	6 pm	On 6 pm registered from HOUSSAIN (O.2.A.37). 12 rounds fired.	Ref. map FRANCE 1". Carmin Sheet 36 S.W. E.W.
20ᵗʰ & 21ˢᵗ July 1915 BOIS GRENIER		Battery did not fire.	E.W.
22ⁿᵈ July 1915 BOIS GRENIER	3.30 pm 4.5 pm 4.15 pm	at 3.30 pm registered GRAND MAISNIL Farm (I.33.D.0.3). 4 rounds fired. at 4.5 pm fired 4 rounds at own trench O.9.C.20 at 4.15 pm fired 4 rounds at LA MOTTE HOUSSAIN Farm.	Ref. map as above & Sheet 36 N.W. E.W.
23ʳᵈ July 1915 BOIS GRENIER	4.30 pm	Fired 3 salvoes of 4 guns each at 4.30 pm at Communication trenches at I.33.B.9.4, I.32.B.1.2 & I.32.B.9.5.	Ref. map. Sheet 36 N.W. E.W.
24ᵗʰ – 27ᵗʰ July 1915 BOIS GRENIER		Battery did not fire.	E.W.

Army Form C. 2118.

WAR DIARY
or
INTELLIGENCE SUMMARY.

(Erase heading not required.)

Hour, Date, Place	Summary of Events and Information	Remarks and references to Appendices
28th July 1915 Bois GRENIER	Capt HALL rejoined from leave	E.H.
29th July 1915 Bois GRENIER	2 Lieut D.G. CAREY ELWES attached to Battery	E.H.
30th July 1915 Bois GRENIER	Battery did not fire	E.H.
31st July 1915 Bois GRENIER	2 Lieut ARKWRIGHT attached to 148th Battery	E.H.

Instructions regarding War Diaries and Intelligence Summaries are contained in F.S. Regs., Part II. and the Staff Manual respectively. Title pages will be prepared in manuscript.

Army Form C. 2118.

WAR DIARY
or
INTELLIGENCE SUMMARY.
(Erase heading not required.)   APPENDIX I

Place	Date	Hour	Summary of Events and Information	Remarks and references to Appendices
			During the month the following Officers were promoted –

To be Capt:– Lt H.S. Pemberton R.A.M.C. (attached)

To be Lt:– 2/Lt A. Beard 148th Bty R.F.A.
C.R. Jackson "
W. Strachan "
L.F. Thompson 99th " | |

121/6561

a2
a36

37th Division

87th Battery R.F.A.

Vol IX

From 1 - 31. 8. 15

CONFIDENTIAL.

WAR DIARY

OF

67ᵀᴴ BATTERY ROYAL FIELD ARTILLERY

FROM 1-8-15 TO 31-8-15

(VOL IX)

Army Form C. 2118.

WAR DIARY
or
INTELLIGENCE SUMMARY.

(Erase heading not required.)

Instructions regarding War Diaries and Intelligence Summaries are contained in F. S. Regs., Part II. and the Staff Manual respectively. Title pages will be prepared in manuscript.

Hour, Date, Place	Summary of Events and Information	Remarks and references to Appendices

(9 29 6) W 4141—463 100,000 9/14 H W V Forms/C. 2118/10

325

Army Form C. 2118.

WAR DIARY
or
INTELLIGENCE SUMMARY. Ect/-

(Erase heading not required.)

Instructions regarding War Diaries and Intelligence Summaries are contained in F.S. Regs., Part II. and the Staff Manual respectively. Title pages will be prepared in manuscript.

Hour, Date, Place	Summary of Events and Information	Remarks and references to Appendices
1st August 1915 Bois GRENIER	Battery did not fire	Ect/-
2nd August 1915 11.30am Bois GRENIER	Registered house at O.9.D.2.9. fired 12 rounds	Ref. map FRANCE "13" Series sheet 36 S.W. Ect/-
3rd August 1915 Bois GRENIER	Battery did not fire	Ect/-
4th August 1915 3.30pm Bois GRENIER	at 3.30pm registered German front line trenches at I.31.D.4.4 × 18.7. fired 12 rounds	Ref. map FRANCE "13" Series Sheet 36 N.W. Ect/-
5th August 1915 3.0pm Bois GRENIER	at 3.0pm fired 12 rounds at House at O.9.D.2.9 and Farm at I.32.C.9.4	Ect/-
6th August 1915 Bois GRENIER	Battery did not fire	Ect/-
7th August 1915 11.30am 12.10pm Bois GRENIER	at 11.30am registered German trenches at I.32.C.9 and I.32.A.4.1. at 12.10pm registered trenches at I.32.A.6.8. and S.3. 24 rounds fired.	Ect/-

(9 29 6) W 4141—463 100,000 9/14 HWV Forms/C.2118/10

326

Army Form C. 2118.

WAR DIARY
or
INTELLIGENCE SUMMARY.

(Erase heading not required.)

Instructions regarding War Diaries and Intelligence Summaries are contained in F.S. Regs., Part II. and the Staff Manual respectively. Title pages will be prepared in manuscript.

Hour, Date, Place	Summary of Events and Information	Remarks and references to Appendices
8th August 1915 6pm Bois Grenier	At 6.0 p.m. registered lines at BONTEMS. O.10.D.9.3. 12 rounds fired.	Ref map FRANCE 1/10000 Sheet 36 S.W.
9th August 1915 2.45pm Bois Grenier	Fired 12 rounds at BONTEMS	Ect
10th August 1915 Bois Grenier	Artillery did not fire	Ect
11th August 1915 3.45pm Bois Grenier	Fired 12 rounds at BONTEMS, at 6.4 p.m. fired 6.45 pm 12 rounds at railway embankment at O.4.C.9.3	Ect
12th August 1915 10.30am Bois Grenier	Fired with aeroplane observation and registered railway crossing at I.34.C.4.1 and road junction at O.4.C.3.1. Fired 8 rounds	Ref map as above and Sheet 36 N.W. Ect
13th August 1915 Bois Grenier	Battery did not fire	Ect
14th August 1915 11am Bois Grenier	At H.S.a.m. fired 8 rounds at wood in O.10.D. Centre a.9.2.15pm fired 8 rounds at house O.9.D.1.9	Ref map Sheet 36 S.W. Ect

Army Form C. 2118.

WAR DIARY
or
INTELLIGENCE SUMMARY. ECB

(Erase heading not required.)

Instructions regarding War Diaries and Intelligence Summaries are contained in F.S. Regs., Part II. and the Staff Manual respectively. Title pages will be prepared in manuscript.

Hour, Date, Place	Summary of Events and Information	Remarks and references to Appendices
15 August 1915 BOIS GRENIER	Battery did not fire	ECB
16 August 1915 BOIS GRENIER	Battery did not fire	ECB
17 August 1915 BOIS GRENIER	at 2.40 p.m. registered German front line trenches at I.31.C.6.0 and I.31.D.8.1 and I.31.D.0.2 and 2.3. Fired 20 rounds.	Ref map FRANCE 1/3arris sheet 36 N.W. ECB
18 August 1915 BOIS GRENIER	Battery zone changed to cover trenches 48 × 49. From I.31.C.4.7 to I.31.D.1.5. New observing station at I.31.A.5.7.	ECB
19 August 1915 BOIS GRENIER	Battery did not fire	ECB
20 August 1915 BOIS GRENIER	9 am C.Y. s.p. - fired with aeroplane observation & registered LES BAS CHAMPS Farm O.9.B.8.7 and House at O.10.D.9.6. Fired 9 rounds.	Ref. m.p. Sheet 36 S.W. ECB

(9 29 6) W 4141—463 100,000 9/14 H W V Forms/C. 2118/10

Army Form C. 2118.

WAR DIARY
or
INTELLIGENCE SUMMARY. *Ecs*
(Erase heading not required.)

Instructions regarding War Diaries and Intelligence Summaries are contained in F.S. Regs., Part II. and the Staff Manual respectively. Title pages will be prepared in manuscript.

Hour, Date, Place		Summary of Events and Information	Remarks and references to Appendices
21st August 1915 Bois GRENIER	6 pm	Tried with aeroplane observation & registered Road junction at 09c47 and THIROUANNE Cross Roads at 015A87. Fired 17 rounds.	Ref. map FRANCE "B" Series Sheet 36 S.W. Ecs
22nd August 1915 Bois GRENIER	3.30 pm 3.45 pm 6 pm	Tried with aeroplane observation and registered LE BAS HAU Cross Roads at O2D16. Fired 9 rounds. at 3.10 pm fired 3 rounds at trees at O1B36. at 6 pm fired 6 rounds at German trenches by request of the Infantry.	Ecs
23rd August 1915 Bois GRENIER	11.20 am	at 11.20 am fired 7 rounds at German Trenches by request of Infantry in retaliation to hostile shelling. At 3 pm fired 1 round with aeroplane observation at House O15B78. Only 1 round fired as it was too misty to observe.	Ref. map as above Ecs
24th August 1915 R.OJ GRENIER		Battery did not fire	Ecs

Army Form C. 2118.

WAR DIARY
or
INTELLIGENCE SUMMARY. E.M

(Erase heading not required.)

Instructions regarding War Diaries and Intelligence Summaries are contained in F.S. Regs., Part II. and the Staff Manual respectively. Title pages will be prepared in manuscript.

Hour, Date, Place	Summary of Events and Information	Remarks and references to Appendices
25th August 1915 BOIS GRENIER	Battery did not fire	ECH
26th August 1915 BOIS GRENIER	Battery did not fire	ECH
27th August 1915 BOIS GRENIER	12 S/M moved to L'HALLOBEAU B25c 4.6. at 12 S/M fired with aeroplane observation following tgts. LES MOULINS DE SORUS FARME O15B7D, CHATEAU DE FLANDRE O15D35 and communication trench I3c CD6. 18 rounds fired	Ref. map BELGIUM-FRANCE 1/3 Series Sheet 36. ECH
28th August 1915 BOIS GRENIER	Commenced preparing a position at H16347. Battery did not fire	Ref. map as above. ECH
29th August 1915 12.45pm BOIS GRENIER	At 12.45pm fired 2 rounds at German front line trench in front of Trench 49	ECH

(9 29 6) W4141—463 100,000 9/14 H W V Forms/C. 2118/10

WAR DIARY
or
INTELLIGENCE SUMMARY. ECH

(Erase heading not required.)

Army Form C. 2118.

Hour, Date, Place	Summary of Events and Information	Remarks and references to Appendices
30th August 1915 Bois GRENIER	Battery attached to 25th Brigade 8th Division for win Enemy purposes. Battery did not fire	ECH
31st August 1915 3.15pm Bois GRENIER 2nd/1st	At 2 N.p.m registered shrine at O.1.D.9.0, 9 rounds fired. At 3.25pm registered House O.1.B.3.6 7 rounds fired.	ECH

121/6983

27th Hussain

by the Butty R.T.A.
Vol X
Sept 15

CONFIDENTIAL.

WAR DIARY

OF

67TH BATTERY ROYAL FIELD ARTILLERY.

From 1-9-15 To _____

Vol X

Army Form C. 2118.

WAR DIARY
or
INTELLIGENCE SUMMARY.
(Erase heading not required.)

Instructions regarding War Diaries and Intelligence Summaries are contained in F.S. Regs., Part II. and the Staff Manual respectively. Title pages will be prepared in manuscript.

Hour, Date, Place	Summary of Events and Information	Remarks and references to Appendices

(73989) W4141—463. 400,000. 9/14. H.&J.Ltd. Forms/C. 2118/10.

352

Army Form C. 2118.

WAR DIARY
or
INTELLIGENCE SUMMARY. E.S.B

(Erase heading not required.)

Army Form C. 2118.

Instructions regarding War Diaries and Intelligence Summaries are contained in F. S. Regs., Part II. and the Staff Manual respectively. Title pages will be prepared in manuscript.

Hour, Date, Place	Summary of Events and Information	Remarks and references to Appendices
1st September 1915. 6.30 pm Bois GRENIER	at 6.20 pm fired 20 rounds at House O2C12.	Ref map BELGIUM and FRANCE "B" Series sheet 9.36. E.S.B
2nd September 1915. 11.30 a.m. Bois GRENIER 2.40pm	at 11.0 a.m registered House L31D90. 10 rounds fired. at 2.40 pm fired 7 rounds at and registered House O2C12.	E.S.B
3rd September 1915. 11.30 a.m. Bois GRENIER	Registered House M31 O18D4 at 11.30 a.m. 10 rounds fired.	E.S.B
4 September 1915. Bois GRENIER	Battery did not fire.	E.S.B
5 September 1915. 4.15pm Bois GRENIER	at 4.15 pm registered house at O2C74. fired 17 rounds.	E.S.B

Army Form C. 2118.

WAR DIARY
or
INTELLIGENCE SUMMARY. Ec/A

(Erase heading not required.)

Instructions regarding War Diaries and Intelligence Summaries are contained in F.S. Regs., Part II. and the Staff Manual respectively. Title pages will be prepared in manuscript.

Hour, Date, Place	Summary of Events and Information	Remarks and references to Appendices
6 September 1915 4.15 p.m. Bois GRENIER	2.9.4.15 p.m. fired 13 rounds at cottage on target registered.	Ref map BELGIUM & FRANCE 2 series sheet 26. Ec/A
7 September 1915 Bois GRENIER	Battery did not open fire.	Ec/A
8 September 1915 4.40 p.m. Bois GRENIER	At 4.40 p.m. registered round at O.2.A.4.4 and aeroplane observation of round fired.	Ec/A
9 September 1915 Bois GRENIER	Battery did not fire.	Ec/A
10 September 1915 Bois GRENIER	Lieut M.D. MOTT, 1 Sergeant, 1 Bombardier, attached for instructional purposes from D Battery 102nd Brigade, 23rd Division. "1 Gunner"	Ec/A
11 September 1915 Bois GRENIER	Battery did not fire.	Ec/A

334

WAR DIARY
or
INTELLIGENCE SUMMARY. S.H

(Erase heading not required.)

Army Form C. 2118.

Hour, Date, Place	Summary of Events and Information	Remarks and references to Appendices
12th September 1915 BOIS GRENIER	Lieut C.E. RYAN struck off strength of Battery with effect from 18.8.15. 2nd Lieut N.S. KYDD struck off strength of Battery on orders to return to the front with effect from 9.9.15. 7.45 pm Then left section relieved at 7.45 pm by a section of the 1st Battery and withdrew to wagon lines.	S.H
13th September 1915 12.30 pm BOIS GRENIER	At 12.30 pm left section marched via STEENWERCK and LE VERRIER to billets at OUSTERSTEEN. Road 1/4 mile North of OUSTERSTEEN. Arrived 3.30 pm. horses in field, men in barns.	Ref. map BELGIUM HAZEBROUCK S-A Scale 1/100,000 S.H
14th September 1915 8.15 pm BOIS GRENIER	Right section relieved at 8.15 pm by a section of 1st Battery R.F.A. & withdrew to wagon lines. Lieut M.D. MOTT, 1 Sergeant, 1 Bombardier & 1 Driver returned to their own unit. "D" Battery 103rd Brigade. Battery Sergeant Major A. BAKER promoted to Commissioned rank and transferred to Base.	S.H
14th September 1915 S.H		

335

Army Form C. 2118.

WAR DIARY
or
INTELLIGENCE SUMMARY. Ec.B

(Erase heading not required.)

Instructions regarding War Diaries and Intelligence Summaries are contained in F.S. Regs., Part II and the Staff Manual respectively. Title pages will be prepared in manuscript.

Hour, Date, Place	Summary of Events and Information	Remarks and references to Appendices
15th September 1915 L'HALLO BEAU 10 a.m. 1.0 p.m.	Right Section and Battery Staff marched and joined Left Section at billets North of OUSTERSTEEN. Started at 10 a.m. arrived 1.0 p.m.	Ref map BELGIUM HAZEBROUCK 1st Scale 1/100,000 Ec.B
16th September 1915 OUSTERSTEEN	In the morning battery had a route march. 2nd Lieut E. N. KENT LEMON struck off Strength of Battery as unfit to return to the Front with effect from 16.9.15	" Ec.B
17th September 1915 OUSTERSTEEN	Brigade route march. Inspected by Brigadier Genl WHITE THOMPSON, C.B. Commanding 27th Divisional Artillery.	" Ec.B
18th September 1915 OUSTERSTEEN 2 p.m. 6.45 p.m. 8.17 p.m. 11.20 p.m.	2 p.m. at 2 p.m. moved to STEENBERBE with a section of 99th Battery R.F.A. under command of Major F.H.S. GILES 99th Bty. R.F.A. to entrain. Reached via VIEUX BERQUIN and LA MOTTE. Entraining satisfactory commenced at 6.45 p.m. and finished 8.17 p.m. Train left at 11.20 p.m.	" Ec.B

Army Form C. 2118.

WAR DIARY
or
INTELLIGENCE SUMMARY. Ec/4

(Erase heading not required.)

Instructions regarding War Diaries and Intelligence Summaries are contained in F.S. Regs., Part II and the Staff Manual respectively. Title pages will be prepared in manuscript.

Hour, Date, Place	Summary of Events and Information	Remarks and references to Appendices
19th September 1915 "In the Train"	Watered & fed without detraining at ABBEVILLE 5.30 a.m. Arrived LONGUEAU at 9.15 a.m. and 9.15 a.m. commenced detraining, detrainment complete with 9.55 a.m. ready to march at 9.55 a.m. marched with Section of 99th Battery to CERISY via GLISY, BLANGY, AUBIGNY, FOUILLOY and HAMEL. Bivouac near SOMME Canal, Men and horses in the open. Arrived CERISY 4.0 pm	Ref map. FRANCE AMIENS 1:2 Scale 1/80,000 Ec/4
20th September 1915 CERISY	Battery rested	Ec/4
21st September 1915 CERISY	Moved horse lines to a field in the village. Men and horses in the open	Ec/4
22nd September 1915 CERISY	Battery rested	Ec/4

337

WAR DIARY
or
INTELLIGENCE SUMMARY. ECB

(Erase heading not required.)

Army Form C. 2118.

Instructions regarding War Diaries and Intelligence Summaries are contained in F.S. Regs., Part II and the Staff Manual respectively. Title pages will be prepared in manuscript.

Hour, Date, Place	Summary of Events and Information	Remarks and references to Appendices
23rd September 1915 CERISY	Reconnoitred gun position East of CAPPY with a view to coming into action of German front line trench. Sent Lieut L. ARKWRIGHT forward to Battery from 20th Brigade Ammunition Column. ECB	Ref. map FRANCE AMIENS 1in Scale 1/80,000.
24 September 1915 6.30pm CERISY 10.45pm	At 6.30pm Battery marched to come into action via MORCOURT, MERICOURT, CHUIGNOLLES & CAPPY. Battery position 100 x 200yds of E in B of E in 8 DU 30 OCTOBRE 4 bis, 3me Tirage. Wagon lines in sunken lane ½ mile East of CHUIGNOLLES. Battery was in action at 10.45pm.	Ref. map as above and French artillery map E in B DU 30 OCTOBRE 4 bis, 3me Tirage, 27 Juin 1915. ECB
25th September 1915 1pm CERISY CAPPY 2pm 4.45pm 8.15pm	At 1pm registered wire to gate NE of BRUSYLVIS observation from trench 250 yards North. Battery fired at wire from 2 to 3.30pm and from 4.45 to 5.15pm. 400 rounds fired. Owing to darkness and long grass effect on wire difficult to estimate. A large gap at 8.15pm to 20° appeared to have been cut. Battery retired at 8.15pm and reached billets at CERISY at 10.15pm.	ECB

338

WAR DIARY
or
INTELLIGENCE SUMMARY.   Sgd/

(Erase heading not required.)

Army Form C. 2118.

Hour, Date, Place	Summary of Events and Information	Remarks and references to Appendices
26ᵗʰ September 1915 CÉRISY	Reconnoitred for gun position East of CAPPY with a view to close support of infantry attack between FEUILLÈRES and HERBECOURT. Position chosen in South East edge of wood 400 yards East of BOIS DE 30 OCTOBRE. In the evening a working party of 1 Officer and 40 men to prepare position went to CAPPY and were billeted in the Château. 2Lieut. M.L. QUINLIVAIN & BULGER posted to Battery from Divisional Ammunition Column.	Ref. map French artillery A bis, 3ᵉ Tirage 27ᵉ Juin 1915. Sgd/
27ᵗʰ September 1915 CÉRISY	Started preparing position	Sgd/
28ᵗʰ September 1915 CÉRISY	Continued preparing position.	Sgd/
29ᵗʰ September 1915 CÉRISY	Finished preparing position. Working party returned to billets at CÉRISY.	Sgd/
30ᵗʰ September 1915 CÉRISY	Battery drill order.	Sgd/

121/3868

27th Division

99th Batty: R.F.A.

Vol I. 26.9 — 31.12.14

Army Form C. 2118.

WAR DIARY
or
INTELLIGENCE SUMMARY.
(Erase heading not required.)

99th Battery RFA

Instructions regarding War Diaries and Intelligence Summaries are contained in F.S. Regs., Part II. and the Staff Manual respectively. Title pages will be prepared in manuscript.

Hour, Date, Place	Summary of Events and Information	Remarks and references to Appendices
1914		
28. Sept. NEEMUCH INDIA	Orders received to hold personnel of Battery in readiness to proceed to ENGLAND at an early date.	
29 Sept. "	Medical Inspection of Battery prior to embarkation.	
30 Sept. "	Orders received to leave married families in INDIA as a temporary measure. 2 ofrs. 3 gunners, and 1 driver in hospital.	Officers of Battery:- Capt. E.O. Anderson Commanding
1 Oct. - 9 Oct. "	Preparations for embarkation proceeded. Lt. King Harman arrived to take over details, horses etc	Lts. Morgan and Wilson
10 Oct. "	Guns and heavy baggage were removed to Railway Station and Entrained 9 p.m. Left NEEMUCH 2.5 a.m.	
7.20am 11 Oct. RUTLAM	Arrived and after breakfast guns etc. were transferred to the broad guage line - time taken 1 hour. Left 2.30 p.m.	
6.45am 12 Oct. PHAGODA BOMBAY	Arrived BARODA 9.20 p.m.; left 10.30 p.m. Arrived CARNAC BUNDA, BOMBAY. and left 8.50 a.m. Arrived to ALEXANDRA DOCKS and detrained 12.20 p.m. Guns etc trained to CARNAC BUNDA and camped there	Troops on HMT. AVON:- 2bn. 95th. 96th. 98th. and 99th. Batteries R.F.A. 4th Battalion Rifle Brigade
13 Oct. BOMBAY.	Personnel marched to docks 3 a.m. Guns etc shipped on HMT. AVON Battery marched. Bv. Woolgar, 2 gunners and 7 wagon bodies transferred troops allotted.	
15 Oct BOMBAY	15. HMT. ARAGON. Vessel moved into the stream.	
16 Oct "	Convoy sailed 5 pm. escorted by HM Cruisers SWIFTSURE and GOLIATH Gnr Jackson awarded 28 days detention by Col. Treager	
17 Oct At Sea	Sea calm for sleeping on his foot.	
18 Oct at Sea	Divine Service. Distribution of comforts supplied by circlins of	
23 Oct PORT SUEZ	BOMBAY Arrived in port	

Army Form C. 2118.

WAR DIARY
or
INTELLIGENCE SUMMARY.
(Erase heading not required.)

99a Battery R.F.A.

Instructions regarding War Diaries and Intelligence Summaries are contained in F.S. Regs., Part II and the Staff Manual respectively. Title pages will be prepared in manuscript.

Hour, Date, Place		Summary of Events and Information	Remarks and references to Appendices
24 Oct.	PORT SAID	Arrived in port. Escorted by French cruiser ST. VINCENT to within 3 days of GIBRALTAR	
25 Oct – 7 Nov.	at sea		
8 Nov.	GIBRALTAR	Arrived	
11 Nov.	do.	Left. Rough weather experienced	
16 Nov.	PLYMOUTH	Arrived in PLYMOUTH SOUND.	
17 Nov.	do.	Disembarked at R.N. Dockyard, DEVONPORT	
18 Nov.	WINCHESTER	Proceeded by train to WINCHESTER and marched from there to MORN HILL CAMP 5 miles E. of WINCHESTER arriving at 10 p.m.	
19 Nov.	MORN HILL CAMP	Process of mobilization commenced.	Capt. Morgan left to join 3rd Bde. Lt. Wilson became Adj. 20th Bde.
26 Nov.	do.	Under a new scheme each battery divided into two to form the nucleus of 4 gun batteries. The right half battery received one gun and became 99th Battery. The left half battery became 136th Battery. These two together with 89th Battery (formed by division of the 98th) formed the 20th Brigade. Mobilization continued.	The officers of the Battery were:- Major E.O. Anderson Commanding, 2/Lt. L.F. Thompson, Q. Ward, R. Rawn.
27 Nov. to 15 Dec.	WINCHESTER		The 20th Bde. was now commanded by Lt. Col. P.E. Gray. The 27th Divisional Artillery by Brig. Gen. A. Stokes D.S.O. and the 27th Division by Major General T.D'O Snow C.B.
16 Dec.	MORN HILL	The 27th Division was inspected near camp by H.M. the King	
20 Dec.	do.	The Battery marched out of WINCHESTER with the Division at 9.18 a.m. and reached SOUTHAMPTON 2.30 p.m. Embarked on H.M.T. CARDIGANSHIRE The battery was complimented by the Embarkation Officer on the speed of embarkation. Sailed 6.7 p.m. Sea Calm	
7 a.m. 21 Dec.	HAVRE	Arrived off coast but waited for tide till noon. Disembarked at 2.30 p.m. and bivouacked on a short with 364th Battery	
22 Dec.	HAVRE	Battery entrained 12 noon at the GARE DES MARCHANDISES. Train left at 4.20 p.m. Halted ROUEN to water horses 8.30 p.m. Left ROUEN 9.10 p.m.	
23 Dec.	On train	Halted at ABBEVILLE 8 a.m. Passed through BOULOGNE, CALAIS, ST. OMER 4 p.m. and ARQUE 4.20 p.m. Detrained and reached ST. OMER and marched to billets in a chateau between SERCOUS and WALLON CAPPEL	The chateau lies 20 Bde. HQ and the Battery. It is situated 9½ miles E.S.E. of ST. OMER Ref. Map BELGIUM, HAZEBROUCK 5A.

Army Form C. 2118.

99 Battery R.F.A.

WAR DIARY
or
INTELLIGENCE SUMMARY.
(Erase heading not required.)

Hour, Date, Place	Summary of Events and Information	Remarks and references to Appendices
24 Dec. Nr. SERCOUS	Remained in Billets; heavy frost during night. Two cases of strangles during among the horses.	
25 Dec. do.	Xmas Day. Divine Service in open 10.45 am. Holiday for men. All ranks received Xmas card from HM the King.	app.
26 Dec. do.	All ranks received Xmas gift of a pipe, tobacco and cigarettes from Princess Mary and Xmas puddings from Daily News Fund.	
27-29 Dec. do.	Treated ~~men~~ and Pleurisy pneumonia, and Pleurisy. 2 horses died from ~~strangles~~.	app.
30-31 Dec. do.	Battery inspected by Lt Col Gray. Weather fine and cold. 1 horse died	

27th Division

99th Batty: R.f.A.
96th ?

121/4256

Vol II 1 — 31.1.15

340

Army Form C. 2118.

WAR DIARY
INTELLIGENCE SUMMARY.
(Erase heading not required.)

Instructions regarding War Diaries and Intelligence Summaries are contained in F.S. Regs., Part II and the Staff Manual respectively. Title pages will be prepared in manuscript.

Hour, Date, Place		Summary of Events and Information	Remarks and references to Appendices
1915			
1st January	SERCOUS	Battery remained in billets. Weather wet and cold.	L.F.F.
2nd	do. 9.a.m.	Brigade inspected by G.O.C. 27th Divl. Artillery at LA BELLE HOTESSE	
3rd	do. 4 p.m.	Order received to be prepared to move early.	Ref. Maps. BELGIUM HAZEBROUCK 5A
6th	do. 11 a.m.	Battery left billets and marched to STRAZEELE arriving at	BELGIUM SERIES13 S.W.
7th	STRAZEELE 10 a.m.	billets there 4 p.m.	
		Battery marched to within 2 kilometres of DICKEBUSH and	
8th	DICKEBUSCH 4 a.m.	bivouacked on a field	Wood referred to is shewn on map BELGIUM SERIES B S.W. 1/20,000 O.7.A. L.F.F.
		Right section replaced a section of a French Battery of 75 m/m guns near N.E. end of L'ETANG DE DICKEBUSCH. Fired 50 rounds at German trenches along front edge of a wood. Range 3000x Cat 154	
9th	do	Left section replaced remainder of French Battery. Fired 30 rounds	
10th	do 4 a.m.	Battery fired at same target 80 rounds	
11th	do	Ammunition expenditure limited to 20 rounds per gun per day.	
12th	do	Ammunition increased to 20 rounds per gun per day. According to	During this time Drivers and Horses were in billets near DICKEBUSCH about 2 miles from Battery L.F.F.
13th	do	Infantry report fire very effective. Fired 80 rounds	
14th	do	Field L5b. rounds. Rain interfered with observation.	
15th	do.	Ammunition limited to 20 rounds per battery. Fired 20 rounds. Fired	
16th	do.	Ammunition easy.	
		Fired 20 rounds. Germans fired very much less	
		Fired 4 rounds.	
17th	do.	Battery relieved by 96th Battery. Left guns in position and retired to rest billets near WESTOUTRE. Billets much more uncomfortable	
18th to 21st	WESTOUTRE	than those in firing line. Several men sick with some feet affected by cold and damp.	
		Remained in billets resting.	

Army Form C. 2118.

WAR DIARY
or
INTELLIGENCE SUMMARY.
(Erase heading not required.)

Instructions regarding War Diaries and Intelligence Summaries are contained in F.S. Regs., Part II. and the Staff Manual respectively. Title pages will be prepared in manuscript.

Hour, Date, Place	Summary of Events and Information	Remarks and references to Appendices
21st January WESTOUTRE	Battery remained in resting billets	
to do		
29th do		
30th – 31st Jan.	Gun positions were prepared near DICKEBUSCH. Battery to relieve a French battery.	Position of battery 200x E of L'ETANG DE DICKEBUSCH LA.

27th Division

121/4507

99th Battery R.F.A. (20th Bde)

Vol III 1-28.2.15

WAR DIARY
of
INTELLIGENCE SUMMARY.
(Erase heading not required.)

Army Form C. 2118.

343

Instructions regarding War Diaries and Intelligence Summaries are contained in F.S. Regs., Part II. and the Staff Manual respectively. Title pages will be prepared in manuscript.

Hour, Date, Place	Summary of Events and Information	Remarks and references to Appendices
1st Feb. 1915 DICKEBUSCH	Guns brought to previously prepared Gunners moved to billets near Guns, wagon line to MILLEKRUISS Lines laid out on EIKOFF FARM and telephone wires to SHELLY FARM Observation post.	LFF EIKOFF FARM shown O3d.3.2 SHELLY FARM " O2d.9.0 BELGIUM Sheet 28 SW.
2nd	Registered zone of trenches O3d.33 to O9a.19 Fired 19 rounds. Fired 34 rounds at enemy's trench mortar reported O3 C40. Lt Mac Neece posted temporarily to H Battery RHA. 2nd Lt Wood posted temporarily to H Battery RHA.	LFF
3rd	Fired 18 rounds at transport reported to be on road running ESE of ST ELOI	
4th	No firing	
5th	Fired 19 rounds at farm and wood O9a.9.5	LFF
6th – 8th	Fired 16 rounds at midnight on trenches near EIKOFF FARM to keep down rifle fire while RE repaired parapets of advanced trenches.	LFF
9th	Battery relieved by 67th Battery. Took our guns in the reserve position.	Guns of battery in reserve zone 500 x S of L'ETANG DE DICKEBUSCH
10th	Battery remained resting in billets	and 400 N of DICKEBUSCH – YPRES road LFF
11th		
12th – 13th	Battery took part in an action described in Appendix I	
14th. 15th.	Battery remained in reserve.	
16th – 22nd	Battery relieved 364th Battery taking over their guns in position	Reference map BELGIUM sheet 28 SW.
22nd	E of L'ETANG DE DICKEBUSCH. Zone of fire O2C83 – O2d.35 Fired 14 rounds, observed from TUMULUS 50x S of ST ELOI	1/10,000
23rd	Registered zone, fired 34 rounds.	
24th	Fired 20 rounds including 6 Trotyl	
26th	Fired 32 rounds. First at 2.15 p.m. on zone of trenches O2C.83 – O2d.35 Secondly at 5 p.m. at battery reported to be O9 C30. Fire not observed in mis cast	Observation from TUMULUS was difficult owing to the fact that a periscope had to be used and that the enemy continually smashed periscopes with rifle fire. LFF
27th	Fired 18 rounds on wood zone. 10 on SW corner of wood O7C53 to O7C5b fire being observed by 39th Battery RFA in the second series and from TUMULUS STELOI in the first series	
28th	Fired 16 rounds on zone O2C83 – O2d.35	

APPENDIX I
WAR DIARY
INTELLIGENCE SUMMARY.
(Erase heading not required.)

Army Form C. 2118.

Hour, Date, Place	Summary of Events and Information	Remarks and references to Appendices
14th Feb. 1915 — DICKEBUSCH	Description of Action which took place Feb 14/15 1915. At 4 p.m. a message was received from 82nd Infantry Bde that the enemy had begun an attack of on trenches 19, 20, 21, and 22 S.E. of ST ELOI. The battery opened gun fire at 4-8 p.m. from the position of the battery in reserve. A quick rate of fire was maintained till 5 p.m. when it was reported that trenches 19, 20, 21, and 22 had been taken by the enemy. The battery was under heavy shell fire during this time but there were two casualties. From 5 p.m. to 3.20 a.m. (15/2/15) battery fire (indistinct) was maintained and searching and sweeping employed. At 3.20 a.m. 4 a.m. and 5.30 a.m. rapid fire was called for to support a counter-attack. At 6.57 a.m. ceased fire. The trenches lost the day before had been regained. 558 rounds were fired.	Br. Gen. Rorgley commanded 82nd Inf. Bde which made the counter attack. Br. Gen. Stokes commanded 27th Divl. Artillery.
15th Feb. — DICKEBUSCH	The following messages were received:— (1) From CMDG 5th Army Corps — To G.O.C 27th DIVN "Well done. Congratulations to General Rorgley and his troops and to General Stokes and his guns." (2) From G.O.C. 82nd Inf. Bde. to G.O.C 27th Divl. Artillery "Very grateful to R.A. All trenches were recaptured. Very grateful for tremendous help."	

12/48/1

27th Division

99th Batty: R.F.A.

O.t.IV. 1 – 31.3.15

VOLUME IV

WAR DIARY
or
INTELLIGENCE SUMMARY.

(Erase heading not required.)

Army Form C. 2118.

Hour, Date, Place		Summary of Events and Information	Remarks and references to Appendices
	1915		Reference Map BELGIUM S.W.
2 pm.	MARCH 1st DICKEBUSCH	Opened fire. Fired 14 rounds on 30d of trenches O2e 38 – O2d 35	Scale 1/20000
12.30am.	" 2nd "	Opened fire on trenches in O2d 43 – O2d76 to support infantry attack. Number of rounds fired 251. The effect from official reports was satisfactory.	L.F.P.
12.12 pm.	" 3rd. "	Fired 26 rounds. Observation – appeared effective.	
3.31 pm.	" 4th "	Fired 14 rounds.	
2.16 pm.	" 5th "	Fired 14 rounds on O2d 34 – O2d76	
6.31 a.m.	" 6th "	Battery opened fire as a part of planned bombardment. At 4.30 a.m. came under heavy shell fire from enemy. Casualties – first an battery – Gnr. Newbie killed – Gnr. Fallers died of wounds – Gnr. Shaw and Gallander severely wounded – Gnr. Haslam wounded. Ceased firing 7 pm. Fired 531 rounds.	L.F.P.
12.5 pm.	" 7th "	Fired on trenches (reported guns) O 14 a 76, O 7d 95, O 8 B 32. 69 rounds.	
7.38 am.	" 8th "	Fired 3b rounds on German support trenches O 2d 43 – O 2d 76.	L.F.P.
10.50 a.m.	" 9a "	Took part with heavy artillery in bombardment of trenches S.of ST. ELOI. Fired 109 rounds. Our infantry evacuated front line trenches and field guns crept exhaustion and retired.	
9.48 am.	" 10th "	Fired 69 rounds with aeroplane observation. Wireless telegraphy was used successfully.	L.F.P.
10.40am.	" 11th "	Fired 95 rounds on German fire and support trenches.	
12.5 pm.	" 12th "	Fired 20 rounds.	These 3 trenches are due S.
10.45am.	" 13th "	Fired 45 rounds on enemy trenches in front of trenches 19, 20, 21 of ST ELOI.	of ST.ELOI. L.F.P.
5.29 pm.	" 14th "	Enemy made large attack on ST.ELOI. Battery fired on German support trench and roads S of village of ST.ELOI. At various times during night at rate of rifle fire was quickened to support counter attacks. At 6.55am. turned fire on trenches S of ST.ELOI. Ceased fire 1.25 pm. (15.3.15) Casualties – Major E.O. Rushmer wounded in arm and leg at about 6 pm. but remained at his post for some time after. Infantry reported fire effective.	

(9 29 6) W 4141–463 100,000 9/14 HWV Forms/C. 2118/10

347

Army Form C. 2118.

WAR DIARY
or
INTELLIGENCE SUMMARY.
(Erase heading not required.)

Instructions regarding War Diaries and Intelligence Summaries are contained in F.S. Regs., Part II. and the Staff Manual respectively. Title pages will be prepared in manuscript.

Hour, Date, Place	Summary of Events and Information	Remarks and references to Appendices
1 p.m. March 15th DICKEBUSCH	Cpl. Betts and Gnr. Smyth killed — Gnr. Pitts died of wounds — Gnr. Blake severely wounded — They were the working detachment of No. 1 gun when a German 6" H.E. hinsinger shell burst 1 yard to the left of the trail.	L.F.P.
March 16th	Captn. Hon. O.H. Stanley took over temporary command of battery at 7 a.m.	L.F.P.
17th	Did not fire. Gun moved to new position in rear of old one and 50' from DICKEBUSCH — YPRES road.	
18th	Registered gun.	
19-25	Battery did not fire. Alternative position prepared N. of DICKEBUSCH.	L.F.P.
25	Right section relieved by section 67th By.	
26	Left " " " " "	
27	Battery moved to wagon line billet 1 mile W. of DICKEBUSCH — BAILLEUL road.	
28-30	Battery remained in rest.	Major A.K. Mann posted to command battery vice Major E.O. Anstyham (wounded).
31	Battery moved to billets 2 kilomètres E. of frontier BELGIUM — FRANCE on BOESCHEEPE — POPERINGHE road.	L.F.P.

27ᵉ Division

264 Batty R+H.

Vol I. 26.11 — 31.12.14

121/3976

20 BNF

WAR DIARY
or
INTELLIGENCE SUMMARY. 364th Battery, R.F.A.
(Erase heading not required.)

Army Form C. 2118.

Hour, Date, Place	Summary of Events and Information	Remarks and references to Appendices
1914 Nov 28th Winchester.	364th Battery formed from left half battery of 99th Battery & found part of 25th Brigade R.F.A., together with 67th & 99th.	Officers posted:— Maj. R.M. Maitz Lieut. A.S. Bellingham. R.F. Gore-Burston. C.W. Shenwill.
Nov 29th to Dec 19th "	Mobilization proceeds under great difficulties, owing to continuous rain, mud etc; sickness among men from India and among horses, due to the camp conditions; the necessity of allowing furlough to men from India; and also to the fact that deficiencies of kit was only received in driblets. The battery was completed in personnel by men from various reserve batteries, most of whom had received very little training as gunners, though fairly efficient. Promotion among N.C.O.'s very rapid and seniore ranks were mostly recruited from young N.C.O.'s with little experience.	
Dec 20th Jan.	Brigade Hospitalled for horsed supply of units at to 82nd & 84th Bdes. Battery marched to Southampton and embarked same day in Transport HUANCHACO, which sailed at 7 p.m., arriving off HAVRE early on 21st.	
Dec 21st 12 noon.	Battery disembarked in BASSIN BELLOT at HAVRE DOCKS and bivouacked in Shed on wharf.	

Army Form C. 2118.

WAR DIARY
—of—
INTELLIGENCE SUMMARY. 364th Battery R.F.A.
(Erase heading not required.)

Instructions regarding War Diaries and Intelligence Summaries are contained in F.S. Regs., Part II and the Staff Manual respectively. Title pages will be prepared in manuscript.

Hour, Date, Place	Summary of Events and Information	Remarks and references to Appendices
1914. Dec. 22nd 1am.	Battery entrained at GARE des MARCHANDISES (Pont-1) at HAVRE.	
" 23rd 3am.	Battery detrained at ARQUES (Refoulement du Nord) and marched into billets at SERCUS, arriving about 12 noon. 20th Brigade Bde. R. Art. also at SERCUS, remainder of Brigade between that place and MALCON-CAPPEL. 20th Brigade comes under Area Commander of 80th Inf. Bde Area. Brigade Headquarters at BLARINGHEM.	Inhabitants very civil and friendly.
" 26th	Battery (in part of 27th Div.) becomes a unit of 2nd Army under Lt. Genl. Sir H. Smith-Dorrien. (2nd, 3rd Corps & 27th Div.)	
" 26th to 31st	Battery remains in billets at SERCUS.	

121/4210

27th Division

364th Battery R.F.A.   20 BDE

Vol II. 1 — 31.1.15

Appendix II — remarks on equipment

" III — remarks on Supplies

" IV — remarks on Operations.

All above worth reading.

WAR DIARY
or
INTELLIGENCE SUMMARY.
(Erase heading not required.)

Ref. maps: Belgium 1/40,000 HAZEBROUCK, 5A.
and Serie "13", 1/20,000
Sheet 28. S.W. and N.W.
Army Form C. 2118.

364th Battery, R.F.A.

Hour, Date, Place	Summary of Events and Information	Remarks and references to Appendices
1915 January 1st to 5th	Battery remaining in billets at SERCUS.	
11 a.m. – 6th	Battery marched to STRAZEELE via HAZEBROUCK and billets there night of 6/7.	
11 a.m. – 7th	Battery marched via BAILLEUL to DICKEBUSCH and bivouaced night of 7/8 in an open field about 1½ miles S.W. of that place.	
5 a.m. – 8th	2 guns marched through DICKEBUSCH and take over the flank emplacements of a battery of 9th French Field Artillery Regt. just E. of DICKEBUSCH VIJVER. The composite battery composed of 2 French & 2 British guns remained throughout 8th, and the French officer handed over the zone, target, pivots of fire and telephone trunk observation stations. Only the French gunners fire.	(belonging to 32nd French Divn.) 2nd Gen. Bombardier proceeds to ST ELOIS to reconnoitre for Brigade observing officers.
5 a.m. – 9th	Remaining two guns take the place of the 2 arabic french guns. Fire is opened on PICCADILLY FARM and French Trench S.W. of it. Carnet & turned on to the line in front of ST ELOI behind & within ½ telephone wires by which German heavy guns shell the tunnelled at ST ELOI.	2nd Gen. Bombier observes from ST ELOI
10th	Left section shells trenches in front of ST ELOI, right section shells PICCADILLY FARM and trench S. of it. Telephone & ST ELOI made well, but shelling by German guns of observing station on tunnelled makes observation permanent. In the afternoon they blow in observing post and render it useless. In addition an unexploded heavy shell falls in cemetery and remains there.	2nd Lt. Showell at ST ELOI

[signature] Maj. R.F.A.

Ref. Map. Series "B". 1/20000
Sheet 28. S.W. and N.W.
364th Battery R.F.A.

Army Form C. 2118.

WAR DIARY
or
INTELLIGENCE SUMMARY.
(Erase heading not required.)

Hour, Date, Place	Summary of Events and Information	Remarks and references to Appendices
1915 January 11th 5 a.m.	2/Lt. Gen. Browne proceeds to ST. ELOI with the object of discovering whether observation can be carried out from the vicinity of trenches. He is accompanied by Gunner Ryan. 87th Bty. who points him out ST. ELOI. Some delay takes place owing to heavy fog in information HQ, and it is about 9am about getting to St. Eloi. Trenches leave the boundary where he was seen by an officer of the Lancers on 12/1/6. A Company's machine gun team & men that represents the H.Q. opponents and is missing. Since he facing taken place on their heaven during the day's service, although communication is obtained with the telephonist at the trenches he is unable to get Gun. Browne as being in the trenches South of trench. PICCADILLY F.M. & trench S. shelled. 2/Lt. Gen. Browne & Morning Report Bug.R.H.A.	Gunner [?]Slane came over and that, Telegraph morning about 9am learning as near as Potchefs mention up mountains. Appeared to be officers. Faint Battalion on the left. Faint Colour of ditto.
7 p.m 9.30 p.m.	* Telephone restored - nothing known First trench fully out into reaches 12 midnight - no rest.	* BM Garrison
3 a.m.	Second search party sent out returns about 9.30 a.m. - no rest. Early taken place in wood in FM PICCADILLY St. - open in ST. ELOI town 87th Bty. Branch up - zero registered - that enemy within 2000 (trenches field)	2/Lt. Garrison 2/Lt. Honnor.
2 a.m.	Third search party sent out - returns about 9am - no rest. Pass reported to find in official report that Lt. Gen. Browne is missing.	Corp. Wells, 2nd Clements, 2nd Cuipon, 2nd Gower, Gnr. Violet, Btr. Salip.
10 a.m.	Battery opens fire this day on zone next post - i.e. trenches from ST. ELOI to F.M. PICCADILLY exclusive of later. Observing station (Tobacco field) heavily shelled with minenwerfer shell falling in air and shrapnel (30 pdr.) shrapnel used no guns.) This must have been given away on 12th by Orderlies carrying loudly 87/85. There, the idea being that very much to take over that gun. Quickly name them in back. Some shall fall to short. This days a/c casualty on left. 2 casualties (Sollier are men wounded) LEINSTERS. 250 yards further back.	

T.M. White
Major R.F.A.

Ref. Map Series "B" 1/20000
Sheet 28. S.W. and Army Form C. 2118.
N.W.
364th Battery R.F.A.

WAR DIARY
or
INTELLIGENCE SUMMARY.
(Erase heading not required.)

Hour, Date, Place	Summary of Events and Information	Remarks and references to Appendices
1915		
January		
14th — 4 a.m.	Entrenched m.g. observing station. Hut by L. Bellingham established there. Observing station heavily shelled – given away this time probably	Cloudy – no aircraft.
10 a.m.	by telephonist going out to look for faults in wire. Line of battery removed from its petrol-witnstanding. Took O.C. 131st upto the pad of their series from apt. in road in order to help him locate a target. Our m.g. observing station which was entrenched after dark that evening.	2/Lt R.H. Pitt joined up – brings 13th A.C. teams up. Division to relieve 2/Lt Shenwell.
15th — 5 a.m.	Occupied new observing station under haystack. This if protection to haystack – comfortable if day – if very difficult – for enemy to spot. Came to conclusion that a German observer, if not observed, were concealed in their shortline between PICCADILLY and ST PAUL. Pitt idea of distributing fire. Shelled several likely spots, to tune of 114 rounds. Daily allowance since 14th only 20. Puckington team in battery late. Enemy shelled old observing station again if haven immediately in rear of haystack, but did not spot new station.	Cloudy – no aircraft.
16th	Haystack again used that spotted – only 12 shots fired this stray – pivot being stopped by order of 13th Div Comd! after that number had been fired.	Cloudy – no aircraft.
17th — 5 a.m. 11 a.m.	Personnel of 131st Battery relieves mine at guns – mine return to billets. 7 fellows after fatting observing officer into haystack station, Capt Hawley the hound of telephone main etc.	Cloudy – a funnel bi-plane up. No alarm.

T.M. Watt
Maj, R.F.A.

WAR DIARY or INTELLIGENCE SUMMARY.

(Erase heading not required.)

Ref. Map. Series "B"
20000 Sheet 28.S.W. Army Form C. 2118.
and N.W.
364th Battery R.F.A.

Hour, Date, Place	Summary of Events and Information	Remarks and references to Appendices
1915 January 18th – 23rd	Battery in 131st Bty billets near HERZEELE, N.W. of HESTOUTRE. Graunfeld and his auxiliary. All men have hot baths in Brewery at BOESCHEPE. Maj: Mids ill, but remains Battery Ship. for billets to larger farms close by. [in billets]	
23rd	2/Lt Bellingham, acting B.C., goes to reconnoitre fresh horse position near Crossroads at HELLEBLAST, S.W. of DICKEBUSCH and enters it on 24th + 25th + 26th.	
24th		
25th		
26th 9 am	Battery starts to march to DICKEBUSCH to relieve 131st Bty, but is stopped by counter order saying reliefs are not to take place for the present, and returns to billets.	
27th 4:30 pm	Battery remains in billets. 2/Lt. Bardwell proceeds to HALLEBAST with 12 men to complete gun position of reserve Bty till 2.A. All telephone operator material ordered up to DICKEBUSCH — Order cancelled just as they are on point of starting.	
28th	Battery remains in billets.	
29th	Battery remains in billets. 2/Lt Bellingham goes up to DICKEBUSCH with 16.C. Brigade to reconnoitre fresh position, the Brigade having been ordered to relieve French batteries in up of present position.	

Ref. Maps. Series "B"
Sheet 28. S.W. and   Army Form C. 2118.
N.W.
364th Battery R.F.A.

WAR DIARY
or
INTELLIGENCE SUMMARY.
(Erase heading not required.)

Hour, Date, Place	Summary of Events and Information	Remarks and references to Appendices
1915. January 30th 7 a.m.	2½ Bellewaarde went up to DICKEBUSCH & mts. on bivouacs to bivouac for the night there in 29th — Park occupied by Major Stokes, Comdg. 27th Div. F. Arty. who signed requisition that 364 & 187 will go into French employment, relieved for time 99th — Making party sent to prepare 99th Batteries position, to return at nightfall to billet.	
31st 6 p.m.	2nd Shewell takes party to prepare Battery support of B. 18th Bty & to 131st Bty returning to DICKEBUSCH over field holds them and to 131st Bty returning to billet with 9 men & part Battery support of 364 B. Battery remains in billets.	Following Appendices attached. I. Remarks on tour. II. " " Equipment. III. " " Supplies. IV. " " Personnel. Thomas Major R.F.A.

War Diary
364th Battery. R.F.A.

Appendix I. Remarks on Horses.—

The 4 heavy draught horses (2 per G.S. wagon*) allowed for the wagons of the train are not suitable for the work. These horses are accustomed to heavy slow work, and the work required of them in bringing up supplies and in keeping up with the movements of a unit or of the train is too fast for them, and soon wears them to pieces, especially on the paved roads of the Continent.

They are moreover accustomed to large quantities of food and to be fed constantly. This it is often, in fact generally impossible to give them. They will not eat more than a certain quantity of oats plain, and the ration of hay has generally been small and indifferent in quality, while it is impossible to give them the "chop" on which they are generally fed in civil life.

It would be much more satisfactory to have 4 light draught horses per G.S. wagon for this work. The work would be done more efficiently and the horses would keep fitter, and the want of hay etc when on the move would be less felt.

T.W. White
Maj. R.F.A.

31/1/15.

War Diary.
364th Battery. R.F.A.

Appendix II. — Remarks on equipment.

A.S.C. harness. — This harness is not suitable. On the narrow paved roads on the continent, with deep mud on either side the driver has not sufficient control with long reins over his horses. The neck collar also is unsuitable. Much difficulty was experienced in getting collars to fit, and even when the collar is fitted, the horse often rapidly falls away and in a fortnight's time the collar is again too large. This necessitates constant refitting and alteration.

Transport. — 2 G.S. wagons per battery is insufficient. One is completely taken up with supplies, and the other with technical stores. The one day's reserve supplies practically fill the supply wagon and therefore it has to be unloaded before fresh supplies can be drawn. The baggage wagon will just hold the stores, provided there is nothing extra; but frequently stores are delivered to a battery from Ordnance, and have to be carried for 2 or 3 days before they can be issued. Under such circumstances I have frequently had to leave stores behind and send back for them. The issue of a one horse light cart per battery may partially solve this difficulty, but I recommend the issue of a third G.S. wagon per battery.

Horse Rugs. — The utility of these is doubtful. In frosty weather they undoubtedly keep the horses warmer, but in wet weather I am inclined to think they increase the chance of the horse catching cold. The horse's own coat makes to my mind a better protection once they are accustomed to standing out. As in wet weather it is in any case impossible to clip, there is the less reason for horse rugs. —

Stationery. — The issue of War Diaries in loose sheet-form is most inconvenient & difficult to keep clean. It would be much better to issue as books with stiff covers and to have the sheets detachable. —

31/1/15.

T.P.M. White, Maj. R.F.A.

War Diary.
364th Battery R.F.A.

Appendix III. — Remarks on Supplies. —

Forage. — The want of soft food for horses has been very badly felt. It is impossible to keep horses fit, even when in regular work, on nothing but oats. Horses will not eat more than a certain quantity of oats, and when in billets, where often exercising is very difficult owing to congestion of traffic on the roads, I have found it impossible to get horses to eat their full ration, simply because I could get nothing to mix with the oats. I have got bran occasionally but the supply is very intermittent and in very small quantities. Bran is indispensable for sick horses. I suggest that bran should form a regular portion of a horse's rations; and if bran cannot always be obtained then that a portion of the ration should be compressed forage, such as was issued during the S. African war and which was invaluable.

Leakage of Supplies. — It is obvious that leakage of certain supplies has been and is going on on a considerable scale. The chief items are tobacco, cigarettes, jam, rum, & preserved meat. At times when we have been unable to obtain tobacco & cigarettes from Supplies, my men have bought from inhabitants quantities of tobacco & cigarettes of British make which are obviously ration ones. The same with jam & meat, though we have not at any time been short of these. I also know that rum has been sold to the troops by inhabitants from jars similar to the ration jars, though I have been unable so far to catch anyone in the act. I have already reported concrete cases of above to my Brigade headquarters, and I believe that steps have been taken to trace the sources of this leakage.

31/1/15.

F. P. White
Maj. R.F.A.

War Diary
364th Battery. R.F.A.

Appendix IV. – Remarks on Operations. –

Co-operation between Infantry & Artillery. –

In the present phase of trench warfare it has been my experience that cooperation with the infantry in my immediate front has been difficult for several reasons.

In the first place the infantry do not seem to be supplied with telephones. Consequently on several occasions to my knowledge there has been no communication by daylight between the trenches and infantry battalion headquarters in rear, so that the battalion headquarters could give my battery no information either as to the effect of my fire or as to what portion of the enemy's trenches, if any, the infantry in front would like fire brought to bear on. The artillery has only just enough telephones for its own work and cannot provide instruments for this work.

Secondly the constant reliefs of infantry, due to the state of the trenches in this weather, have made cooperation still more difficult. Reliefs take place at night – it is difficult to find officers in the dark – and the infantry coming out have naturally only one desire – to get away back to their billets as quickly as possible. Consequently it may be two days after before a battery commander can get any comments on the work of the artillery from the infantry. Events are then no longer fresh in the mind of the commentator, & his comments are of the less value accordingly. Where our own trenches are so close to the enemy's, prompt information is essential. The issue of telephones to the infantry, and instructions to them to send back daily reports of our artillery work from their point of view would be of immense value.

Allowance of Gun Ammunition. –

To tie a Battery Comdr. down to a daily allowance of ammunition seems to me unsound. To tie him to an average would be better. If he was allowed so much a week and it was left to his discretion how much he fired each day, the result would be the same, and, I think, the value received greater

27th Division

121/4610

20 B/E

364th Battery R.F.A.

Vol III 1 - 28.2.15

364th Battery. R.F.A.

WAR DIARY
or
INTELLIGENCE SUMMARY.
(Erase heading not required.)

Army Form C. 2118.

Ref. Map Sheet "B" Sheet 28
N.W. and S.W. 1/40,000
20000 & 40000

Hour, Date, Place	Summary of Events and Information	Remarks and references to Appendices
1915. February 1st	Battery remained in billets near HERSHENY (WESTOUTRE.)	
2nd 3 p.m.	Battery marched into new billets near crossroads at MILLEKRUIS, N. of DICKEBUSCH. Maj. White arranged with Commandant of Group of 58 S. Bat. went to French Hill entirely to inspect posn. that night.	High wind and rain all day.
9 p.m.	Guns arrive to explore grounds - harspird Hershery have received orders to remain till next day. Tent being broken, 6 empty emplacements (6) + live guns been installed this position by H.29.d.6.5. was quite close to the crest and had been heavily shelled in front made - Consequently shell holes [?] made in difficult to get guns into.	Position as before except this lived guns left.
3rd 8 a.m.	Battery takes over guns of 67th Bty in position at H.29.c.8.2. and hands over guns & position to 67th Bty (in reserve.) Zone allotted in new position from FARM EIKHOF in O.3.d.3.1. to N.E. corner of O.3.d. and next lie west. Germans biplane constantly over position all morning. French remaining 6 guns stay in position till evening when milk[?] fire opened on zone but [?] is corrected as telephone broken down. Zone was fired.	Lieut. Harrison Lieut. O.C.A. Artillerie arrived from J Battery R.H.A. for temporary attachment. W.M.W. May. R.F.A.

364th Bty R.F.A. Army Form C. 2118.

Ref to Scenes "B" Sheet 28
N.W. 1/40000 and 28 S.W.
1/40000 and 20000

WAR DIARY
or
INTELLIGENCE SUMMARY.
(Erase heading not required.)

Hour, Date, Place	Summary of Events and Information	Remarks and references to Appendices
1915. February 4th	11am. Fire opened on zone J continued till line ranges formed. 14 sh/gun. Observed firm point in wood on canal in I.33. c.5.9.	Fire - not much done.
	2pm. A German machine gun reported to the mountains near O.8.a.8. Fire was laid out from mg. & observed from T. Patrol. Observation impossible from this observing station.	Fire on machine gun.
	11.30pm. Fired from O.3.d.8.0 to O.4.c.4.3 laid on by order of O.C.18th Div. from mg. 8chofs, no grins no shrapnel. This night Germans attacked on line of 28th Div in our left, who had just taken over from French division. Battery kept attacking to assist all night - hostile hammered.	
5th	8am. Orders to endeavour to prevent noise of that machine could not yone allotted to batteries from O.8.a.7.6 to O.2.a.7.2, letter in two also immediately of 15th of 57 ELOS.	Lieut. A.S. Bellingham joined. 1 gun J Battery R.H.A. to temporary attachment to learning. Fine & sunny.
	12 noon. 20 rds fired to get his range. Corrected on meet gun. Observed from Wieltie School N. of ROORMIZEELE which is only the highest zone could be seen. The ground sloping away to west in left. R.J. Partout at YPELOS in front - effect satisfactory.	
	5 pm. R.J. Partout report German guns about O.3.d.3.3. Battery gets sprayed him, more fontus. infantry range cannot seen at line too much too night. Too dark to dig more. 284th Btn. in this at attacked or Counter attacks but by 24th Battery on right East no found.	

Army Form C. 2118.

364th Battery. R.F.A.

By Map Sheet "B" Sheet 28
1/40000 and 1/20000 N.W. and S.W.

WAR DIARY
or
INTELLIGENCE SUMMARY.
(Erase heading not required.)

Hour, Date, Place	Summary of Events and Information	Remarks and references to Appendices
1915 February 6th. 8 am.	8 rounds Shrapnel fired for more accurate correction of fuses ranges. Observed from mound at ST ELOI by Maj. Pilot.	Fine rain all morning. Cleared in afternoon.
3 pm.	2nd Lieut. Start-Wright N.A. gun could be brought back without danger of hitting pilots who were Chief of Battery, Maj. Pilot and 2nd Lieut.	
3.30 pm.	Wire reported that O.2.L.A.2. [illegible] report as to effect was [illegible]. Wire visible from tower of MESSCHAETE. Request to but expected fallen to the whole lot. Lieut. S.H. Pitt returning from ST ELOI. Several lots of German guns, Halver heavy. Their lands into road 6/7 carrel in square 0.1.A.Y.B. when it returned from march. Report sent to DIV. ARTY ko GPR to communicate to 28th Div. 100 whose zone this was in.	
7th 12.15 am.	8 Shrapnel fired on wholl zone. They followed by 8 Shrapnel for harassing, of O.2.D.A.2. effects fired at motor Turkish (?) at O.2.D.A.2. Both were observed from ST ELOI by and S.O.B. Phabefield.	[illegible] Rain [illegible] apparent effect of firing [illegible] difficulties the report in not [illegible]. Fine.
8th 2/6 pm.	8 Shrapnel fired on Trenches in zone. Observed from ST ELOI by 2nd Lt. H-B-Hill.	Fine morning.
5 pm.	12 Shrapnel H.V. Target fired at [illegible] supposed to be in wood by Canal in O.4.a.4.1. This fired on response to message from Whitty in Breach support at ELZENWALLE that they were being heavily shelled from E. Bank when fired 'yesterday after 6 p.m. fired at SHELLEY FARM O.2.L.6.B4. Could only be observed if high. Could not very well be Effective as not on small lines from map.	

364th Battery, R.F.A.
Ref. map Sheet "B" Sheet 28.
1/40,000 and 1/20,000 M.R. and S.K.

WAR DIARY
or
INTELLIGENCE SUMMARY
Army Form C. 2118.

Hour, Date, Place	Summary of Events and Information	Remarks and references to Appendices
1915. February. 9th 10 a.m.	Fire opened on FARMHOUSE /0.3.A.4.2./ where ascended to draw fire given by Lt. KAVANAGH R.I. Artillery. Worked of German guns not then seen. 26 rds charged fuzes then ceased fire.	Equally wire is between enemy fire.
1 p.m.	Fire opened on trenches immediately S.E. of ST. ELOI to prevent out 17, 12 and 21 Trenches which E.O.C. 8th Arty. reported had suffered with H.E. & shrapnel burst on accurate sweeping & supported by bits Twenty. Heavy rain then made observation impossible. Ceased fire from ST ELOI by Oliver Rushbrook.	
12 noon	8 rds shrapnel fired on roads leading to trenches in view. This on account of his being found by 29th Bty. His accurate work about to other Batteries. Spoke up for his & assured not battalion was W.A.K & chiefly D.S. instantly quiet in response to swings by W.E. & Infantry to keep down heavy rifle fire on working party E. of ST. ELOI. Upon his switch back to HALLEBAST - OUDERDON road junct. Bty went back to open fire, & their shrapnel emerges to victory.	
10th 12.30 p.m.	5 shrapnel fired to make sure lines apparently which on zone observed by Lt. Mandrell from ST ELOI, which & distilled by German to about an hour from Mauser to 12 mm. B.E. of busy. Front goes from Lt. Bushwell. E. ST. ELOI for instructions on observation. German aeroplane (2) came over fulling bound twice during alarm. Telephone relay station shifted from PORMIZEELE to house in road leading to W. POTSDAM.	Fine & still.

M.W.M.
Major R.F.A.

WAR DIARY or INTELLIGENCE SUMMARY

Army Form C. 2118.

364th Battery R.F.A. "B" Brigade
Ref. Brigade Orders "B" Brigade
N.W. and S.W. 26000 27000

Hour, Date, Place	Summary of Events and Information	Remarks and references to Appendices
1915 February 11th 10 p.m.	Fired 1 round of 730# Howitzer Battery into St Eloi from a German trench S.W of St Eloi. Gun itself appeared to explode. Incident reported to Brigade & noted.	None to make returns to Experience.
1 p.m.	12 sharpnel fired on zone. Than 2 target trees & hut platform in trenches H which were in full pair germs & immedly. Burn behind it & put one round in and one exactly, another on top trees, both guns fired - two were immedly ordered - Mr. Gunn & Liz scouts sportively. shots at platform - danced by you note at St. Eloi.	From platform and was careful mud pit and rifle cells.
12th 1.57p.m.	Instructions received from O.C. & O.C. 91st Battery. F.O.C. Bret Arty wished to turn on B.nk & need winning from O.9.a.8.2 to O.9.a.5.57. No sharpnel was. Beavers spins at St Eloi says it looked most splendid. Word sounded Bath turn to hand. to Ph.AL.blad at 1.57 to 2.04.	Air Ld. same might Bomber enfluded till 12 hrs. Yuspras. Then departure.
11.45 p.m.	Keatings messages from O.C. Royal Irish Regt. at St. Eloi Red-Germans Bund shelling ST ELOI 1 the would like battery to retaliate. 2 shrapnel fired on trenches in zone. Lt. Pritchard unable to get up his wound but waiting going to Germans shall fire falling on it	
3.30 p.m.	Officers of R. Very Corps & Lt. Inspector R.M. observing officers stow at Battery & arrange to have a battery to give performance has brought a fires a new model of the flash. Three guns for regiments, as follows :- Points roads O.8. d. 7.6. O.15.c. 8.3. O.14.a.7.6. O.10.d.5.2.	Electric peripheral apparatus fails to let you hypothesises arrangements to make.
(a) Gun. O.15.c. 8.3		
(ii) Gun. O.14.a.7.6		
(iv) Gun. O.10.d.5.2		

364th Battery R.F.A.
Army Form C. 2118.

WAR DIARY
or
INTELLIGENCE SUMMARY.
(Erase heading not required.)

Ref. Map Sheet "B" Sheet 28.
HOOGE and 28000 S.W. & N.W.

Hour, Date, Place	Summary of Events and Information	Remarks and references to Appendices
1915. February 13th	Aeroplane did not turn up owing to misty weather. N.E. half of small wood in O.8 engaged by order of O.C. 27th Div. L. Arty. — 14 shrapnel & 8 T. lyd. fired. Observed by 27th Sherwell from STEL01.	Misty morning — Rain later. Cleared in afternoon for 2 hrs but rain again in evening.
14th 12.25 pm	N.E. half of wood in O.8 engaged by orders of F.O.C. 5th Divl. Arty. Fired 1, shrapnel & 4 T. lyd fired in above. same manner.	
4 p.m.	Germans shell trench E.M. ST ELOI, and following shelled were infantry attack, our LEINSTERS kept out of train. Battery gave full artillery support by it our own & destroying belts to the E. so below. M.G. A.M. kept fire on ridge & N.E. trench. Battery assisted in fighting engagement by support concentration by 2 BLFs and R.G.P.R. (to hold em. particularly during counter-attack by 3.54 & 3.5 am on 15th), with Troop battery.	Detailed details of this action in Appendix E
4.30 am 7 am	Specially called the attention on Faulk etc. and following bringing field, and 7th shrapnel, ... Battery kept up fire of 14 F personnel field howitzer, until bridge in front of attack at about 1.30 .... Satisfied behind the file, with shell stopped all general guns one shell making direct hit on M.C. 2 guns shelling the sergt and 2 of the whole detachment, grounded of 3 Huns I name ..... mustering for attack roundly hit in the front of his burning fires & am. V.M.A. Battery in sections at HERVOUTRE .... position by 6 am on 15th. the day night guns being brought back & position to HERVOUTRE and (was any to Mulland) and Mulland toward morning. No 4 gun damaged in the engagement but position giving to touch of the buffer. This morning being recovered 7/15th by 26 Battery gun on the limbers.	
15th	7/14th Batty 2nd Brig B.J.D. drawn out by the 2nd Brigade.

R.F.A.

WAR DIARY
or
INTELLIGENCE SUMMARY.
(Erase heading not required.)

Army Form C. 2118.

364th Battery, R.F.A.
Ref. Map Sheet "13" Sheet 28
1/40,000 & 1/20,000
S¹ Wd. N.W.

Hour, Date, Place	Summary of Events and Information	Remarks and references to Appendices
1915. February 15th	Premises replaced & round examined. Round found near DEREBUSCH Church at 4pm. Information received that Capt. A.S. Bellingham attached to Bde. T.H.R. accidentally wounded by bomb.	Cloudy - Stormy rain - hail in afternoon.
3pm	Information received from Infantry that Lieut. T.L. Cox-Cherrie, adjoining force 11th Jan. is alive and a prisoner of war in Germany	
9.40pm	Shots (shrapnel Bosch) fired in direction of line opposite E of ST ELOI. Enemy stopped almost at once, a bow. at about 1st line of Infantry. Round apparently caused by heavy crump-shells fire.	
16th 10.45am	Cross heads at O.E.O.I.9.8 ranged on by shrapnel (2" Mortar) in aeroplane. Close range found with 12 into shrapnel	First spent fired in conjunction with aeroplane.
4pm	Attempt made to range on gun emplacements located by aircraft at O.Sc.6.3. Shots that had been fired, shortly held the spotting owing to presence of several German aeroplanes. This afternoon a German observation balloon, sausage shaped, was up over German lines for about 2 hours.	Fine throughout - Afternoon.
9.20pm	1 shrapnel fired on receipt of message for support from Infantry E of ST ELOI. Shrapnel almost at once local very short was apparently registered & the message for general support by all batteries was sent by mistake.	

(Signature)

15.

Army Form C. 2118.

364th Battery R.F.A.

Ref. maps: Series "B" Sheet 28.
S.W. and N.W.
alt: 28970 HAZED

WAR DIARY
or
INTELLIGENCE SUMMARY.
(Erase heading not required.)

Instructions regarding War Diaries and Intelligence Summaries are contained in F.S. Regs., Part II. and the Staff Manual respectively. Title pages will be prepared in manuscript.

Hour, Date, Place	Summary of Events and Information	Remarks and references to Appendices
1915. February.		
17th 3.30 pm	12 rds shrapnel fired on work moving from O.F.a.9.6 to front trench at 0.9.a.6.3 along which Germans were reported to be moving troops. Observation not possible, many a splinters — ST ELOI could be seen of the bursts.	Cloudy – raining – strong wind
18th 2.15 pm	5 shrapnel fired at guns emplacements located by aircraft at 0.15.a.6.3. at position observing from aeroplane. Wind very high and drifting clouds made observation impossible. Ruby (?) light above 0.P. whitish colour could not be distinguished. Very light above — Observed in machine only sand mound against clouds.	Very high wind – broken sky – also fog clouds forming sunshine.
3.30 pm	6 rounds shrapnel fired at buildings in 0.9.d.9.8. where guns reported. Target could not be seen from observing post. So fired the fired from map.	Officer posted from 7th Div in place of 2d Lt A.F. Bellingham, 6.1.84 R.H.A. Name not given.
19th 11 am	N.E. end of wood in O. Engaged with 5 shrapnel + 6 Trotyl C. Observed by Lt Randell from ST ELOI.	
11.45 am	Trench SE. of ST ELOI, the point of view I. Cavell where troops reported engaged with 8 shrapnel, ignition of house observed from ST ELOI.	
4.30 pm	Guns reported at 0.15.6.6.6 engaged with 10 shrapnel + 6 Trotyl C. No observation, no target visible from ST ELOI.	

WAR DIARY or INTELLIGENCE SUMMARY

Army Form C. 2118.

364th Battery R.F.A.

Ref. map series "B" Sheet 28.
1 / 10,000 and 1 / 20,000   N.W. and S.W.

Hour, Date, Place	Summary of Events and Information	Remarks and references to Appendices
1915 February 20th		
10.7 a.m.	Observing aeroplane became our high off Hillopens tempted to burst beneath him it so causing on burst at 0.13.c.8.3 hurting it. Shrapnel fired. No further signals received therefore were unable to prospect were tire. Happened after Half-machine was not sent to prospect were tire.	Fine 44/43 in morning mild. Some duel rain in afternoon. Cloud increasing. Spice still bright.
10.45 p.m.	Aeroplane returned. beautiful message received giving O.14.a.6.6. as our target. This happened on red line. 4 rounds fired with 3 shrapnel.	
12.42 p.m.	Trenches S.E. of ST ELOI in front of our 20 and 21 engaged with 8 shrapnel and 1 Trolgl. At mar. 1 Trolgl found by 2nd Plat from ST ELOI.	Trolgl — 1 killed.
3.48 p.m.	N. edge of wood in O.9.c, where guns reported, engaged with 13 shrapnel, & 6 Trolgl. Observing officers at ST ELOI unable to see burst. so burst fixed entirely from map, resembling fire used.	
21st 1.48 p.m.	Zone from O.8.a.7.8. to O.2.d.7.2. shelled with 14 rounds chiefly with object of correcting lines before handing over. 6 gr& Hy, and finally air 2zle 4 render to observing officer 99 L (2nd Thompson) who accompanied 2nd Shenwell to ST ELOI.	Fine — foggy all morning. cleared some after noon. Brightest of the even remaining with some clouds & mist.
2.12 p.m.	Trenches S.E. of ST ELOI in front of our 19, 20 & 21 hinder shelled with 4 shrapnel & 44 Trolgl; also with about 4 objt and also in accordance with G.O.C. 27 Dvn! Artyg; instructed to shell these trenches daily. Blue 4 Trolgl. 36 burst well, the others were very high.	Trolgl — erratic bursting & / Augt.

364th Battery R.F.A.
Army Form C. 2118.
R/Maps Series 'B' - Sheet 28.
1/40000 and 1/20000 N.W. and S.W.

WAR DIARY
or
INTELLIGENCE SUMMARY.
(Erase heading not required.)

1915. Hour, Date, Place	Summary of Events and Information	Remarks and references to Appendices
February 22nd 10 a.m.	Billets, guard, targets etc handed over to Battery becoming resting Battery (orders of 99th Brigade) (not other guns) Inf: first reconnoitred ground S. of ST ELOI with a view to the possibility of putting a gun up there to enfilade trenches S.E. of mound in the event of our making G attack there. First results recommended incomplete.	This 6 weeks mostly stormy - fine no rain.
23rd 5.30 p.m.	Resting. Gun & man parties. Rein suddenly at 11 p.m. line billets. Reconnaissance guns moved to emplacements next to left. Party sent to mound at ST ELOI to repair parapet.	Fine - alternate cloud and sunshine.
24th 11 a.m. 4 p.m.	Telephone line from Infantry Batt: HQ to mound at ST ELOI doubled and sent through - divide by guns connected with 24 hrs Inspired. Inf: First reconnaissance positions N.W. of DICKIE BUSCH to B49/W. Second line of defence Guns allotted. Carried on same day. Inf: Wite reconnoitres left position for gun to enfilade ST ELOI trenches from N.E. Doubtless get in before reconnaissance completed	High northerly wind - cleaning. Streets of mud, slush, snow.
25th 9 a.m. 9 p.m.	Inf: White & Lt Milne (P49) complete reconnaissance for the right position. Position for gun found & could back by Infantry - I. 33. d. 3. 5. Party (97th+ 99th) under Cpl Bay finishes ST ELOI mound parapet personnel.	Snow & sleet with high wind in morning. Weather cleared in afternoon.
26th 27th 28th	Work in gun position continues. ditto. ditto.	Cloudy - cold wind veering to S. Some march. Snow. Fine - wind still high.

W.M. ?
Major R.F.A.

Army Form C. 2118.

WAR DIARY
or
INTELLIGENCE SUMMARY.

(Erase heading not required.)

Hour, Date, Place	Summary of Events and Information	Remarks and references to Appendices
28th Feb 1915 DICKEBUSCH	Commenced firing at 11.30 a.m ceased at 12 N/6 m. 16 Rounds Shrapnel fired at Trenches in Battery Zone. At 3.10 p.m 11 rounds of shrapnel were fired and enemys communication trench running from O 13 a 4.2 to O 7 c 4.3 was again registered. The firing was observed by standing officer of the 39th Battery R.F.A.	Ref map BELGIUM & FRANCE 3"Sones Sheet 28 S.W Scale 1/20,000 Ect

War Diary for February 1915.
364th Battery R.F.A.

Appendix I. – Night action of night 14/15 Febr 1915 near ST ELOI.

Date Feb.	Time.	
14th	3.47 p.m.	First message saying "Support Infantry" received from LEINSTERS via 67th Bty observing officer at SHELLEYS FARM. Fire opened.
"	3.55 pm.	Second message "S.O.S" received from Royal Irish Fusiliers at ST ELOI via 364th Bty. Fire was opened with one round Gun Fire, followed by Battery Fire 5 secs.
"	4.15 pm.	Rate of fire reduced to 10"
"	4.20 pm.	Rate of fire reduced to 30"
"	4.30 pm.	Rate of fire reduced to 1 minute
"	4.40 pm.	Shells fell all round 364th Battery – apparently these were from 30pr light field howitzers (4.2 in) – and one bursting on No. 2 gun, killed 3 men of the detachment & wounded 3 others, also smashing the dial & telescope sights, rocking bar, sight-clinometer & elevating gear. The detachments were withdrawn from the guns temporarily.
"	4.50 pm.	Telephone line from battery to ST ELOI broken.
"	5.11 pm.	Telephone line mended & communication with ST ELOI reestablished.
"	5.15 pm.	Battery switched on to ground immediately in front of trenches 19 & 20, which had been taken by Germans. Rate of fire increased to 20 secs.
"	5.31 pm.	Rate of fire reduced again to 1 minute – Orders to hold battery ready to support counter attack.
"	7 pm.	Battery switched back to normal zone between the ST ELOI – MESSINES and ST ELOI – OOSTTAVERNE roads.
"	8.30 pm.	Rate of fire reduced to 2 mins. – Information received that trenches 19, 20, 21 and 22 had been taken by Germans
"	9.39 pm.	Firing stopped pending counter attack. – End of first phase

Appendix. I (continued.)

12.25 am. Rate of fire quickened to 1 min. — Approach roads to ST ELOI swept.

12.30 am. Order received to harness up horses.

2.34 am. Message received that counter attack postponed from 2.30 am to 3.30 am.

3 am. Rate of fire quickened to 10".

3.20 am. " " " to 5".

3.30 am. Elevation raised by 200ˣ.

3.32 am. Counter attack postponed till 4 am. Rate of fire reduced to 30", & quickened again at 3.55 am.

4.7 am. Message received that counter attack not started. Rate of fire reduced to 10" and at 4.25 to 30".

4.40 am. Firing stopped.

4.48 am. " taken up again at 10".

4.54 am. Counter attack starts.

5.6 am. Rate reduced to 30".

6.34 am. Message that trenches 21 & 22 retaken.

6.57 am. Firing ceases.

7.32 am. Message that all trenches retaken. End of second phase.—

List of Casualties night of 14/15 Feby 1915.

Killed — No. 44667 Sergᵗ A. H. Dyer. } Buried on E. side
No. 65911. Bombᵈʳ G. Wiltshire. } of DICKEBUSCH
No. 57212 Gunr S. Constable. } Churchyard.

Wounded — No. 51560 Corpˡ S. Ransom. }
No. 51300 Gunr W. Shearing. }
No. 93695 Gunr G. McWade. }

Other Casualties during month of February 1915.

Died — No. 23885 Gunr MacFarlane. J. } Buried at
(of heart failure & tuberculosis.) } H.31.b 2.5. in
} corner of roads.

R. M. White
Maj. R.F.A.

121/48/1

27th Division
36th Battn. R+A.   20 BDE
Vol IV   1 – 31.3.15

364th Battery. R.F.A.

Army Form C. 2118.

WAR DIARY
or
INTELLIGENCE SUMMARY.
(Erase heading not required.)

Ref. Map. Sheet "B" Sheet 28.
1/40000 and N.W. 1/20000

Hour, Date, Place	Summary of Events and Information	Remarks and references to Appendices
1915 March 1st		High wind - showing storms
9 p.m.	Preparations made to support attack by 6th Division on trenches in sqr. J.14, 20 & 21. Maj. White, in comd. the Brigade, reports with O.C. No. 1 (164)? & 6 & 139 Pm. Batteries (2nd & 7th Bty) at ROOTMIZEELE. O.C. Archibald commands the battery.	at intervals from St. Eloi front - Bright mostly at intervals - occasionally obscured by clouds. More cloudy towards morning.
2nd 12.30 am	On signal given by 67th Bty. Battery opens Battery fire slow on German support trenches. Fire continued at intervals ranging from 5 mins to 2 mins till 2.35 am when it stopped. Lt Thompson (07+13ey) observed for Bty from pumphouse at ST. ELOI. Information re German attack also received from O. Pryor (87+13ey) at SHELLEY'S FARM. Telephone wire cut by shell at 1.30 am and communication re-established at 2.5 am. Battery was heavily shelled, & detachment withdrawn temporarily into shelters, but no casualties & no damage done except one direct hit on one experimental pattern dug-out in rear of the German shells apparently from field gun (15 pr.) light field howitzer (30 pr.) and one 5.9 inch gun. Some 3rds were fired and buried themselves in the mud. There were mostly small shell. 125 rounds shrapnel were fired by battery. Some 26 yds of German parallel taken by 1st + 17 FR Rifles. Very small volume of German rifle fire, battery was not hit. Gunners freshly.	
7 am.	Normal state of readiness resumed. Nothing to record. Battery resting.	Overclouded - Fine rain over all the day.
3rd		

[signed] R.F.A.

364th Battery, R.F.A.

WAR DIARY or INTELLIGENCE SUMMARY.
(Erase heading not required.)

Army Form C. 2118.

Ref. maps Scale "B" Sheet 28, and N.W. and S.W. 1/40000 20000

Hour, Date, Place	Summary of Events and Information	Remarks and references to Appendices
1915 Present to		
10 a.m.	Took over guns & positions & zone from 67th & 135th (honoured) & found 75 rounds of 9.2", 757s & Hills brown & battery in action zone.	Cloudy, trouble - occasional Sun.
12 noon	Ends of Johnson's & Target fired at 5 of was struck 21 yards. Observation from O.P. at OY ELD and at CAPT JAMES. H.R.A. Found 22 — found 4 adequate — Practice good, without 4 hits body observed. Battery ordered to limit roundabout.	
1.5 p.m.	8 Shrapnel fired on Germans improving trench 19.20, 4.22, (in Square O.2 d.)	
2 a.m.	4 P.B.T. fired to assist fire for 116th Heavy Battery but got no hit, so firing was stopped	
12.15 a.m.	4 4 (white 80.5) Howitzers 3rd Regiment Division, at Michigan trenches trying to [illeg] to bombard N of 9th Division and of Shrewell moved into trenches before day & 31 a.s. Bombardment commenced. Infantry routed 15.15.20 inclusive before daylight.	Nightrise & wide [illeg] mist after sunrise and a few days to penetrate shortens started all day.
[3rd Cavalry Div area — appears on sheet 20]		
7.45 a.m.	Battery (also 3 & 5) opened fire on German trenches towards [illeg] 16,17, and 18+19, at battery fire 30 per 1 minute, slowly day at the rate of 10.30 per minute, when half dropped to 6/min.	
12 noon	and some of 12 heavy short bombs assisted by 116th Heavy Battery and a section of 93rd Co's Battery. Enemy occasional trouble, he about 6 from 12 a.m. to 5.30 p.m.	
7 p.m.	where battery fire ranged from 30 & 16.2' at longest & nearer to recuperation & Infantry by this infantry. No firmly claimed admit given. Rifled at 5.30 shrapnel & found 157 H.E. Great shell in and about guns, Normalities 9.3f, 20 opm orders, had 2 killed & 3 wounded.	
7.30 a.m.		
+ 8.10 a.m.		

[signature] R.F.A.
Mis

364th Battery. R.F.A.

WAR DIARY
or
INTELLIGENCE SUMMARY.
(Erase heading not required.)

Army Form C. 2118.

Ref. Map Sheet "13". Sheet 28.
45.00 and N.W. S.W. 26700

Hour, Date, Place	Summary of Events and Information	Remarks and references to Appendices
19/5. March 3rd (omitted in preparation) 12.30 p.m. 3 p.m.	Trenches opposite 19.19.4.7.20 shelled without retaliation – 10 shells fired. September 21 shelled – 24 shells fired at Trig.Pt. – Several hits obtained. Combined observation by Capt. Pay on mound at 21 ST.ELOI and infantry in trench 22.	Cloudy. Would – no wind.
7th 5 a.m. 10.40 a.m. 11.10 a.m. 1 p.m.	12 shrapnel on trenches opposite 19.19.4.7.20 – no observation. 8 shrapnel on gun emplacements at O.P.C. 3.1. – no observation. 8 shrapnel on gun emplacements at O.15.a.4.1. – no observation. 7 shrapnel 1 & 8 Trig.Pt. on infield near trench 21. Combined observation with – several hits noted.	Cloudy – some light rain. Wind from N. to N.E. Wind veers to N. at 2 a.m.
4.15 p.m. 4.30 p.m. 4.35 p.m.	5 shrapnel on 2 small roads in O.9.a – observed by Lt. Thompson (39th) at ST ELOI. 7 shrapnel on road in O.9.C. – no observation. 5 shrapnel on gun emplacement at O.15.b.6.6. – no observation. The above fired in accordance with orders to expend enemy's batteries firing up to a limit of double the daily allowance of ammunition.	Orders received that in future daily allowance of ammunition doubled. Also that Trig.Pt. would be used till further orders.
8 p.m.	Lt. Pitt takes working party to improve mound at ST.ELOI, & returned about 2 a.m.	

F.M.Nicht
Major R.F.A.

371   364th Battery. R.F.A.   Army Form C. 2118.   21.

WAR DIARY
or
INTELLIGENCE SUMMARY.

Ref. Maps. Series "13" Sheet 28.
1/40000 N.W. and S.W. 1/20000

(Erase heading not required.)

Hour, Date, Place	Summary of Events and Information	Remarks and references to Appendices
March 8th	Day passed quietly. On occasions with R.A. Div'l Arty orders a few rounds were fired at intervals during the day – total expenditure 30 shrapnel.	Cold wind from N.N.W. Fine & unusual sun.
9th	Quiet day – no shooting. "Brent-Archibald" (attached) R.H.A. leaves with orders to report himself at VIEUX BERQUIN. Lieut. M.W. Hadlock (Temp'y Commission) joined, having been posted in place of 2/Lt. Bellamy (invalided home, accidentally wounded). (109)	Rain, milder.
10th 2.3 p.m. 3.30 p.m. 4.30 p.m.	10 shrapnel on trenches in front of 119, to prevent rein[forcing]. 8 on trenches in front of 17.7.18 in 99 & 139's zone, fatigue being out the time firing in NE aeroplane. 26 rds on trenches in O.J.C. in front of 22 and 23, this battery having been taken over the previous night by 57th Div'n from 28th Div'n at Meteren – occasionally aimed bursts for attraction of enemy observing stations.	Rain, mild.
11th 11.30 am 11.30 am 2.30 pm 2.55 pm	Registration of enemy's works opposite trench 23, in O.J.C. – 12 rds. Fire directed on to parapets for the most. – 18 rds. 30 rds shrapnel fired on N.S. corner of parapet for purpose of putting wire. Elevation raised on to maintain of work "parapets bombardt." – 60 rds fired. There was all part of a combined artillery operation rehearsed by Bt (Cap't) in which battery 27th 4/9th Div'ns took part. Total rds fired during day by battery 144	Very misty morning – mild. Later clearer after 11 am. Report out to G.O.C.R.A. re appearance of enemy motors or catapult throwing large bombs fired from front of 18.
12th	Quiet day – The shooting [?Practice] combined artillery operation took place on HOLLANDSCHESCHUUR F.M.E. position, but 364th Bergade did not take part in it.	Misty morning – Cleared soon after. Bank field.

[signature] R.F.A.

WAR DIARY
or
INTELLIGENCE SUMMARY.

(Erase heading not required.)

Army Form C. 2118.

364th Battery R.F.A.
Ref: Ordce Seris "B" Sheet 28
1/40,000 and N.W. and E.W. 1/20,000

Hour, Date, Place	Summary of Events and Information	Remarks and references to Appendices
1915 March 13th		
12.15 p.m.	12 rds fired on battery at O.9.c.3.1. This battery had been shelling our trenches near ST ELOI for some days – apparently 151st Battery. Hostile had not been seen up to date. Lt Pitt at ST ELOI W.Ing O.P. he said on this morning Enplacement had been located some time earlier by R.F. Capt. Clowston was actually on front crest north, but well through tree, but some rounds at rear burst on plain where flash was seen.	Frosty morning – cleared about 10 a.m. – Wind veering to N – Colder.
2.20 p.m.	25 rounds fired on zone batteries by forward Trenches 22 + 23 in O.3.c. This formed part of combined artillery operation. Lt Pitt observing manned at ST ELOI, reported that a heavy howitzer (bigger than the 5.9 in) was firing. This is the first been of such armament since end of January.	Fine – mild. Frosty morning & evening. Apparent return of 8.2 howitzer.
14th		
10.15 a.m. 3.10 p.m.	Engaged guns at O.9.c.31. 6 shrapnel. Repeated at 11.45 a.m. and again at 3.15 p.m.	Frosty & mild.
5.10 p.m.	German attack on horned at ST ELOI and neighbouring trenches. No message received upon in order today to mine being out, but 19th Brigade is well & message was taken up on horse. Turn gun fire. Firing continued all night – and transport supplied ammunition to batteries carrying at 7.25 p.m. on 15th. – Battery shelled at various times – casualties 2 nco's + files wounded. Lt Shemwell commanding the battery, Major White no commanding the Brigade, Brig at VOORMEZEELE writ Br Gen Wingley (comdg 82nd Inf Bde) at VOORMEZEELE Account of action in Appendix VI Capt O. Say 1, 2nd Home Counties Bgde R.F.A. (Territorial) Joining with 20th Bde R.F.A. Ammun Column, attached to Battery Temporarily.	Action of 14th March – see App VI.

363

Army Form C. 2118.

364 F Battery R.F.A.
Ref. maps: series "B" Sheet 28.
1/40000 and N.W. and S.W. 1/20000

WAR DIARY
or
INTELLIGENCE SUMMARY.
(Erase heading not required.)

Hour, Date, Place	Summary of Events and Information	Remarks and references to Appendices
1915. March 15th	Action at ST ELOI Continued. Total number of rounds fired from 5.15pm on 14th to 6 p.7.25pm on 15th inst 1344.	Strafing and mud.
16th 5pm–5.15pm	12 shrapnel fired at gun target at 0.10.a.7.6. } Flashes had been seen from left 12 " " " at 0.9.a.0.0. } litter position on The 15th. by observer in aircraft. Search for next evening station. Pris. Daniell part S. of POPERINGHE tried in interim.	Muddy – less mud.
17th 1pm	Trenches in front of 17 and 20 engaged – 4 shrapnel. Plan of proposed at ST ELOI making adequate observation impossible. Search for next evening station continued. Lt Col Gray retired Casualties Command of Brigade.	
18th 1am	Cooperation with my Bn-Battalion of left section handed over to 19th Brigade R.F.A. together with next telephone line leading to 16/17. – Battery in future only has to keep touch with left battalion.	Mud – not much mist except in early morning.
4.30pm	Brig. Matth at Staunton House party contains telephone lines laid out on night of 16/17.t (WHITE HORSE CELLARS in ST ELOI's Command of BREASTWORK), not known meaning it may to men becoming entangled is a daylight connect on St Etienne's wire into BREASTWORK and minimum time during day, manage in firing line garrison. No hot-horses front under strafing, Regiment cannot be seen sufficiently. Established first in front of trenches 19 and 20.	

[signature]

374

24

Army Form C. 2118.

36th Battery. R.F.A.

WAR DIARY
or
INTELLIGENCE SUMMARY.
(Erase heading not required.)

Ref. Map Sheet "B" Sheet 28.
Ypres and N.D. and S.W. 1/20,000

Hour, Date, Place	Summary of Events and Information	Remarks and references to Appendices
1915 March 19th / 1 a.m.	Maj. White, after two months complete laying down to hospital at BYEASTMORE. Having established new in touch with Battalion head-quarters of infantry battalion in trench area opposite to the 2 SHELLEYS FARM, some 30 yards further.	Cold wind from N.N.W. Frost began to fall about 2 a.m. and continued in driving showers with occasional spells of sun, all day, and being rep'd at 19/20.
	Day passed quietly. Battery did not fire.	
20th	Day passed quietly — Battery did not fire — Maj. White reconnoitring and made a rest/alt observing station for battery in H position (firing on by-zone) at H 35. C. 9.1.	Snowy & cold. Wind chipped. Some mist in evening.
21st 10.15 am 6.12 / 3 pm	Registration of main German trench in front of 19 and 20, near SHELLEYS FARM. Observed by Lt Shewell from trench 21, near SHELLEYS FARM. Persisted on 7 th trides at one.	Sunny & cold — wind sliped 7 pm S.W. much milder.
22nd 4 pm 3 pm	New dividication station at H 35 C 9.1. taken into use. Some of 15 rounds fired on left zone. C.O. and Adjt 23rd 13th R.F.A. come to see position milk seem to taking over shortly.	This evening — mild.
23rd 8 am 2.35 pm	O.C. 108 th Battery comes to see position etc, milk near taking over. 14 shrapnel fired on 19 +20 and main trench in rear. + 20 rest mod snapped. Relieved by Lt Sheldrick from trench 21.	Overclouded — mild
24th 11 am	8 shrapnel fired on guns in battery at O.B.a. 7,5, from which flashes had been seen. 27 trd Arty H.Q. got moved to RENING HELST, and from 12 noon came under G.O.C. 3rd Div. Arty, pending relief.	Mild — light showers.

T.M. White
May. R.F.A.

364th Battery. RFA
Ref. Map Sheet "B" Sheet 28
1/40000 and N.W. and S.W. 1/20000

WAR DIARY
or
INTELLIGENCE SUMMARY.
(Erase heading not required.)

Army Form C. 2118.

Hour, Date, Place	Summary of Events and Information	Remarks and references to Appendices
1915 March 23rd 3am.	Major Pott, taking 2nd Ballon of 19th Bty to Trench 21, lost his way & was unable to get in before daylight, so returned. Consequently no 6 Reserve Officer in Trench this day. Bombarding (20th Bde) relieved by 3rd Div (1st Bde).	Early morning thick mist & hail frost shower. Late Review. Late cold northerly mind. Snow.
9 p.m.	Day passed quietly - Battery did not fire. One section No 5th (Bty) (23rd Bde) arrived in relief 17th mm. Emplacements of left section guns, which were then removed & handed over to 99th Bty, & other guns belonged. Reported section returns to Major Lin under 2nd Maxwell.	
26th 8 am.	Orders received that relief are cancelled and that 23rd Bde guns will be replaced again by 20th Bde.	Cloudy - cold - occasional shower.
11am.	Orders received that 20th & 10th note battery relief will be reversed out on 27th, each battery reassuming its own gun posn. 20th Bde relief rec'd under L.O.R. 3rd Div 160/61.	
11.30am.	Guns reregistered on trenches in front of BREASTWORK 23 (O.3.c) 17 note (0.2.b.9.d) (note).	
3.20pm.	Guns reregistered on trenches in front of BREASTWORK.	
7.30pm.	Action 10th Bty withdrawn trustorme to their battery.	
27th	One section 67th Bty takes over their empty element.	Slight frost at night
	Present 67th Bty takes over position 364th Personnel takes over	Fine - cold - westerly wind.
9am.	take over gun & C position from 99th Bty	Alternate sunshine & cloud.
10am.		
3pm.	Registration. 1 gun in B.2. Camp at (1.9 Hill)	
	1 STE401 in 1.6.2. Camp at (1.9 Hill).	
5.15pm.	Engaged guns reported in O.9.C.F.6, in a behind wood. Searching fire 200 yds in depth employed (2 rods). No accurate observation possible, though burst could be seen through trees.	Frost setting in

WAR DIARY or INTELLIGENCE SUMMARY.

364th Battery, R.F.A.
Ref. Maps: Sheet "B" Sheet 28
NW and SW 1:40,000 & 1:20,000

Army Form C. 2118.

Hour, Date, Place	Summary of Events and Information	Remarks and references to Appendices
March 28th 3 pm	Registration series of 12 rds fired on trenches S. of ST ELOI. Intermittent harass'g fire of guns 2½ from ordinary positions and to incomplete registration of other 3 guns on 17½. Report received in morning of heavy German guns having been seen in aeroplane approaching VOORMEZEELE from S.E. probably 8.2 inch. Instructions to look out for it, & attempt to locate position.	Bright — Sunny — v. misty. Cold — frosty mainly. Frost at night.
29th 30th 10 am 3.35 pm 5.30 pm	Day bright & quiet. Battery did not fire. Capt Ing (attached) rec'd orders to join his batt. Sec'n 6. 8 rds on trenches S. of 57 E.10 1. 12 rds on guns at O.15.c.6.7.7. by map — no observation possible. 4 rds on trenches S. of 57 E.10.1. Observed from cottage at H.35.c.9.1	Bright — Sunny — cold. N. wind — frost at night. Bright — Sunny — cold — wind still N.W.
31st 12 noon 3.45 – 4.30 pm 9 pm	Orders received that activity by 23rd & 13th Bde R.F.A. will not be carried out, as formerly detailed, in respect of 31st Mar/April & 1st April. 3 rds 2nd gun, 3 gun targets at O.9.a.3.0., O.9.d.3.3 and O.9.b.9.1. Third fire from 5.9 howitzer rifled guns, which shelled N.W. corner of trench in Bagneux. H.2.9.d., some 400 yds in front of battery. Probably German Observation Balloon which was up had caught flash of guns & shells were perfectly visible from Batt., went to shelter. Gun in line. Fire section 10g t 134. Taken of emplacements of 4th section, which not drawn to keep in line with 3rd Sect. Batt.	Bright sunny — milder. Full moon. App. VII — Remarks on No.7. shed sight. App. VIII — Transferred to TMS. [signature] Maj, R.F.A.

364th Battery. R.F.A.
War Diary - March 1915.

Appendix VI.
Account of action of 14/15 March 1915 at ST ELOI.

14th

5.10pm. — The batteries of 19th Bde R.F.A. on our right were heard to open with gun fire. No S.O.S. message had been received by battery, but according to instructions gun fire was opened, followed by battery fire 5 secs, at about 5.15pm.
Capt Fry was observing that day at the MOUND at ST ELOI, but no communication could be got with him or with either of the battalion headquarters at BUS HOUSE and WHITE HORSE CELLAR.

6pm. Maj. White, who was commanding the brigade ordered to join Bt. Gen Langley, Comdg 82nd Infy Bde, who were holding the left section, at VOORMEZEELE. Lieut Sherwell assumes command of the battery.
About this time the enemy shelled the battery, both with H.E. and shrapnel, most with 5.9 inch shell, but also with field guns (15pr). The shelling continued for about an hour, & 2 rank & file (names below) were wounded by shrapnel.

7pm. Capt Fry reported at VOORMEZEELE about this time, having fallen back with the retiring infantry from the MOUND, and helped to rally them at the support trenches.

7pm 14th to 7.25pm on 15th } Battery continued to fire at varying rates during the night and next day, altering range and rate of fire to support the counter attacks, first of the Royal Irish and Leinsters, supported by 4th K.R.R. Corps, and then that of Rifle Brigade (4th) and P.P.C.L.I. The former took place about 2am & the latter about 4am on 15th, & both failed to retake the mound.

15th

6.30am. Battery switched onto MOUND for about ½ hour, & then resumed its original zone.
In about 26 hours the battery fired 1344 rounds.

Names of Wounded:-
No. 54597. Bombr. G. Wells.
No. 76868. Gunr. P. Cassim.

T.R.M.White
Maj. R.F.A.
Comdg. 364th Bty. R.F.A.

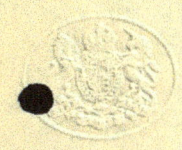

364th Battery. R.F.A.
War Diary - March 1915.

Appendix VII.

Remarks on No. 7. Dial Sight.

The lower minute scale, attached to the carrier, is unnecessary, often inaccurate, and frequently confusing to the layer.

There is often a large amount of backlash in these, and the milled head can be turned nearly half a degree sometimes without affecting the centre arrowhead. These scales are not required, as minutes can be put on the scales marked on the milled heads of the top scale, which turns the circular degree plate. The use of these has the advantage that the same head is used for putting on both degrees & minutes, & it greatly reduces the likelihood of layer's error. I recommend that the lower scale plate & milled heads be removed.

P.W. White
Maj.

Comdg 364th Bty R.F.A.

In the field.
31/3/15.

364th Battery. R.F.A.
War Diary – March 1915.

Appendix VIII. –

Amendment to Training Manual Signalling.

The System of allotting Station calls for batteries R.F.A., laid down in App. VI T.M.S. 1907 (Reprint 1911) does not contemplate the possibility of more than 259 batteries, which number has now been greatly exceeded.

If it is considered necessary to allot a permanent call to every battery, I suggest that some system be authorised as soon as possible.

At the same time I would suggest that the necessity is open to doubt. I have not yet had occasion to use such a call. The necessity would apparently only arise when a battery is detached for special service with other troops.

For communication between a Brigade (Artillery) Commander & his battery Commanders the letters A, B, C and D added to the Brigade call would seem to suffice.

Would not this also serve the purpose for communication with other troops & help to solve a difficult problem.

T.W.W. White
Maj.
Comdg 364th Battery. R.F.A.

In the field.
31/3/15.

121/5166

29th Division

364th Batty R.F.A.   20 BDE

Vol V   1 – 30.4.19

364th Battery. R.F.A.
Ref Map Series "B" Sheet 28
L1 and N.W. and N.E. 1
1/40000   20000

WAR DIARY
or
INTELLIGENCE SUMMARY.
(Erase heading not required.)

Army Form C. 2118.

Hour, Date, Place	Summary of Events and Information	Remarks and references to Appendices
April 1st 5am 6am	Battery Commdr. and Staff relieved by the Composite Battery of 1 Section 433 E Battery 109 F Battery (Major Fisher). The information given B.C. who then took Command. The Battery then marched to rest billets near ABEELE, about 3 miles S.W. of POPERINGHE, between Reninghelst and ABEELE — POPER- -INGHEM road. R.H. Section left in action, with 2/Lt Channell attached.	Fine – still mild – cold at night.
9am	Reinforcements replaced by another section 109 F Bty – withdrawn from action and marched back to rest billets, arriving about 1am on 2nd	
2nd 6.30pm	Battery resting in billets – Reconning of horses. Fingers. Orders received that Battery will take up position of 6 guns Battery at T.18.c.2.2. (E. of YPRES) by relieving on nights of 5/6th and 6/7th inst., 4th(?) B.C. and one other Officer will reconnoitre it & obtain all information from French B.C. on 3rd or 4th Sunday as best.	Fine, mild. Strong gale of N.W. tempest, bringing very heavy rain with it.
3rd 6.30pm	Battery resting. Inspection of men & horses carried by Capt. Gen. Sir 94 Plumer, Comdg. 5th Corps, who expressed approval of workdone by Battery during Sunday & Monday. Further orders etc. to be on to position as before.	Mild – overcast – clearing off from Westwards.
4th	Battery resting. Maj. White + 2/Lt Pearsall proceeded by horse to POPERINGHE by motor bus from there to YPRES, thence on foot to the position to be taken over from French Battery of 42nd Rgt. (90 Capt.) Position of Battery, Observation Station & fuze battery reconnoitred. French Officers were very kind & hospitable. The thought that his position not being even my been & hospitable,) & it was very dirty & unacceptable.	Overclouded. Mild during & occasionally – dull. T M W maj. R.A.

379
28.

WAR DIARY *or* **INTELLIGENCE SUMMARY**

Army Form C. 2118.

364th Battery, R.F.A.

Ref. Maps: Sheets "B" 1/40,000 Ypres 28 and S.E.
and 1/20,000 Ypres N.E. and S.E.

(Erase heading not required.)

Instructions regarding War Diaries and Intelligence Summaries are contained in F.S. Regs., Part II. and the Staff Manual respectively. Title pages will be prepared in manuscript.

19/5

Hour, Date, Place	Summary of Events and Information	Remarks and references to Appendices
April 3rd 6 p.m.	Left section with Maj. & Lt. Pitt marched via VLAMERTINGHE YPRES and took up position at I.18.c.2.2. Relieving one section of 149th Battery. — Found that no approaches to Battery position existed & had to adapt all the available cover, & make the shelters up by hand. Right section & first line wagons of 149th were relieved by section at ASELE. Battery position alongside 149th Battery. The trench had proper observation station some y[ds] behind. While trying to reach trench at dawn found it impossible — see zone of our batteries from the ridge in advance, had to crawl on on one's stomach from gun position to trench & remain there all day. The trench had lost its parapet in most places, knocked down by shell gallery on it. One was quite safe behind the parapet though behind, though some pot shots from the battery.	Fine & fairly warm morning. Cloudy up till about 4 a.m. when ...
4.30 p.m.	Registration firing east (zone 1) Registered on church tower of ZANDVOORDE village. No. 2 gun about 3° by y[d]s.	
7 p.m.	One of the horses of Major's limber. Ammn exhausted & sent out and fired in retreat. Horses sent back to firing battery teams at I.S.c.3.0. Only the guns were left in their positions. Had no opportunity of protection of any kind. R.V. Fraull	This strenuous morning + night. Cooled over in the morning exhausted to some ex... shock, in airing all night
6 p.m.	Right-section firing battery of 6th. First line wagons & transport wanted from ASEELE were then at Shorwall & Haddock Limbers wagons dropped at H.10.b.3.6. where their lindly mules alongside ammunition column. ... gun good one major hip-shot getting into position about to take ...	

364th Battery R.F.A.
Army Form C. 2118.
Ref. Map Series "B" Sheet 28.
N.W., N.E. and S.E.
and 1/20,000

WAR DIARY
or
INTELLIGENCE SUMMARY
(Erase heading not required.)

1915.

Hour, Date, Place	Summary of Events and Information	Remarks and references to Appendices
April 7th 8 a.m.	The remaining French section pulled out at 12 midnight. The battery was shelled by field guns (about 30 rds) at about 2 p.m. No damage.	High wind — unclouded. Several heavy showers.
11 a.m.	After considerable trouble the trapped gun was manhandled out of the mud into position. A good many 15lb shell dropped	
12 noon.	around, but not very close.	
4.30 p.m.	Repn station sent (Mode) of left section field on zone. The whole zone of battery covered about 10½ deg top of ZANDVOORDE tower.	
7 p.m.	The remaining two batteries of reinforcements were mainly getting empty, being now empty, returned to major thus.	
8th 10 a.m.	Orders received that at 67e, 99e + 364th batteries allotted to right section (27th Division's line. 145th Bty to left of 1st Brigade on centre section) +19th Bde on left section. 82nd Bty 132 to that night. Section, 8th centre, + 80th left — 364th being left battery of right section, is affiliated to left Battalion of 82nd or Irish Brigade, which on this day was Royal Irish Fusiliers.	Fine — alternate sun + cloud. High wind veering to W.
12.30 p.m.	Rept. Station posted (15 rds.) fired on zone to no burst. 2d Haddick as to limits of fire.	
1.15 p.m.	German section of 2 guns reported at J.26.c.2.1. Endeavour O.C. B34 to engage it. Right section thereof got it by map and 15 rds fired in bursts of 2 at 1½ minutes interval. The battery mess killed by field guns just before this from two directions, from my report of from left — first just after a few rounds from a howitzer gun fell on left plat. of battery, one almost in a Belgian battery in rear about 200 yds to our left. Many thousands of 30f howitzer bursting on percussion. No damage.	

T.M. Millet R.F.A.
Maj.

WAR DIARY or INTELLIGENCE SUMMARY

Army Form C. 2118.

384th Battery R.F.A.

Ref. Map Series "B" Sheet 28 N.W., N.E. and S.E. 1/20,000

12/5/15

Hour, Date, Place	Summary of Events and Information	Remarks and references to Appendices
(Cont'd) 6 p.m.	Orders received laying down zones of battery. — The only change in our front taken over from French was that the width of zone was enlarged about 2 deg. to the right. The battery now covered the ground in front of trenches 17 to 25 inclusive.	Fine — mist — hot wind fairly cold from N.W.
6.7 a.m. 9 a.m. 2 p.m.	Germans active on battery several times fairly high. 2nd Lieut. Stenwell goes to reconnoitre new map position at H. 15. Battery shelled by field gun from direction of ZANDVOORDE — tried to explode an 18 ads on J.26.c.2.1. Shelling stopped after about 1½ hours. One man wounded.*	* No.52498 Bombdr A. Poole
4 p.m. 8 p.m.	Ran telegraph registration on buildings at J.27.c.7.9 and J.26.d.8.3 (14 rds.) Enemy battery prepares gun trenches half way east of Chateau Knost marsh to ring weapons. Most YPRES in H.18 under 2nd Lt Stenwell. 2½/8th Ldn's +OXF+YPRS., have assisted with guns. Officers' mess established in house on YPRES — MENIN road at J.17.a.6.8. This with view to making 2/Battery headquarters mathematic position. Lieut. F.R.E wrote Bdn. Hd.Qs Offr Bde's of Rfr. at ordinary arrangement of tel. from this time.	
11 a.m.	Buildings at J.27.c. 7.9 fired on to confirm registration 8 p.m. yesterday, of officer (10 rds.)	
3-5 p.m.	Any shots went through windows 17 to 25 to try/find observing station in truss building. It was impossible on account of zinc landing directly only 3 were fired. One struck tree behind gun with intention of	Fine — coldish wind from NW alternate breeze + cloud.

W M Millet Capt R.F.A.

382
31.

3621 F Battery R.F.A.   Army Form C. 2118.

Ref. map Series "B" Sheet 28 - 1/40000
and Sheet 1 N.W., N.E. and S.E.
and Sheet ? ?

WAR DIARY
or
INTELLIGENCE SUMMARY
(Erase heading not required.)

Date	Hour, Date, Place	Summary of Events and Information	Remarks and references to Appendices
1915 April			
10. (contd)	6.15 p.m.	At Strooyken (M8) heavy attaining station built close woodthe numbers of German infantry could be seen moving to ZANDVOORDE billets (on the FREEZENBERG road. Battery fired 12 rds., which scattered them.	Fine cool with seven cloud.
	11.30 am 12.15 p.m.	Battery was shelled by field guns from direction of R6N ZILLEBEKE. 20 common shells.	
11.	11am 11.30 am	Enfilade fire on J.31.c.3.5, a target given by B Bty, R.A. Field fire on J.31.c.3.6, a target moment on French obsce. We killed a number from information obtained from Flank of J.31.	
	1.30 p.m.	Our own artillery at German observation balloon at various etc 2. Fell long ways short. This balloon partially ascends from S.W. of TEN BRIELEN.	
	6.36 p.m.	Germans again seen in ZANDVOORDE. Had scattered them. Observing officers favoured to think there was an evening shift. We think stores then. Motor parties carrying up material were seen as well as carts.	
		Battery stand by to brake with aeroplane, which however did not come, being engaged with 18th R19 - 13th & R.F.A. The battery nearly shelled, but German aeroplanes were active in the evening. 3 of them ?? of ??	

[signature] R.A.

364th Battery, R.F.A.

Army Form C. 2118. 32

WAR DIARY or INTELLIGENCE SUMMARY

Ref. maps. Series "B" Sheet 28.
1/40000 and 1/20000 N.W., N.E. & S.E.
N.W., N.E. & S.E.

(Erase heading not required.)

1915

Hour, Date, Place	Summary of Events and Information	Remarks and references to Appendices
April 12 / 11.25 a.m.	Spent by shell from a 77mm battery firing from direction of N.E.W. ZILLEBEKE full near battery. Gun supposed at 12.5.5 fire by a similar battery from direction of ZANDVOORDE. Battery unable to make self conspicuous at moment.	Fine - mild - occasional intervals. No wind.
3.45 – 5 p.m.	Aeroplane turned us & two targets. Two targets were engaged, effective fire being attained on both - very successful at J.36.A.3.2. and J.32.B.5.5. This aeroplane was working with 1st Brigade Point Battery. Battery up & above along the line, & then which of fire when behind the Australian battery dummies. Their practice along well. Barrack fund.	
5.15 p.m.	Since 12 shell from 77mm battery at last range as found over battery falling near on Ypres road or MENIN road. Major Luis more shelled 4min to change to H.15.a.5.55 - Battery office staff was brought up to better connection to all batteries at I.4.d.7.6.	
13 / 11.5–11.20 a.m.	6 rifles were fired in 2 bursts of 3 each. on guns reported at J.26.6.5.3.2. No observation is possible in this target.	Fine - cool wind from N.W.
1 – 1.15 p.m.	Two registration series of 4 rounds each fired on buildings at J.27.c.5.5. and at ZANDVOORDE village, but of which one retreats from the observing station. Again endeavoured to find a better observing station, but failed.	
3.20 p.m.	German 77mm guns shelled no. with about 18 rds from direction NEW ZILLEBEKE. Bearing of 1st shell scrap gun 180° magnetic. Two gun emplacements were hit but no damage done. All H.E. shell, bursting after graze action. fuze apparently. —	

T.M. White
Major. R.F.A.

WAR DIARY or INTELLIGENCE SUMMARY

(Erase heading not required.)

364th Battery R.F.A.

Army Form C. 2118.

Ref. Map Sheet "B" Sheet 28.
and 1/20000 N.W, N.E. and S.E. 1/40000

Hour, Date, Place	Summary of Events and Information	Remarks and references to Appendices
April 14th 12 noon	8 rds fired on J.33.a.8.5. by order of Brigade Cmdr. We were notified what the target was.	Heavy clouds – N.W. wind – stormy rain at intervals. Cleared in afternoon & fine night.
5.15 p.m.	Shots fired on guns reported in J.32.d.57. which had been annoying bomolers in HERENTHAGE Wood about J.20.	
15th 2.30 p.m.	The morning was again spent to-day to H.10a. S.E. front. Alternative position of Right section reconnoitred. 12 rds on guns reported at J.32.d.5.0. The same target was engaged on 14th.	Fine – mild.
2.40 p.m.	The above target again engaged with 8 rds. Work continued on alternative position for left section by men sent up from ammunition column.	
16th	This position was J-1.17.t. 3.10. Warning received of impending attack by Germans on night 15/16. Gas officer ordered to be awake all night. No attack took place.	
10.35 a.m.	O.C. 1st Brigade R.F.A. asks for fire on Battery employing HERENTHAGE Freiture. 6 rds fired on J.32.6.8.9. supposed to be alternative position.	Fine – mild.
2.15–2.30 p.m.	15 rds fired on P.3.a.6.2 – 6 rds on J.33.K.65. – and 6 rds on J.27.d.2.1. all by order of O.C. 20th 73rd R.F.A. Natives of targets not known.	
7/am	3 rds fired on ZANDVOORDE village on receipt of information from observing officer that considerable movement had gone on there. Report sent in of Battery when photos were seen on 15th by 2nd R.F.A. Weather cloudy at J.34.c.3.8 and J.27.c.7.2. Work continued on alternative positions.– Attack again expected.	

T. M. White
Maj. R.F.A.

364th Battery R.F.A.

WAR DIARY
or
INTELLIGENCE SUMMARY
(Erase heading not required.)

Army Form C. 2118.

Ref. Maps Series "B" Sheet 28 - 1/40000
and 1/20000 M.M., N.E. and S.E.

1915	Hour, Date, Place	Summary of Events and Information	Remarks and references to Appendices
April 17th	3 a.m.	Kept station prior to new position in angle of road at I.17.B.3.10. Big waggons came when officers had been to reconnoitre position.	Fine morning - night cold.
	3.30-4 p.m.	Left station reported on zone from new position - unable to observe from trench 22 by Maj. White. Still much at angle of descent - it was possible to bring "burst" to about 250 yards beyond our trenches. Orders received to bring 1st echelon of waggons this up to farm at I.11.a.1.5. This consisted later on account of ammunition. ZWARTELEN. Battery fired in support of attack by 5th Div. on hill 60 near coming this at 7.30 p.m.	
18th		A good deal of gun firing, bombing & heavy grenades went on all night. The 7th station was shelled by 77 mm guns (about 18 rounds) one shell striking a dugout vacated that morning. The left section. No casualties.	
	8 a.m.	A german aeroplane was seen to fall to the N. of us, apparently brought down by one of our own planes.	Fine morning - night cold.
	8.30 a.m.	Continued firing. Battery did not fire.	
	6.15-6.25 a.m.	Pt 8 p.m. the battery stood ready in close support unmolested - another attack by 5th Div's taking place at this hour. Battery did not fire, but the left section was shelled for 10 minutes (about 40 shells) by a 15 - field howitzer (30 lb) battery with shrapnel and no casualties. One man slightly wounded in hand by splinter, outside Bty Hd Qtrs, two shells were fired.	
	10 p.m.	Firing night - 5th Div Arty fired at intervals all night. All limbers & ammunition wagons with 6 teams & some extra drivers, & conducting personnel, came up to farm at I.11.a.1.5. forming 1st echelon of wagon line.	*No. 69815 Cpl. A.L. Dickinson R.F.A.

*M.M.. R.F.A.
Major. R.F.A.

384

384th Battery, R.F.A.

Army Form C. 2118.

Ref. Trench Series "B" Sheet 28. 1/40000
and 20000 N.W., N.E., and S.E.

WAR DIARY
or
INTELLIGENCE SUMMARY
(Erase heading not required.)

Hour, Date, Place	Summary of Events and Information	Remarks and references to Appendices
1915. April 19th		
11.5 a.m.	Right section new position was shelled, about 12 shells from 77mm guns & 3 from a G. howitzer howitzer in turn (range of guns). Remainder in good line rate in reply H (917.F.3.6) were shelled by 77mm guns, about 25 in all, several of them bursting over the guns.	Sun becoming lighter and not so cold.
12.15 p.m.		
4.25 p.m.	Reported to R.13 Battn repeated an observation station, in forward station I.31.6.5.7., to Brussels forward post so as to say.	
5-5.30 p.m.	10 rds fired from No.3 gun in retaliation to get corrections on ZANDVOORDE village.	
5.50 p.m.	Road junction in front of left section shelled by 15p.t. howitzers, 17 shells burst found (shells of the machinery the guns).	
7.45 p.m.	77mm guns began to shell YPRES—MENIN road to a burst station 40 yds in front of left section, continuing at intervals till about 10 p.m. Probable number of these shells were blinds, certainly 60%	
20th		
3 a.m.	Right section moved into new position in garden at I.W.C.4.2.	Over clouded - Wind moderately veering to S. Very draught at night.
1.20 a.m.	2 rounds fired into ZANDVOORDE village by order of J.C.20th Bde.	
2.30 to 3.30 p.m.	Target (guns) at J.33.d.9.3. registered by wireless aeroplane — using 14 rounds, the last 6 of which were signalled effective and the last 2 lite.	
3 p.m.	Counter Attack by Germans on Hill 60 (15th & 13th Bde, 5th Divn) on our right started. Fighting continuing late into night. Battery took no part in support of 5th Divn — YPRES—MENIN road in front of 15th section especially the left was continually shelled up till 10pm, many bullets & splinters reaching the emplacements. Several infantry were killed & wounded on the road.	

T.M.M. Lt R.F.A.
Mjr. R.F.A.

364th Battery R.F.A.

Army Form C. 2118.

Ref. map Series "B" Sheet 28 - 1/40000
and 1/20000 N.W, N.E, and S.E.

WAR DIARY
or
INTELLIGENCE SUMMARY
(Erase heading not required.)

1915	Hour, Date, Place	Summary of Events and Information	Remarks and references to Appendices
April 21st		Artillery duel general at dawn, - mainly 5th Div-n: our lighter batteries were turned onto gun targets in 5th Div-n zone in support. Our battery was given a target - guns at R.1.a.9.5.	Cloudy - cold - very thin train at intervals - Cleared later - this frosty night.
	10.50am	Opened fire on it at 10.50 am at a slow rate of fire, continuing	
	2.30-4pm	till 6pm, firing 75 rounds during that period. Worked aeroplane registered gun target at R.1, F.3.7, using 18 rounds to do so, & giving no effects, but hits towards end of series. Evening harassed quickly, excepting a somewhat violent shelling 6/14 8th 134 in front of us about 6.30pm, 9-12 rounds on the YPRES—MENIN road.	
22nd		Capt. J.B.C. Madge, 106th Bde R.F.A., West-Avining, joined the battery for attachment for a fortnight in order to gain experience. He was taken up to nearby station & day batteries R.17 - R.25.	Fine - still - coldest night.
	12.30-2.30pm	19 rounds fired on zone in front of Bn-d.s for verification of line transport, and distribution of direct range.	
	3pm	3 rounds fired into ZANDVOORDE village on receipt of information from observing officer that waggons were moving there. The range observed gave cts/vel.	
	5.30pm	Heavy cannonade & rifle fire opened away to the N., in direction of ST JULIEN, & continued till about 9pm.	
	6.15pm	77mm guns from S.E. shelled YPRES—MENIN road, & continued to do so till midnight after dark.	
	7.15pm	99th Battery, 300 yds M.S.W. of us was somewhat severely shelled.	
	9.30pm	Regt Lt-Section ordered to man guns round the ready to line N. in direction of WIELTJE in square C.28 to support Zouaves.	
	10.30pm	Left-Section ordered to leave guns on to YPRES—MENIN road, & be ready to fire down it towards GHELUVELT.	

T.M. Mott, R.F.A.
Mjr.

WAR DIARY
or
INTELLIGENCE SUMMARY

(Erase heading not required.)

364th Battery, R.F.A.   Army Form C. 2118.

Ref. map. Sheet "B" Sheet 28 - 1/40,000
and 1/20,000   N.W, N.E, and S.E.

Hour, Date, Place	Summary of Events and Information	Remarks and references to Appendices
April **22nd (cont.d)**	The order to harass enfg. roads start to major being about 9 p.m.	
23rd 1.30 a.m.	S.O.S. R. was received from 62nd Inf. Bde., artillery reflective fire out in front of night station. Guns were ordered to open again to S. and N. in turn about 20 rds. The order 40th was then sent; 62nd Bde. informing us that the infantry had not developed into an attack, as had been feared.	Morning clear. Rain N.E. Wind veering to E. & little brighter up towards clouds. Very cold. Whole again enjoy lit.
3.5 a.m.	62nd Inf. / 1st Bde. again asked for artillery fire on front of night station. 20 rds. more fired.	
	The infantry H.Q. continued all night and shortly before 4 a.m. we were ordered to turn one gun to the N. again.	
4 a.m.	This was done and continued firing slowly interchange of N.E. meanwhile forming station. Shelling of the YPRES-MENIN road continued intermittently all night & large number of shell falling near battery.	
	Rest of day passed quietly, with occasional exchanges of shell fire away M.Batteries directly. About 8 p.m. we were told to turn guns S. again onto our own zone.	
5.30 p.m.	Ordered fire on Zn. by request of infantry.	
7 p.m.	77mm guns from near KLEIN ZILLEBEKE shelled road near Bty. H.Q.	
	Infantry broke out again beyond WELTJE in the evening, being very heavy till dusk & then dying away somewhat. It started to shell with fresh vigor about 3.30 a.m. on 24th. It seemed to move gradually in distance, & at we assumed no counter attack was [?] generally.	
	Machine guns were harassed about 8 p.m.	

[signature] Maj. R.F.A.

389
85

WAR DIARY or INTELLIGENCE SUMMARY

(Erase heading not required.)

364th Battery, R.F.A.   Army Form C. 2118.
Ref. Maps Ypres "B". Sheet 28 - 1/40000
and 1/25000 N.W., N.E., and S.E.

Instructions regarding War Diaries and Intelligence Summaries are contained in F.S. Regs., Part II. and the Staff Manual respectively. Title pages will be prepared in manuscript.

Hour, Date, Place	Summary of Events and Information	Remarks and references to Appendices
April 1915		
24th		
3.30 a.m.	Fighting to N. broke out again. Shells began falling in front of Left Section, some 17mm fired from direction of THELUVELT and some "Woolly" or 5.9 in howitzers from direction of ZANDVOORDE. Several shells found, bearing Turkish inscription found in town. Remainder of morning passed quietly for battery, though fighting to N. went on intermittently.	Fine - clouding over later. C.S.L. Edmond L. Paul duty night.
2.45 p.m.	Battery intended orders to bring moved to N. and then in villages of ST JULIEN. 4 rounds ending E. side S.E. of St. This latter changed to move in Square C.10 and 11, and later back again to Square C.12 at turning on the carpet. Continued up to about 5 p.m. — return left section turned round again to S. and fired on its own zone in Squares J.25 + 26, about 42 rounds. 4.22 rounds were fired by Battery altogether this day. Horses had been harnessed up all day & about that came up to field by night section near YPRES — MENIN road. — Lieut. Starrdell reconnoitered line of probable retirement via railway St. of YPRES, & took later 4 from back to field at Forw'd Column. Those returned soon after 12 mn.	
25th		
3 a.m.	Orders received that major would retire within British lines. Also that hostile attacks made take place from G.N., but that if our brigade only left the road buffers in their remainder attempting to their own zone. R.J. F. Section accordingly returned to S. again.	Cloudy — light rain — wind dropped.
10 a.m.	Front 20 rds fired on zone by request of 82nd Inf. Brig. in response to shelling of our trenches by Germans —	
10.45 a.m.	Ends fired on zone again for Saint nearer, by request of R.J. Zuihill. Four gun targets engaged with Black card as follows: - Right Section P.1, a. 7. 9. — J. 31. C. 3. 5. — J. 31. c. 7. 6. Left Section J. 31. 6. 3. 5.	
11.30 a.m.	First line majors sent back to Ammo Column trenches	[signature] R.F.A. Maj.

WAR DIARY or INTELLIGENCE SUMMARY

Army Form C. 2118.

384th Battery, R.F.A.

Ref. Map of Series "B" Sheet 28 – 40,000
N.W., N.E. and S.E.
and 20,000

19/5

Hour, Date, Place	Summary of Events and Information	Remarks and references to Appendices
April 25th (cont'd.)	Remainder of day passed quietly for battery. Fighting continued to N, but very little more came through to us. Two German biplanes over our positions from 6 to 7 p.m.	Weather cleared towards evening – Finer still bright by de.
26th 7 a.m.	Biplanes over us again for an hour or more. Battle field continued to the N. A little west of it. About this time we heard that French were about to make counter-attack from Canal with PILCKEN as its objective. To judge by firing this started about 8 a.m. Battery still faced to S, covering its own zone.	Fair – not too much – clouds high & travelling fast.
11.45 a.m.	Enemy Genl. resumed command on handing of centre section. Dwelt fire along the zone; left section also supported guns which enfiladed centre section trenches from J.26.c.3.6. (160th Fd 28 nds)	
1.55 p.m. to 4.15 p.m.	At 1.45 p.m. orders received to support general counter-attack by French, Lahore division, & Canadian division, with fire. Battery fired on 6 zones, firing at a rate of about 20 rds an hour; left section also firing intermittently on guns at J.26.c.3.6, and my left section taking H/E 67th-184d zone (i.e. 5 day minenwerfer) in addition to its own. Enemy 15 ctm were very active continually to the N of Ypres over an hour. (160th fired 36 nds)	
4.15 to 8 p.m.	Fired separate gun targets engaged with a few rounds each with the object of keeping down their fire. They were allocated as follows: – F.1.c.3.7 – I.36.d.7.8 – I.36.d.7.3.5 – I.36.d.3.2 – J.22.c.3.6. There were last heard opened fire on our howitzer guns about 6 p.m.	
5.30 to 6.30 p.m.	Gen 5"9" howitzer & cutter made a few 4.2 howitzers firing in bursts, started anew, just beyond 67th 184d, apparently from direction of ZANDVOORDE. About 6.30 p.m. a 77 mm Battery shelled zone behind left section with some violence for 10 or 15 minutes; apparently from direction of GHELUVELT. I/blieved. There guns in square J.23. Cd. About now we heard that French attack, which failed at first, was now making headway, & that Lahore Division were progressing favourably.	

W.M.W. R.F.A.

WAR DIARY or INTELLIGENCE SUMMARY

364th Battery, R.F.A. Army Form C. 2118.

Ref. Map. Series "B". Sheet 28 — 1/40,000
and 1/20,000 N.W., N.E and S.E.

19/15

Hour, Date, Place	Summary of Events and Information	Remarks and references to Appendices
April		
27th	At about 3pm or 2nd Lieut Sherwell, with Capt. Venters & "B" Battery, relieved 2nd Lieut Cunningham, 67th Bty, at forward observing station G.N., near MILTIGE, remaining out on 27th.	Dull, cloudy - clearing somewhat towards noon.
Noon	Battle ridge meeting up to trench 23 on R.J. division had been continuation of a hand to hand mêlée in this front.	
12 noon	Battle pouch at isolated intervals of trench mortar.	
12.15 pm	Orders received to turn night station to Majors to support front attacks, also to return to trench running E & W from ST JULIEN to cross roads at D.7.c.1.7. at slow rate; found 10 rds in boxes in shaft.	
12.3 pm	Ft. station bust into ground from cartel of square C.16 C.C.16.c.8.8 (probably)	
1.15/1.37 pm	Ft. 15/pm the 16th "Ops" fire now received 32 rds were fired.	
2.15 to 2.30 pm	Rapid station again opened fire on road running E from ST JULIEN at a rate of 20 rds an hour.	
2.30 to 3.20 pm	Bty ½ action, concentrated on village of ST JULIEN and were ranged by Lieut Sherwell from forward observing station.	
3.30 to 7 pm	Rapid action again this exhibited fire along road from ST JULIEN to D.7.c.1.7. from support received from Maj. Hardinge-Newman R.F.A about 3pm. Then went forward in attempt to locate of the field near along the head and thought ST JULIEN. Fire was opened at of 10 rds on toils. Total number of rds fired from 2.15 to 7 pm was 134.	
7 pm	Rate of fire from night action dropped to 10 rds an hour. Passed ??? at 7.30pm to 15 rds an hour.	
	The battery was not shelled to-day. German hostile active all day. From 7pm on 27/4/15 to 5.72 noon on 28/4/15 hostile station continued to fire on salva target at varying rates (2.19 rate).	
28th		
3 am	Maj. White went to observing station to carry out reconnaissance, leaving Lieut Sherwell to command battery all day. —	Fine, clear, not fairly mild.

A1. 392

364th Battery, R.F.A. Army Form C. 2118.
Ref. Map Sheet "B", Sheet 28 - 1/40000
and 1/5000 N.W., N.E. and S.E.

WAR DIARY
or
INTELLIGENCE SUMMARY
(Erase heading not required.)

Hour, Date, Place	Summary of Events and Information	Remarks and references to Appendices
1915 April 28th (cont'd) 12 noon.	Right section's target changed to N. edge of wood at C.10.d.6.6. on which they continued to fire at varying rates till 8.30 p.m. (180 rds)	
12.15 to 7 p.m.	Left section tried to keep a trench in motion in front of trench R.25 just (112 rds) Infantry seemed pleased with results.	
2.30 p.m.	German support trenches in front of C.3 shelled by direction by request of infantry (Brade)	
6 p.m.	Fires at J.28.c.3.6. engaged (Brade) Infantry said we stopped their firing.	
	A German aeroplane (biplane) was brought down by rifle fire about 1 pm near N. observing station - pilot unknown but wounded.	
	Orders received for move of left section to N⁰ of YPRES. Detail received later about 10 p.m. — an officer to relieve N⁰13 F.A. LAHORE Div⁴ near ZILLEBEKE.	
8 p.m.	About 12 noon Bty Hd Qs. were shelled by 77mm from direction of KLEIN ZILLEBEKE. One H.E. shell pierced roof of stable housed inside, killing 2 horses & wounding the other 2. Three men officers' chargers —	
	All preparations made for move of left section & officers' orders for that detailed all mfhr. Precaution in with guns all ordered & with exception of 100 rds for right section. Orders to move never came. Left section gun limbers brought up as there to carry on with.	
29th	Morning quiet as far as battery was concerned. Continued shelling by enemy of large line area E. of YPRES, i.e. POTIJZE, WIELTJE etc and all bonds behind own lines. Also of YPRES itself.	Line, Enemy & Frame [signature] 364 F.A. Maj.

393
42

WAR DIARY
or
INTELLIGENCE SUMMARY
(Erase heading not required.)

Army Form C. 2118.

364th Battery. R.F.A.

Ref. Maps Lorise "B" Sheet 28 – 1/40000
+ N.W., N.E. and S.E. 1/20000

Instructions regarding War Diaries and Intelligence Summaries are contained in F.S. Regs, Part II. and the Staff Manual respectively. Title pages will be prepared in manuscript.

1915.

Hour, Date, Place		Summary of Events and Information	Remarks and references to Appendices
April 29th (cont'd)	1 pm	Fired on at C.16. a. 6.7. registered by forward observing officer (Fido).	
	2.30 pm	8 rds fired along zone in front of Trenches 18.17-25 by request of infantry.	
	3.10 am 5.50 pm	Fired at J.26.c.3.5, engaged by request of infantry (8 rds) Same point engaged again (8 rds). These guns had been annoying our infantry in the trenches.	
	10 am	Lt. White, Lieut. Haddock thirty laid lines to next observing station at farm at C.22.b. 7.7 and fortified an observing post there, Lt. Haddock remaining out to observe on 30th. —	
	11 pm	Orders received that no move in relief of 18th B'de R.F.A. would take place that night. —	
30th	9.30 am 11 am	6 rds fired on guns at J.26.c.3.5 by request of infantry in trench 18.13. Right section took over task of keeping up slow rate of fire on triangle of roads E and N.E. of ST JULIEN from 6th. This had been going practically continuously for 7 days. —	Heavy mist came on at 4 am. dispersed gradually - clear by 11 am. & noon fine.
	10 am	Very heavy rifle & gun fire on left front. BESINGHE started about 10 am started about 1½ hours. Apparently in French area.	
	12.30 pm	Fired at C.16.b. 5.2. and C.17.a. 4.3. reported by Lieut. Haddock forms annoying station (14 rds)	
	5 pm	Fired at C.16. a. 6.7. registered also (2 rds.) By Town rifle & action had quite 54 rds on triangle started mentioned above.	

[signature] R.F.A.
Maj.

394
A3

364th Battery. R.F.A.   Army Form C. 2118.

Ref: Map Series "B" Sheet 28 – S.W.
and 28.NW. N.W, N.E, & S.E.
1:20000

WAR DIARY
or
INTELLIGENCE SUMMARY
(Erase heading not required.)

Hour, Date, Place	Summary of Events and Information	Remarks and references to Appendices
April 30th	Orders for move in relief of 18th Bde. R.F.A. finally cancelled, but Battery told to hold itself in readiness to fall back through YPRES to somewhere W. of that place. This order was only verbal & replaced another received shortly before to effect that 364 & 114th Btys were to remain in their position, & 67th & 99th were to fall back. The next order apparently contemplated the whole Brigade falling back. Details were to be received later.	
10 p.m.	First section turned round to S. again on its own zones, to open fire. Up to 12 mn no further orders received.	
7.30 – 9 p.m.	A number of large kensifero shells (5.9in) were falling over right section, apparently meant for 99th Bty in S. end of wood. No casualties. Two horses slightly wounded. H-Staff & a mare limber harnessed.	

signature
Maj: R.F.A.

2nd Division

364 In Bath R.F.A.

20 ODE

121/5614

Vol VI 1 — 31.5.15.

WAR DIARY or INTELLIGENCE SUMMARY

Army Form C. 2118.

364th Battery R.F.A.
Ref. Ypres Sheet 28 — 1/40000
and 1/20000 N.W., N.E., & S.E.

Hour, Date, Place	Summary of Events and Information	Remarks and references to Appendices
1915 May 1st		
7.30 am	Right Section ordered to turn N. again, in expectation of another attack by French on hill 29 mm left.	Misty early – sunny warm.
10.30 am	Several rounds, mainly shrapnel, registered in squares C.9, C.10, and C.15.	
6.12 noon 1 pm	Warning received of attack at 2.44 p.m. by French & Lahore Division on hill 29 in square C.15.a. Rgt. Section to help support attack.	
2.50–3.30 pm	Trenches from farm at C.15.b.3.8 to C.15.b.10.8 shelled (115 rnds)	
3.30–3.55 pm	Fire switched onto hill 27 in C.15.a. & b. (36 rnds)	
4 pm – 7.25 pm	Fire switched back again to trenches as above + continued at varying slow rate till 7.25 pm. (50 rnds)	
7.15 pm	By request of infantry 13 rnds fired on point at J.26.c.3.6 by left section. Three fused were said to be shelling till 60.	
	About this time Germans commenced bombardment with heavy guns, 10 tr 8.2 in & 5.9 in howitzers chiefly. Their main objective seemed to be 67th Bty in railway, not several of their shots fell near one or other of our positions. No casualties. The main lines were not shelled today. Lieut. Pitt, Sergt. Wilkin & 3 men went on forward control duty on YPRES — MENIN road at 8.30 pm, dealing with men of LAHORE DIVN. & other troops.	
2nd	Morning + afternoon passed very quietly. Battery did not fire.	Cloudy – fine rain afternoon. Cleared in evening. Light N. wind colder.
— 5 pm	Heavy rifle + m.g. fire broke out 1.M. 73, about 5.30 pm went next German station 1x21. Germans had been used asphyxiating gases. Battery (Right section) opened fire at 5.10 pm, on twice attacking. Battery 200–300 yards S. of trench in C.15.b.6 and 2.17.d.	

T.M. Bt.
Maj. R.F.A.

WAR DIARY or INTELLIGENCE SUMMARY

Army Form C. 2118.

364th Battery, R.F.A.

Ref. map. Series "B" Sheet 28 — 1/40,000 and 1/20,000 N.W., N.E. and S.E.

1915

Hour, Date, Place	Summary of Events and Information	Remarks and references to Appendices
May		
2nd (cont.) 5.45 p.m.	Fire was kept up to S. of road Ell Ste Stan. (Ironside) when it was switched onto hill 27, from farm at C.16.a.8.7 to road junction at C.16.b.4.6, & continued till 6.50 p.m. (70 rds.)	
6.50 p.m.	From 6 p.m. till nearly 7pm three separate field batteries shelled round about Bt Hd sections & Bty HQ, from N.E., from KLEIN ZILLEBEKE and from FREZUENBERG directions. They fired from 50 to 60 shells, continued at very slow rate about 25% more third. Shrapnel 25% were third.	
7 p.m.	Fire reopened at slow rate (30 rds an hour) keeping up till about 8pm	
8.30 p.m.	Orders received for move of whole Brigade to N. of YPRES on night of 3/4 May. Verbal orders received on telephone for move to take place at 11 p.m. on night of 2/3rd. Brigade to rendezvous at crossroads in square H.12. Batteries to march in independently.	
9 p.m.		
1/2 m.n.	Battery marched via YPRES, & got through with one man + 2 horses slightly scratched. Still were falling on road continuously at a few minutes interval, especially near railway crossings & the MENIN GATE.	
3rd 3am.	Brigade, having assembled at rendezvous, proceeded to temporary bivouac in fields in H.9.d.	
2pm.	Battery went into its new 2nd line billets at small farm at H.15.a.5.5. Two telephonists had been left behind to keep up as much Fort ? Castle was opposite. This done they followed the battery & at the MENIN GATE of YPRES, which was bombarded continuously, one was killed by a splinter from a heavy H.E. shell. Remainder of day battery rested quietly. Lieut. F.B.L. Hudson, R.F.A. (T.F.), RN. Rees. Bury, attached for experience and instruction, returned to England.	* No. 75356 Gnr. F. York

Forms/C. 2118/11.

395

364th Battery, R.F.A.   Army Form C. 2118.

Ref. Map Series "B" Sheet 28 — 40000
and 20000 N.W., N.E., & S.E.

WAR DIARY
or
INTELLIGENCE SUMMARY
(Erase heading not required.)

1915.

Hour, Date, Place	Summary of Events and Information	Remarks and references to Appendices
May 4th	Day passed quietly. Battery resting. In evening Maj. White & 2nd Lt Pitt reconnoitred gun positions S.W. of YPRES in Square I.13 and 19.	Warm morning — Clouded over later — Light shower in evening. Clear night.
5th	Battery resting. Maj. White, accompanied by Lieut. Haddock, went out by order of G.O.C. R.A. & reconnoitred position for battery 27th Div'l Art'y, to cover front from LILLEGATE to road bridge over CANAL near LANGHOF. (Area given Square H.17,18 and I.13 and position half of Square H.23, 24 and I.19.)	Fine, warm.
6th 2pm	Orders for 20th Brigade to prepare 4 gun positions at H.18.6.5.8 (34^c) & three others in H.18.d and 24.b. Maj. White, accompanied by Capt. Melson (Adjt) showed battery commdrs these positions. Letter went to reconnoitre S° and E aspects of YPRES for Hamburg fire positions. This letter by order of G.O.C. R.A. 27th Div'n.	Fine, warm.
8pm	Working party under 2nd Lt Pitt commenced work on position H.18.6.5.8, returning at daylight. Maj. White took 2 teams to marking ammtn new station. Shrapnel in 2 magns of 908th Bty who had had horses killed these Magns. Approx. position of 908th Magns were CANAL BANKS Hospital buildings by 2nd Lt in their show of shrapnel. Fixed 4th gun position. Ammunition battery still resting.	
7th	Maj. White spent day under orders of G.O.C. R.A. 27th Div'n reconnoitring positions for attack of Div'l Party in Square 7 (Sheet 28) round about BUSSEBOOM to cover line running from N. to S. along E. edge of Square 9 from G.12.b.8.6. G.P.30.a.8.4. Battery resting. Working party under 2nd Lt. Haddock continued work on position at H.18.6.5.8. returning at daylight.	Fine, warm. [signature] Maj. R.F.A.

349
A7.

364th Battery. R.F.A. Army Form C. 2118.

Ref. Map Sheet "B" Sht. 28 – 1/40,000
and 1/20,000 N.W., N.E., and S.E.

WAR DIARY or INTELLIGENCE SUMMARY

(Erase heading not required.)

1915.

Hour, Date, Place	Summary of Events and Information	Remarks and references to Appendices
May 8th. 5 a.m.	Owing to the change of Lieut. F.O.C.R.A. and Brig. White to Remounts. Additional position L.M. of Ypres. Henderson at gun & took over command of Brigade from Lt. Col. Gray, who went to hospital. Lt. Sherwell takes over Command of Battery.	Fine, warm – fresh easterly breeze.
7 a.m.	Heavy cannonade W.E. of YPRES Repair.	
10 a.m.	Orders to harness up & be ready to move received. News received of German attack on night 7/8 & 8th of April 27th Div's. In order to be ready to cover withdrawal if necessary, Battery commander went out to reconnoitre position devised on by F.O.C. Yates observing. Station. 364th Battery Position at H.24. d. 9. 8. Battery remained harnessed up all day.	
9 p.m.	Battery Staff making position out to prepare position. Own making party under Lieut Platt preparing position for section in parallel at H.18. d. 9.5. No. 3 gun sent up to 39th Bty to replace one of theirs damaged by shell.	
11:30 p.m.		
12 m.n.	Orders received to take these batteries up into position before daylight to cover G.H.Q. line M.27 ZILLEBEKE Lam LAKE to YPRES–MENIN road that evening. No room for 364 Bty. till area clear of 3rd Div Batteries.	
9th 1 a.m.	67th moved up to H.24.b. 9.8. 99th to Sp. Wt. Section position at H.18. d. 9.5 & 7.1. 364 F.Bty. remaining in reserve.	Fine – Cold N.E. Wind.
3 a.m.	Lieut Sherwell reconnoitres position for Battery (3 guns) which can be occupied in daylight by unlimbering & behold H.24. 6. 5. 9. Day passed quietly – Battery waiting.	

T.M. [signature]
Major R.F.A.

WAR DIARY
or
INTELLIGENCE SUMMARY
(Erase heading not required.)

Army Form C. 2118.

364th Battery. R.F.A.

Ref. Map Series "B" Sheet 28 — 1/40000
N.W., N.E. and S.E. and 1/20000

Hour, Date, Place	Summary of Events and Information	Remarks and references to Appendices
19/5/15 Eng.		
10th 11am.	Major White went to forward observing station at School at I.9.c.6.1. Sent G.O.C's 621st & 80th Inf. Bdes. Orders asked for more artillery support for his Brigade near HOOGE. Maj. White returned & said G.O.C. R.F.A. who ordered him to take on 87th & 99th at extreme range.	Sunny, warm — wind moderate.
4.5am	Orders for 148th & 364th to go up at night to position E. of CANAL.	
6.30am	Orders for 99th to relieve 98th Bty 14th Brigade. Going to 99th Wood's horses, 364th attempts to take up 4 howitzer support to 99th next position in action at I.11.c.2.2. There 99 up under Q.M. 87th Spent working party goes forward to 364th position at I.13.d.2.3. & finish emplacements etc. made by 99th. 364th arranges to take over ammunition left by 99th in their old position. Battery goes up into position at I.13.d.2.3. (3 guns only.)	
12 mn.		
3-4.5am	Battery open fire on German line from S.E. corner of wood at J.13.a.7.8. to MENIN-YPRES road inclusive at J.13.a.10.2. Anticipated attack by enemy not taking place, battery stops fire at 4.15am. (8 rds.)	
11th 10am.	Battery open fire on same target in reply to bombardment by enemy of our trenches near HOOGE. Slow rate kept up till 12.55 p.m. When "stop" ordered. Observation from Hill 40 between MENIN road and ZILLEBEKE LANE. (4.5 rdr.)	
4pm.	Order received from R.O.E. May not to fire any more to conceal guns thoroughly. This apparently due to some complaint of 5th Div. of our having divulged minute area. Remainder of day passed quietly. Cover for men & guns improved.	

[signature] R.F.A.

364th Battery. R.F.A. Army Form C. 2118.

Ref. map. Sheet "B" Sheet 28 - NOTED
and 25000 N.W., N.E. and S.E.

WAR DIARY
or
INTELLIGENCE SUMMARY
(Erase heading not required.)

Instructions regarding War Diaries and Intelligence Summaries are contained in F.S. Regs, Part II. and the Staff Manual respectively. Title pages will be prepared in manuscript.

Hour, Date, Place	Summary of Events and Information	Remarks and references to Appendices
1915		
Aug.		
12. 8 am. 3.2.5 pm.	Zone on MENIN road T.W. 9 & 6 fired on by regiment of Infantry (23rds) Zone fired on again (14rds). Remainder of day quiet - Position improved.	Overclouded - but moon & still. Clouds finally due to smoke from burning YPRES.
13. 10.15 am.	One section fired on E. edge of LANE WOOD in I.12.b by regiment of O.C. 161/1364 R.F.A. (31 rds). Copy in reports received of Cavalry being shelled out of Trav Farm between VERBRANDEN and BELLEWARDE LANE, 47 Bn. having fallen back to a line running D. & S. through RAILWAY WOOD in I.II.6. F.O. telephone wires in front continually cut all day, & communication very precarious. Bright power-& trench mortars from Trav Farm much. Barbara enforced by O.C. 161/1364 R.F.A. (this boys that cavalry attacks by cavalry about to take place. Just for support from 25th Btn on road between & Treven in I.8.6.	Steady rain all day. S. wind. Very misty. Later rather rather during night.
12.15 am ? 7.35 pm	Battery now fire at intervals on road, hearing fire up till C.4.d, quickening when heavy fire heard. Harping fire up till 7.30 am (227rds). Heavy half last was successful. Now hostile *L.B. telephone meddling line near Hill 40 (I.8) Heavily warn had was by splinter of Shell.	*Nr. 59374 Corp. L.B. Venter
14.	Morning passed quickly - Now gone to be covered by 1468 & 364 from heights on 1st received. The main force was from centre of Square J.19, R.W.19, 148-115 position being in J.30 & that on J.19.C. Had streaming stations & line to SANCTUARY NOT taken over from 146th R.F.A. in afternoon... in this, as 5th Div still reported to be keeping 148 - 69 took up post in this, as 5th Div still reported to be keeping.	Rain early morning - Event turned various. Clouds broke up more later, fine afternoon. Pill evening it.

F.M. Mack
Major R.F.A.

364th Battery. R.F.A.
Army Form C. 2118.

Ref: Infy Series "B" Sheet 28 - 1/40,000
and 27000 N.W, N.E and S.E.

WAR DIARY
or
INTELLIGENCE SUMMARY
(Erase heading not required.)

Hour, Date, Place		Summary of Events and Information	Remarks and references to Appendices
1915			
Aug			
14th (cont'd)	2.30 p.m.	By arrangement with O.C. 12th Bde R.F.A. intermittent fire was opened on points opposite arc of action likely trees behind German huts in I.S.U. and J.I.a. — Neighbouring Brigades were engaged with an average of about 6 intervals between 2 & 0 rounds & 13 shrap (33 rds)	Fine but cloudy — moonrise.
	4.30	O.C. 12th Bde. reported no. of impending German attack on cavalry H.Q. monitoring. Battery fire so not was started on ground behind enemy trenches in I.S.U. and I. gradually slackening. Th on fire to front slowly 13 rnds/ Th/attack apparently did not develop fully. —	
15th		Fine, gone taken over at daylight. Lines laid to trenches and observing officer sent out to report to zones and attack took with Infantry battalion in trenches (Royal Scots) Trouble experienced all day with broken cables — but S.E.W. & 3.30 p.m. Hnes - reposition could begun.	
	4.35 p.m.	No reply fired for Infantry cooperation.	
	5.30 p.m.	Epilogue — in little trenches shelled (I shrap & 7 shot,) & one other. Lt-attack. Lieut Col Roy from I Battery R.H.A arrives to take over command of Brigade...	
16th	10 a.m.	Major Whit returned to command of battery.	
	7 a.m.	9 rds fired on SHREWSBURY FOREST (orders dictated by requirement of Infantry) who reported points back making hostile fire.	Fine — sunny — warm.
	2 p.m.	Attempted to destroy cottage at J.25.a. I.8. with 18 shrapnel & 4 shrap fired to do much damage though half coll moved it. — Range to last - 2800 yrs. Enemy infantry seen this place.	

1247 W 3299 200,000 (E) 8/14 J.B.C. & A. Forms/C. 2118/11.

WAR DIARY or INTELLIGENCE SUMMARY

Army Form C. 2118.

304th Battery R.F.A.

Ref. N. of France "B" Sheet 28 –
and 2/20,000 N/17, N.E. and S.E.

Hour, Date, Place	Summary of Events and Information	Remarks and references to Appendices
May 17th 9 a.m.	Tried to range into battery Iris to B gun – had been returned from Sgt. Bty & came off on night of 15th about 9 pm. Rain prior to this No. 1 howitzer (Sanfield)	Cloudstorm in early morning. Steady rain began about 6.15 am. Stopped about 2 pm.
2.15 & 4pm	Registration completed, weather having lifted slightly & rain stopped. Otherwise still difficult to observe results fired.	
18th 3 a.m.	Major R.W. White went to the trenches for purpose of observation. (Observation French in 11 French holds by Royal Irish Fusiliers) Major White left his principal O.P. and this was sent after him. However to see the French opposite. Major White looked over the French parapet, after he had looked for about a minute & was stopping down off the shooting ledge when he was killed by a bullet. The bullet entered his left eye & he died about 3 minutes after being hit. The body was brought down by a carrying party & was buried at H.24 a 7.8. Ref. map Belgium Sheet 28 N.W. 1/20,000 Clonave. The Rev. arrived 7.30 am 19-5-16.	*Lt. Col May RFA, Capt E.W.S Wilson Capt E.C. Hall RFA Lt Pemberton RAMC & 2/Lt Sherwell & Commy Sarn RFA were present
12.30 pm	Opened fire on Clonmel wood at request of Infantry. 24 rounds were fired but not observed as no officer was forward.	
1.30 pm	2/Lt Haslehurst goes out to forward trenches 2/Lt Sherwell arrives from Wagon Lines & takes over command of the Battery	Sherwell 2/Lt RFA

364th Battery R.F.A.
Army Form C. 2118.
Ref Map Series "B" Sheet 28 - 1/20,000
N.W., N.E. & S.E.
and 1/20000

WAR DIARY
or
INTELLIGENCE SUMMARY
(Erase heading not required.)

Hour, Date, Place	Summary of Events and Information	Remarks and references to Appendices
1915 May 19th 3.45 p.m.	Infantry requested fire to be opened on two workers in the enemies lines reported to be making gun emplacements & Shrapnel and 6 H.E. were fired & three direct hits were obtained with H.E. Observed by 2Lt Haddock in the forward trenches	Weather - cloudy ground very wet
20th 5 p.m.	21 rounds were fired on our zone & lines & ranges being corrected	
21st	Very quiet day - no rounds fired	
22nd	Still very quiet - battery did not fire	
23rd	Zone changed - new zone covering channel round in J.19.C.	
3 p.m.	New Zone registered. 12 rounds being fired observed by 2Lt Sherwell in forward trenches	
4.7 p.m.	Order received from Brigade Office to fire one round gun fire. The rounds 4 - were fired immediately	
24th 3. a.m.	Fire opened on our zone on order from Bde office on account of German attack N. of Menin Road. Our zone was reported quiet an intermittent fire was kept up & 126 rounds in all were fired Hill 40. was very heavily shelled & an Eplve one periodical observing officer being 2Lt R.F.A. in trenches.	Observed by 2Lt R.F.A

53

364th Battery R.F.A.
Ref Map Series 'B' Sheet 28 - Gen'l
Sheet 36 - part

Army Form C. 2118.

WAR DIARY
or
INTELLIGENCE SUMMARY
(Erase heading not required.)

Hour, Date, Place	Summary of Events and Information	Remarks and references to Appendices
1915 May 25. 2.45pm	Major O.M. Harris D.S.O. R.F.A. assumed Command. Lieut Bevitt wounded in shoulder by Shrapnel Bullet. A few Shrapnel & one H.E. burst in and about the Battery position	
26th 3 am.	Relieved by Northumberland R.F.A., & rendezvoused at the bridge Line - marched with the Brigade via BAILLEUX to NIEPPE arriving at 2 pm & went into billets for night.	weather been v bright hot.
27th 12.30pm	O.C. & 2/Lt Shuwell & Lieut Dwab via ARMENTIERES to reconnoitre position & observing stations Run to BOISGRENIER H.30f. Battery arrived & into position at 9 pm.	
28th	Ranges registered on various parts of the enemy's trenches, support trenches & observation houses. Ranges about 2800 x 3000 (approx)	
29th	Continued registration. 10 rounds	
30th	do. 10 rounds	
31st	do second line, communication trenches. 19 rounds	

O.M. Harris Major RFA
OC 364th Bty R.F.A.

171/6034

2nd Division

864th Battery: R.F.A.   20 BDE

Vol VII   1. — 30.6.15.

27t Division

WAR DIARY or INTELLIGENCE SUMMARY

364th Battery   Army Form C. 2118.

Ref. Map Series 8 Sheet 36 NW SW / 20,000

407

June

Hour, Date, Place	Summary of Events and Information	Remarks and references to Appendices
1st	Position handed over to Maj. Hill of 131st RFA who was shown over observing stations, later station of 131 Bty ranged by Maj. O.M. Harris on the German trenches.	
9.30 p.m.	Guns withdrawn & marched to Armentières through Houplines. Lt Shrivell went on in advance to find whereabouts of billets etc. whole battery went to wagon line in Houplines [I.86 D.0.87] for the night. Battery in billets 2 A.M.	
2nd 7.A.M.	Col. Key, accompanied by Major Harris, reconnoitred for a position finally selecting one at C 27 b 9.9 along the Ridge. Working parties were sent out & emplacements for a section prepared, the right section moving in.	
9 p.m.	Working parties & night on remaining emplacements to be position generally.	
3rd	Right section were ranged by Major Harris from observing station in Mairie [C.21 b 5.2] following firing points ch. - Turin Frye Bridge were registered Frelinghien ch. Indian Trench [C.17 a 4.7] — Stop Farm [C.17 b 2.4]. Total rounds fired 24. German 2nd line [C.17 b 5.8] — German 2nd line [C.17 a 4.7]. The battery was shelled whilst firing by a 77mm firing H.E. shell. Several rounds burst within 10 yds of guns, no damage being done. Digging continued all day. The left section was brought in during the night.	

O.B. Farwell 2/Lt R.F.A.

June 405

364th Battery RFA
Army Form C. 2118.

WAR DIARY
or
INTELLIGENCE SUMMARY Ref. Map Series "B" Sheet 36 NW3 SW3
1/20,000

Hour, Date, Place	Summary of Events and Information	Remarks and references to Appendices
4th 9 A.M.	Left Section guns ranged by Major Harris from Mairie the following points being registered. Comm. trench 4° left of Staff farm — Brewery, Felinghien Road Junction [? 17 a 4.7]. One of the latter shell fell in centre of road. Digging continued all day.	
5th Morning	The observing station (Mairie) shelled by 4.2 How. 135 shells were fired to 9.0 were direct hits but the main objective i.e. the tower was not brought down until abt 135th round had been fired. The position at this time was extremely strong. A 6 Pr communication trench was dug along line of guns with traverses leading to each gun. The trenches gave very useful protection as most of the hostile shelling & rifle bullets came from right flank. The hostile trenches in this direction being only 1,300 yds distant.	Weather very fine
Afternoon	Orders received to relieve 131 RFA in Bois Grenier. 2 BCS Sherwell RFA took the left section to Bois Grenier & relieved section of 131 RFA. The guns were in action at 10 p.m.	OCS Farewell 2 Lt R.F.A

WAR DIARY
or
INTELLIGENCE SUMMARY

(Erase heading not required.)

362ⁿᵈ Battery R.F.A.   Army Form C. 2118.
Reg. Map. Series "B" Sheet 36 NW } S/W
                                    2.0,000

Hour, Date, Place	Summary of Events and Information	Remarks and references to Appendices
1915 June 6th	2/Lt Shewell relieved 2/Lt Allan 131 By in the Trenches leaving 2/Lt Ritt in charge of section of 362ⁿᵈ. Major O.M. Harris & 2/Lt Halbach came on with the remainder of the battery, the battery relief being finally finished at 10 P.M. with all guns of 362 & 131 ready to shoot. The battery did not shoot.	Weather fine
7th 8th	The battery did not shoot. Very quiet days spent in strengthening the position, both from point of view of action from rifle & enemy.	
9th 3.45 p.m.	2/Lt A. Ritt goes to Rosetta in ammunition limber. All guns ranged on signpost form D.2.a.3.7. Burst fits of combat with all guns. Communication French rather gone also ranged on I. n.o.o.p.t.	
10th	Battery did not shoot, very quiet day	
11th 11am 1.30 pm	Approach communication trench in I.3.1.d & 0.1.b. Range to Sniper reported sniper in a tree in line found, infantry report sniper in a tree in 0.1.b.6.9. Three shelled with high bursts of shrapnel, enemies artillery very quiet as was the case on the previous day. Fifhal round fired fine. Working party reported in I.3.4.a. Rounds fired fine	11.6.15 2/Lt W.W. Halbach proceeds to England on sick leave. Weather continues to be fine
12th 2.15 pm	Working party dispersed in front of enemies trench at I.3 & c.5.a	
13th 6.15 pm	Wire in front of enemies trench 3 total for the day 8. major fired 20 rounds fine. Enemies Artillery still quiet. Battery did not fire.	O.M. Shewell 2/Lt R.F.A

364 Battery R.F.A. Army Form C. 2118.
Reg Map Series "G" Sheet 36 S.W.3
1 / 20,000.

WAR DIARY
or
INTELLIGENCE SUMMARY
(Erase heading not required.)

Hour, Date, Place	Summary of Events and Information	Remarks and references to Appendices
June 14th 11.45 a.m.	Series & ranges to German parapet & barbed wire etc. being obtained	
6.30 p.m.	A company of infantry opened fire in retaliation to German shelling. 7 Cal. rounds fired B.10.	
15th	4x 4.2 How 6" & the enemy shelled an infantry working party working just in front of O.P. (Subs School H 30 D 7 A) 21 rounds were fired all falling into the cemetery at H 3055.2 on the edge of which the work was being carried on. No damage or casualties.	
6 p.m.	Enemies wire in I 33 & regd wire dealt with being obtained. Enemies artillery quiet.	
	14.6.15 Major D.M. Across O.S.O. took over command of "A" Group. 2/Lt. Sherwell assumed command of a detachment from R.G. Huh reported for duty on attachment from A/62 Bty. 2/Lt. Athwing of 14H. and 2/Lt. Am Col Charles A/62 Bty. 2/Lt Personally to take place of 2/Lt S.U. Pitt who has temporarily gone to post to C.	Weather very fine
6 p.m.	Wire in front of Subsections 51, 52, 53 very carefully registered Enemy replied on our trenches & communication trenches. During the firing an enemy aeroplane came over battery & was shelled until it flew away.	
7 p.m.	Infantry asked for support 2 rounds were fired Total rounds for the day 12. 12 rounds were fired by the enemy from 8 yds field gun & Leerotropmy in subsection 53.	

F.W. Sherwell
Lt. 2/c R.F.A.

364th Battery R.F.A Army Form C. 2118.
Ref Map Series "B" Sheet 36 NW & SW 3
———
24770

WAR DIARY or INTELLIGENCE SUMMARY
(Erase heading not required.)

Instructions regarding War Diaries and Intelligence Summaries are contained in F. S. Regs, Part II. and the Staff Manual respectively. Title pages will be prepared in manuscript.

Date	Hour, Date, Place	Summary of Events and Information	Remarks and references to Appendices
April 17th	5 a.m.	Enemy shelled our trenches in vicinity of Water Farm very heavily. 72 shells from 2 eight gulls how were fired. Infantry requested support & 6 rounds were fired.	Weather very fine
	9 a.m.	Enemy shelling and entering, 6 more rounds were fired in support of the infantry.	
	5.30 pm	Later (in the Evening) 6 rounds from a 5.9 how were fired by the enemy at the cross Roads at 4.30 & 9.15. No damage.	
18th		S.W.W. Haddock returned from England arriving at 6 A.M.	
		The gun being at Water farm observed by O.P. Stinwell & reported to be in hedge O 3.d. Transport load moving in German lines brought by infantry to be on the Bois Blanc road. This was however almost entirely wrong & the more likely one being that running Chaulnes–LaVallée + Halmghem.	
	5 pm	The Battery did not fire. Enemy shelled to tronquet Farm with small pieces. Bréaux with 5.9 how firing 8 rounds. This Gun has a habit of throwing odd rounds on the country.	
19th	3 p.m.	Five rounds fired at Nos Farm. Believe Ro obtained. This farm had not been shelled for some time & probably used as a Coon one post by the enemy.	
19th	9 am–1 pm	A section of a 5 how, in neighbourhood of gris Pot very heavily shelled by enemy. Not 5.9 Hows about. (Co shell fired) No change firing Unit however. Many aeroplanes seen during the day.	

Dot Howard
Lt. R.F.A

WAR DIARY
or
INTELLIGENCE SUMMARY

Army Form C. 2118.

362 Battery R.F.A.
Ref Map Serie "B" Sht 36 NY9 S.W.
2 0,000

Hour, Date, Place	Summary of Events and Information	Remarks and references to Appendices
June 20th	Battery did not fire enemy front lines. During this period a considerable amount was fired at the parties to give better cover from Aeroplanes and for safety. Ground being oven soft & dry in ground position made very stiring from a defence point of view. Enemy aeroplane shelled gun pit during the day. Two rounds were fused after & burst to the S.E of Hooge-Church. Shells this neighbourhood at Anthony's both a few feet bearing & time between flash & report the position of the gun worked out to be at I.11.2.3.6.3.9	
5.30 pm	In accordance with the general orders issued to the batteries of "A" group to take part in defensive operation in conjunction with 14 Infantry Bde 28 rounds were fired with intent of cutting some of the wire infront of subs 50 & 51. To damage the parapet in suiting 52. 12 extra rounds were allowed for this purpose. The total amount of wire was cut out of the number of rounds used 14 from small to allow of any real damage being done the parapet in front of 52. Too hit & close in 20 rounds but the damage done was insignificant as only shrapnel shell were available the nearest left with about 20 rounds from a sight fuzed gun probably the one at O.3.d. German working parties were heard by F.O.O in places where we had shelled during the night. Transport again head on Paradis - Warrington Street	Weather fine
10 pm		

O.C. Sherwell
2/LtRFA

413

369th 9 R.Z.A — Army Form C. 2118.
Ref Map Series B Sheet 36 A W ?
                        S W ?
                     1/20,000

WAR DIARY or INTELLIGENCE SUMMARY

(Erase heading not required.)

Hour, Date, Place	Summary of Events and Information	Remarks and references to Appendices
June 22nd	Very quiet day. Battery did not fire. No shelling by enemy.	Weather still fine
23rd 9 a.m.	Enemy reported to be running on the Harzecourt – La Vallée road. 8 rounds were fired.	
12.30 pm	Some snipers annoying the infantry from support. Turn La Belle Suboisin. 51.8 rounds were fired at them. Several hits on bank were obtained & thirty-four little could be seen direct. Bn's Pot shelled during the day by some Sqd through F.O.O.	Weather very much [?] little could be seen
24th 10 a.m.	Infantry reported enemy to be running troops in sub. 50191. Snow with rifle grenades & 6 rounds were fired. One shell burst. Riflemen ran over trenches. 7 rounds were fired later in the day to check enemy at ranges, all proving correct. We had [?] [?] enemy Brig. Enemy did not shell during the day.	Mist travelled country observation F.O.O. very difficult
3.15 pm		
25th 5.15 pm	Bn's Pot again shelled. About 6 rounds (shrapnel)	
11 pm	4 rounds fired on parcel [?] of Infantry	
12 pm	4 rounds fired on the rear of Trenches & later, in key lines & ranges. Ensaé behind our own Trenches was [?] at 1.15 p.m. Most probably the [?] the guns were fired at 1.17 pm. Most probably the shell struck a tree in the flight.	
7 am	A certain amount of hostile shelling during night. 7 rounds felt gas fire day but travelled from ??	Thundery — Thunder showers at intervals. Bright spells in between showers & wind

O W Learwell
2/Lt R.F.A.

4/14

364th Battery R.F.A. Army. Form C. 2118.
Ref. Map Series B "Sheet 36 NW & SW
$\frac{1}{20,000}$

WAR DIARY
or
INTELLIGENCE SUMMARY
(Erase heading not required.)

Instructions regarding War Diaries and Intelligence Summaries are contained in F.S. Regs., Part II. and the Staff Manual respectively. Title pages will be prepared in manuscript.

Hour, Date, Place	Summary of Events and Information	Remarks and references to Appendices

June 27
Quiet day, no movement in German lines except for six horse team seen on La Houssoie – Escobecques Rd. Snr Pot & St Anne were again shelled by 5.9 How about 6 rounds being fired.

28th
11 AM.
Zone called so as to include sub-sectors A9 & 10 cut our Subs 5.9. New lines & range sheet obtained. Registered La Houssoie – Escobecques road. Regr.s fire. The road is very difficult as it is slightly sunken

12.15 pm.
& has green screen which is very difficult to distinguish owing to very close similarity in colour to their surrounding fields. Total rounds for day 15.

29th
8.15 am.
Series & ranges to barricade I 31 a checked

3.45 pm.
Lines & ranges to Petillieux farms & trenches in Subs A9 registered.

5.35 pm.
F.O.O. reported German working party with wagon galloping by. Two rounds were fired & the wagon let off at a gallop – the men m.o. & saw the Fay falling off. Enemies artillery shewed considerable activity on afternoon & evening, about 40 shell in the Rue Deleble in H 17 & 23 & also Sig Pox & Persone 5.9 How T4.2 How arrived out the shelling. Total rounds fired today by us 19.
No B Farm at I 31 c 2.4 & trenches in zone to check.

30th
8.30 am
St R.G. Will return to Bde. Sr.n.s. Manager. H.C.P.B.D. Burns reports for temporary duty

Weather wet, rain falling for good part of day

No.8 farewell R.J.A. N.S. R.J.A.
Orders 364 ? ? B.S.

27th/5 Division

121/6357

386th Battery R.F.A.
—
6   Vol VIII

20 BdE

1-31-4-15

WAR DIARY or INTELLIGENCE SUMMARY

(Erase heading not required.)

364 FBG R.F.A.   Army Form C. 2118.
Ref. Map. Series "B" Sheet 36 NW
                                        1
                              Scale 20000 SW

Hour, Date, Place	Summary of Events and Information	Remarks and references to Appendices

July 1st

2nd
5.30pm / 5.p.m. — Battery did not fire. Quiet day. Enemy shelled JUNK shoots subsections 5.52, 5.3 with 77m firing 28 shells. House in 0.9.d.2.8 registered. 7m Hour rain & Grenades in zone in order to check enestrange on new zone which exploded subsections A.9. Civilians were seen working at 0.1.00.2.8. Total rounds fired 24.

3rd
8.a.m. — Barricade across road at 1.32.a.5.3. to Grenades opp subsection 0.2 re. registered or charge of zone. Enemy fired a 6" shell at 0.00 Grenades — 4 77m shell at Rbad (H.1.d.1.0.5) & about 10.4.2 How shell in square H.1.6 probably searching for A/53 By which was firing at the time. Total rounds fired by us 1/10.

8.30pm / 9pm — A big white light was seen high in the air & it was not known whether it was fired from a plane or whether it was a Parachute flare. Lt. Pitt returns from leave & proceeds to H.Q's "A" Group.

4th
7/10pm — The 54 Ruelle road from 1.34.d.4 to 9.2 was shelled by up all the shells bursting well off the actual road. As can be seen but they bring the road give an accurate idea of the position. This shoot was in conjunction with the 11th D A/53 & 1895 who shelled other points. The order to fire was given when over 50 Germans had been observed making certain that portion of the road clearly, making place on the road, a good deal of movement was taking place on the enemy been infected.

3pm / 4pm — soldier working party before. 10 men seen at 6.5.a. Enemy shelled L'Amal with 5.9 Hows firing 6 shells. Rounds fired 12.

Weather bright
wind normal

Orig forwarded
2/L. R.F.A.
O.C. 364 FBG R.F.A.

Army Form C. 2118.

364th (?) B/R.F.A.

Ref Map Series B "Sheet 36 NW & SW"
Scale 1/20,000

WAR DIARY
or
INTELLIGENCE SUMMARY
(Erase heading not required.)

Instructions regarding War Diaries and Intelligence Summaries are contained in F.S. Regs., Part II. and the Staff Manual respectively. Title pages will be prepared in manuscript.

Hour, Date, Place	Summary of Events and Information	Remarks and references to Appendices
July 5th 9.15 am / 11 am	Road at O.P.8 of registered. I.D.M. examining gun emplacements No. 1 & 2 wheeling being to O.P.8 stopped immediately to observe situation. Waiting party at 9 a/c 10.9 observed total rounds fired 12.	
6th 10 am	Crossroads at O.9.d.9.2 registered. Le Briseur Rgar sighted it. Front line trenches. Total rounds 12. Civilian working party seen at O.9.d.1.0.0.	
2.30 pm	Enemy shelled End of comm trench (Shaftesbury AV) with 77 mm gun. 8 fell.	
3 pm & onwards	Enemy shelled L'Armée with 5.9 How. 15 shell.	
7th 5.15 pm	The Battery being on the extreme right of the 27th Div. orders were received to register the guns of the left battery of the 8th Div. (33.B.5, 88 W Bde 8th Div) Lt. Stanwell listed the line to Brewery 4.36.b.7.2 — the O.P. of the 83rd Bty. Direct hits on the parapet were obtained & the ammo at ranges registered. Rounds fired 11.	
11 am	Wentworth was seen at O.9.a.10.0.0 with 77 mm gun. 20 shell. Enemy shelled Locality I.B.i.a with 77 mm gun — 8 fell.	
6.25 pm	Shaftesbury Av shelled by 77 mm gun — 8 fell.	
8th	Battery did not fire.	
9th	Bois Grenier & I.O.5 shelled by 6.9 How. 6 shell very quiet day. very much. Battery did not fire.	
10.a	Road at I.9.a.7.5 shelled by 4.2 How - 20 shell. Most of the shell fell about 20 yds short. Some however fell close to some of the house of Breweries. Situation still very quiet. Battery did not fire. Enemy Artillery silent.	Div. 8 forwarded Div 2/P R.F.A

418

364th Battery R.F.A. Army Form C. 2118.
Ref. Map Series "B" Sheet 36 NW
                               36 SW
Scale 20000

WAR DIARY
or
INTELLIGENCE SUMMARY
(Erase heading not required.)

Hour, Date, Place	Summary of Events and Information	Remarks and references to Appendices
July 11th 12.30 p.m.	Enemy shell Subsection 50 with 77 m/m gun – 30 shells. Battery replied with 12 rounds into opposite parapet. Small gathering party observed 5 men seen in vicinity of Ferme de Flâtre.	
13th 4.15 p.m.	Battery did not fire. Enemy shelled House at I19.c.6.5 with about 20 rounds from 77 m/m guns. No damage.	
5.30 p.m.	Wagon + 4 men recd at O.9.d.1.9.0. 2nd Lt Shenwell proceeds to England on leave. 2nd Lt. Pitt assumes command.	
13th 4.30 p.m.	Working party digging Trenches near farm at O.11.b.3.8 shelled and party dispersed. 8 rounds.	
4.45 p.m.	Wagon accompanied by 5 men in uniform (undress) observed coasting down ridge at O.16.a.2.7. Two rounds fired & burst well ahead of gallop in direction of ESCOBECQUES. Enemies Artillery silent.	
14th 8 a.m.	Two rounds fired at wagon on road at O.16.a.2.7. One of which hit corner of wagon. Horse bolted leaving man on road probably wounded. He crawled away later.	
12.15 p.m.	House at O.9.d.1.8. This House is considered a good idea of observation. 6 rounds fired.	
5.30 p.m. etc.	Enemy shelled Brig Pot with 5.9 & 2 Hours firing about 20 rounds. Some hereover but hit majority of rounds fell short. Front turn shelled by 17 m/m. House observed hit Culvert Farm (I.31.a) 15 attempts. One 5.9 shell hit culvert farm (I.31.a).	

2nd Lt Shenwell R.F.A.
O.C. 364th R.F.A.

419

WAR DIARY or **INTELLIGENCE SUMMARY**
Army Form C. 2118.

364th Battery Reg. Map Series "B" Sheet 36 S.W. N.W. 1/20,000

Hour, Date, Place	Summary of Events and Information	Remarks and references to Appendices
July 15th 12.0 pm	Enemy shelled observing station & 5 rounds were put in the gm HOUSSAIN (O2b.3.7) in retaliation. A wagon seen on the ridge at O.6.a.2.7 was sent off at the gallop by a single round. Rounds fired 6.	
16th 2.30 pm	At the request of the infantry 3 rounds were fired at a 15t fuze app in enemy trench approx subs 53. The barrage was not put but was short on Hill. Rounds safe in the French. Enemies artillery quiet. Battery did not fire. Enemies artillery quiet.	
17th	do	
18th	do	
19th 10.30 am	Lieut Arkwright leaves the battery. Enemy shelled road at H.30 to 6.7 & 10.10 with 4 rounds. From A.A. How. Enemy aeroplane dropped darts in vicinity of GIRLS SCHOOL but none were fired on. Battery did not fire.	
20th	Enemies artillery quiet. Major O.M. Harris D.S.O. reassumes command of the battery. Lt. Burns leaves the battery which is relieved in its present position by the 131st Bty & takes up its new position at H.24 & 5.1. This position had been begun a few days previously.	
21st 5.30 pm	The Hôtel d'Artillerie registered with Nos 4 & 2 guns from the new position. No.1 gun, which had been examined by the I.O.M. informed wanting, was not used. Enemies artillery quiet.	Signed S.S. Sorwell 2/Lt R.F.A.
22nd 5.30–6.0 pm	Ranges & lines to the following points taken. Comm French Behind HOTEL - Comm French Relief DISTILLERIE - comm French behind Maxim House - Barricade mirrored at T.21.C.7.3. Enemies artillery active many 90 rounds fired at BOIS GRENIER P.O.T. Trenches at H.31.C.d. Rounds fired by battery 12. Lt. Sherwell returns from England.	

WAR DIARY or INTELLIGENCE SUMMARY

364th Battery R.F.A. Army Form C. 2118.
Ref. Map Series "B" Sheet 36 NW / SW 1/20000

Hour, Date, Place	Summary of Events and Information	Remarks and references to Appendices
July 23rd 5.30 & 6 pm	The following points were registered. Barricade across railway N of canal — Enemy's trench 2°50' 2ff (N) of railway barricade — Enemies trench 4°15' L 08 Barricade. No of rounds 2.B.7. Enemy fired 7 rounds from 5.9" How into Suio Pat.	very windy.
24th	Battery did not fire. enemies artillery quiet.	
26th	Maj. O.M. Harris receives orders to take over command of "X" Battery R.H.A. Capt Cameron R.F.A. arrives to take command of the battery. Maj. Harris took Capt. Cameron to trenches & shot at the following points in order to show Capt. Cameron the lines. The Hotel — Distillery & Managers House. also German Renah across railway & possible formation of subsections 59 & 60. Rounds fired 7.S. Pat with 6 rounds from 4.2. Enemy shelled Suio Pat with 6 rounds from 4.2 How.	
26th	Maj. O.M. Harris D.S.O. leaves Capt. O.S. Cameron R.F.A. assumes command. Battery did not fire. Six rounds from 4.2 How fell in Bois Brenier Trenches appear in subs 39 shelled by 77m Battery probably in O.8d. 12 rounds.	
27th	Battery did not fire. Six rounds from 5.9" How fell in Suio Pat.C. Sels probable at I.23b 8.9.	
28th 12 noon	Line ranges of Wine Stophouls ourtrenches registered. Wire from I 21.8 9.8 & I 21d 1.8. Trenches by German House registered. 12 rounds fired. Enemies artillery quiet. Enemy shelled Bristol & L'Aromi lively during the afternoon with 6.9 & 4.2 How. 37 rds.	referred R.F.A Referred R.F.A

364th Battery R.F.A.
Army Form C. 2118. NW
Reg. Map Series "B" Sheet 36 SW
1/20,000

WAR DIARY
or
INTELLIGENCE SUMMARY
(Erase heading not required.)

Instructions regarding War Diaries and Intelligence Summaries are contained in F. S. Regs., Part II. and the Staff Manual respectively. Title pages will be prepared in manuscript.

Hour, Date, Place	Summary of Events and Information	Remarks and references to Appendices
July 30th	A very quiet day. Battery did not fire & enemies artillery was quiet.	
31st 11.30 am to 1 pm.	Wire opposite subsection 60 registered with 4 rounds in view of operation to be carried out next day. Enemies artillery quiet.	L. Blackwell 2Lt R.F.A.

121/6754

27th Division

364th Batty RFA
Vol ix
August 15

20 BDE

Army Form C. 2118.

WAR DIARY
or
INTELLIGENCE SUMMARY
(Erase heading not required.)

364th Battery.

Instructions regarding War Diaries and Intelligence Summaries are contained in F. S. Regs., Part II. and the Staff Manual respectively. Title pages will be prepared in manuscript.

Hour, Date, Place	Summary of Events and Information	Remarks and references to Appendices
BOIS GRENIER. Aug 2nd to 4th.	Fired a few registering rounds on Aug 2nd & Aug 4th.	
Aug 4th 4.30–5.30 p.m.	Some German L.2" How. shells fell in front of the convent at BOIS GRENIER. No damage.	
Aug. 5th.	Nothing of importance. L-Bienvillé reported shrunk near GRAND MAIRIS — fired 18 rounds at enemy trenches near Salient. The battery position was protected by screens. Our Battery commanding 3rd Corps, who entered himself very pleased with the projectile dug into etc.	
Aug 6th.	Nothing of importance — German shells Dis. bursting party near Convent & 1 shrapnel burst into Convent. No damage.	

1247 W 3299 200,000 (E) 8/14 J.B.C. & A. Forms/C. 2118/11.

WAR DIARY or INTELLIGENCE SUMMARY

364th Battery

Army Form C. 2118.

Hour, Date, Place	Summary of Events and Information	Remarks and references to Appendices
BOIS GRENIER. Aug. 7th, 8th, 9th	Nothing of importance. Registration continued. Germans have shelled our communication trenches intermittently.	
Aug 10 6.72 th	Nothing of importance. On July 9/12 & a new O.S.R. was recommended in der Bottom, a better view of the German trenches obtain to the old. New Station to be at — Arrangements here also made whereby the Battery fires on duty west guard about lat. 138 od. 138 od. he normally rest.	
Aug 13th 9-14 th	But next the guns in action during the period when 133 & or duty. 364 Battery has been made with an aeroplane battery. The pilot of plays will air observation have attended twist into Dr L'angeles where were last visible from the O.S.	

1247 W 3299 200,000 (E) 8/14 J.B.C. & A. Forms/C. 2118/14.

WAR DIARY or INTELLIGENCE SUMMARY

Army Form C. 2118.

364 Battery

Hour, Date, Place	Summary of Events and Information	Remarks and references to Appendices
Aug 16 – 17.	Nothing of importance. 364 Battery has Bo.Sh. of 133 B.G. for a week on 16th.	Very heavy thunderstorms for 3 days –
Aug. 18 – 19.	Nothing of importance. We have been shooting with aeroplane a little, but have not had very conclusive results. Everything on our front has been very quiet.	Weather improved.
Aug. 20th. –	Fired on the Artillery I.27.b.3.5 by Infantry (Buzaphone L.) There is a rifle battery in the battery – Put 4 shell right in a snipping asked. Same thing occurred near BETHUNE No. I.21.b.2.4. Fired at aerial torpedo with aeroplane – observing etc. Sgt. O.K. F.O.W. Shurwell is employed at the wireless station. When aeroplane is up. The camera only 2 out of three for sporty. 1st Obs Sh. of ad- fires – Bone for house. at Douffon Line.	

WAR DIARY
or
INTELLIGENCE SUMMARY 36 L Battery
(Erase heading not required.)

Army Form C. 2118.

Hour, Date, Place	Summary of Events and Information	Remarks and references to Appendices
Aug 20 th Comp.	Reconnoitred a hostile gun battery in Caur we have before buit on BOIS GRENIER line – Pos at H 11 d 6 3. Place not yet fixed on Obs. Stn. A phone has been out along the avenue com. Trenes to find all artillery Telephone wires in to. The firm is cut up to the trenes up each on top of the trench. Very quiet along the front, he has 3 4.2" shells over the Battery the evening – some old bits into the guns. The hostile hangars. been found. Ranges found. 2 telephones wanted here to-day.	
Aug 21 st.	Reconnoitred a new position for the battery again – this time at H 11 b 4 8. in the one in piually field on L 205. Quite liked. Arranged to fire on some Germans who find higher put behind trench S.Q.	SW Someren known.

Army Form C. 2118.

WAR DIARY
or
INTELLIGENCE SUMMARY 364 B Battery

(Erase heading not required.)

Instructions regarding War Diaries and Intelligence Summaries are contained in F.S. Regs, Part II. and the Staff Manual respectively. Title pages will be prepared in manuscript.

Hour, Date, Place	Summary of Events and Information	Remarks and references to Appendices
Aug 21st.	Registration for the last two days have since all rounds shown by the forme been — about 75' in BOUD.	Fine weather —
Aug 22nd.	Registered the trenches at the Sulenterganni. Also fired at German House by request of the Infantry as this has contained a persistent sniping. This was stopped after a few rounds L. 4.15" Rounds also his on German House. Fired on Rotering at ½ midnight. Reported no hostile rifle gate Breslan there. A great Kay. Battery did not shoot. 3 recconnoited Bo. Shot I 7 d 7.10 for our new position. Also enquired arrangements for our firing	Fine weather may be early state.
Aug 23rd.		

Army Form C. 2118.

WAR DIARY
or
INTELLIGENCE SUMMARY 364 Battery

(Erase heading not required.)

Instructions regarding War Diaries and Intelligence Summaries are contained in F. S. Regs, Part II. and the Staff Manual respectively. Title pages will be prepared in manuscript.

Hour, Date, Place	Summary of Events and Information	Remarks and references to Appendices
Aug. 24th to 28th.	There has been little of importance as the 133rd Battery are on duty at the Obs Stn. The battery has continued up to date, by brother-in-law with two blinds & O.K. has been blamed, more rarely no practice has been blamed. The (Adjutant) No Shi is complete at J14.d.6.9. for g.p.g Trench 2' deep for D 6" Cable. Trenches have been dug from No Stn to Head DESPLANQUE FARM. Wait is putting on at rear gun horses. H.11, 12 & 8. I have reconnoitred & been allotted a second Obs Stn for rear gun Pos at J 18 & 4.6. The waggon train have been moved today to winter Position at - H 24 c 5 - 2. Horse standings, shelters for men have to be made by the men at happen time -	Weather has been very fine - hazy early & late.

1247 W 3299 200,000 (E) 8/14 J.B.C. & A. Forms/C. 2118/11.

WAR DIARY or INTELLIGENCE SUMMARY   364 B Battery

Army Form C. 2118.

(Erase heading not required.)

Instructions regarding War Diaries and Intelligence Summaries are contained in F. S. Regs., Part II. and the Staff Manual respectively. Title pages will be prepared in manuscript.

Hour, Date, Place	Summary of Events and Information	Remarks and references to Appendices
Aug 24 – 28/8/1917	4 Experimental Series were fired on 28th Inst with S.S. Fuze Ammunition – Shooting was irregular, elevation erratic, with 1 round II, III, IV & V 80 fuze lemon. The Greater however varies with the Elevation – 122 fm 3000. 126. 3300	
Aug 29th	138 4600. Fuzes burnt off evenly – Gunwirth Shrumel to the mile wagon Por at A 24 C 5.2. there were there for a furling life. At 6 pm we received a message from 11. W35 to say that Trench 60 was being reinforced. Nos 5 Pont – 3rds from fire into German Trench. Bombing ceased.	
Aug 30th	Received orders at 20.07 See No 2 to that we were to dig & purchase a fresh forn Posn at H 24 a 6.6. In lieu of fresh position. Stopped, as other unit. No S.O.S. – 2 waggons from the B amm. column re-filled for O.S.P. – a large	

WAR DIARY or INTELLIGENCE SUMMARY

Army Form C. 2118.

431

Hour, Date, Place	Summary of Events and Information	Remarks and references to Appendices

Aug 30th

Quantity of material from B.E. Park - Brass and all. Used for went into 2 whips answer from 8am to 2pm. 2 km to 7 km. 8pm to midnight, on our flat in the cornfield underneath at trees.

The whip was followed by the guns in our heard from here ready to fire if required.

Waggons were kept 400 yds in rear from there to the highway far back cover & swung to a building in the ground we can dig very deep. The limber is to the Bttn a man low cover - easy for concealment.

Section showing our ground level / front. Very covered. Very many of the trees in that neighbourhood have had branches & are very brunch in the middle of the field. Excellent for cover.

Army Form C. 2118.

WAR DIARY
or
INTELLIGENCE SUMMARY

(Erase heading not required.)

Hour, Date, Place	Summary of Events and Information	Remarks and references to Appendices
Aug 31, 1917	Work on position continued. Enemy came to infront - send every opportunity. Aeroplanes very pleased. Tel- egraphers made. 8 casualties. 2 Bn Staff, but have reported a definite decision get it. This also noted several.	weather cloudy to threatening but fine - Lost -

432

121/6983

27th Division

364th Batty. R.F.A. LoBIE

Vol X

Sept. 15

WAR DIARY
INTELLIGENCE SUMMARY 364 Battery

Army Form C. 2118.

Hour, Date, Place	Summary of Events and Information	Remarks and references to Appendices
September 1915. 1st	Work continued on new from Preston. The B.O.C.T.P. Boy's feet very sore & inflated this afternoon. Sephiah himself lamed. The only trouble is the impossibility turning to the dug along the two B. guns, altho' amount of natural bank cover. Lt Shervel had fever & is in bed. I have shewelmin of the heap endeavouring to find on Nevery Station for the new Zone. He had to wait a little long between showers — the right end good then. The Right Section moved after dark down to the new position. Work continued on new position.	Cloudy, rain most of the afternoon, 1CPL.
Sept 2nd	to get as to the Stain. Refurbished some of the trophi this afternoon. Another to be doubled B 3 holes at PETERIE. Shrapnel a splendid & fire, but is unfortunate has tendency a unful landmark. one fired 3 Premature. Observed 2 mend the R.F.A. at work at BOIS GRENIER	Showery, cold.

WAR DIARY or INTELLIGENCE SUMMARY 364 B Battery

Army Form C. 2118.

(Erase heading not required.)

Hour, Date, Place	Summary of Events and Information	Remarks and references to Appendices
Sept 3rd/15	Registered from the field's School in the morning & OP & forward OP in the afternoon. 2 am - There was to have been registration by aeroplane in the afternoon but - photographic strip went to incorrect 2 am - I think we went over to sleep with the right section.	Rain from 9am till noon.
Sept 4th/15	We for various today to see the tramont home Obs. Sta. I have been at work on a new piece there. The trench between the guns is being completed & the front received is much improved. Speaking to OC Sec is by telephone or visual. Registered S. trench target with aeroplane. Boche put in about 20 shrapnel to the right of the battery, about 75 very close on range.	Rain during afternoon

WAR DIARY or INTELLIGENCE SUMMARY

Army Form C. 2118.

Hour, Date, Place	Summary of Events and Information	Remarks and references to Appendices
Sept 5th 15.	A quiet day. Germans fired a S.G. "flare" into our wire today. We have applied one for a long time — there was continued firing.	Fine day
Sept 6th 15.	Reported fading the front line Trench from BYRES school in the afternoon. BOIS GRENIER was observed this afternoon about 3 (10 S.G "shells") fired from he had one Prisoner who in the right of the battery — the fuze of one came into the Breastwork. The Germans now lately sent an Bo Sh of an very pleased with the view obtained from it. The light was very good for observation. Given hazy most of the day, & everything was quiet — but for one or two shellburst to a G am. Attended a conference of B.G. Combo at B.E.H.Q. Thorn.	Fine day

Army Form C. 2118.

WAR DIARY
or
INTELLIGENCE SUMMARY 364 Battery

(Erase heading not required.)

Instructions regarding War Diaries and Intelligence Summaries are contained in F. S. Regs., Part II. and the Staff Manual respectively. Title pages will be prepared in manuscript.

Hour, Date, Place	Summary of Events and Information	Remarks and references to Appendices
Sept 8th 15"	Very quiet. Barrister difficult. Out enemy's battery and yesterday have been doubtful to form returns. We had to change all our H.E. then put it back, then send it off again. No one seems to know how the matter stands now.	Fine day.
Sept 9th 15" Sept 10 to 16"	Battery did not fire. Observed over my Obs. St. I at 1.1 at 77 to 73/1104 B.Y. Battery did not fire. Received orders to move a gun to H.29 for experimental firing with H.E. Put no 4 detachment to be put the piece ready. and started D/O & Battery came they were 12 men over (to the attached for instruction from —	Fine day 6 hrs
Sept 11 16"/15"	Battery did not fire. Moved no 4 gun to H.29. Reconnoitred Telmets 58 for a place to shoot at the German Parapet.	Fine day E Wind —

1247 W 3299 200,000 (E) 8/14 J.B.C. &A. Forms/C. 2118/11.

WAR DIARY
or
INTELLIGENCE SUMMARY 364 Battery

Army Form C. 2118.

(Erase heading not required.)

Hour, Date, Place	Summary of Events and Information	Remarks and references to Appendices
Sept 11th	A great many of the battalion line are being relieved by Hitchener Batteries. The Major (Major Cond) B/103 arrived this evening to take over of this Position at 7 am is 707. We four fortris about 2 am.	
Sept 12 to 15	10th fining fires 9 rounds of HE on Tanck Rchoits 58 with very fair effect. There were two S batteries bring it cross fires B/103 had the muzzle blown off. Field wire was then ready for us to come firing before came tonight. Firing No 1252 rounds sounds to fire. Nothing returned from our one firm. 9 minutes B/103 in their registration knock out fresh and cornet	Firing Bty E Wd

WAR DIARY
or
INTELLIGENCE SUMMARY 364 BFy

Army Form C. 2118.

Hour, Date, Place	Summary of Events and Information	Remarks and references to Appendices
Sept 13th to 75 —	We received 250 rounds of BHE to fire one of which has to be holed. Fired such rounds when bulged under in front of the church (rounds R.A. runout — firing ceased.)	
Sept 14 to 75.	Continued bombing over to 13/10 3 Lt Sherwell shift thereon attached Comdt of B. Guns on firm at BDC St. MAUR. Fey. Also rec'd in 1 detailed report 2nd Shore the incident in dront. Received OP from over 2 return line two Brackets at 8 pm Burned at Buggin line from STEENWERK 10/pk	
STEENWERK Sept 15th OUTERSTEEN	Bracketing at 10 am Burned STEENWERK 10am in front of B. De Staff Buckers not expected in so noom —	OUTERSTEEN
Sept 16 & 17 & 18.19 OUTERSTEEN.	Remained in bivets — he had some muscles to instruct him and gave him to bring the Various stores etc. for that meeting well together Classes in aircraft rifles — Running a Country correct —	

Army Form C. 2118.

WAR DIARY
or
INTELLIGENCE SUMMARY 364 Artillery

(Erase heading not required.)

Instructions regarding War Diaries and Intelligence Summaries are contained in F. S. Regs., Part II. and the Staff Manual respectively. Title pages will be prepared in manuscript.

Hour, Date, Place	Summary of Events and Information	Remarks and references to Appendices
Sept 19th 15	Marched at 8 am to STEENWERCK 12 miles. Billeted on the way. Rested 20 min left knee - 8 to 9 pm. Marched off at 11.20 am. arrived miles at 6 pm. Got billets. Received blankets & kits 3 pm. On 20th 18 yards — 153 yards of ground to march to East — great drill — men arrived. Well found entered into Stationary watch nearing arrived at rendezvous.	fine weather
Sept 20 to 22nd Oct 1st	Stayed during time as rehearsed Bt Staff. Lost men. 2 Lt Stanhope wounded as rejected to reconnoitre front. B. Capt'n. Visit from Artillery accompanied relief. Battery did a fair Through the two days engagement.	
Sept 23rd		
Oct 24th	New Command 2 Lt Stanwell & 2 Lt Patrick & 14 infantry 20 came in morning to replace men — infantry for battery. Battery moved to the right of Arthur	

Army Form C. 2118.

WAR DIARY
or
INTELLIGENCE SUMMARY

(Erase heading not required.)

364 Battery

Hour, Date, Place	Summary of Events and Information	Remarks and references to Appendices
Sept 26th 15 CHPPL	Concentration 2-2.30 pm & 4-4.45 & 5.15pm. Bombarded hostile trenches and batteries in morning from guns south of autoroute & from 2 howitzer here to 4th 15th. Fired 401 rounds. One gun out of action 20 mins but came into action a few minutes later.	Rain
Oct 1st Sept 26th	Army SOS 1 am. Cut [?] on 2 B Battery's front [?] [?] trenches and to anticipated [?] attack. Points 4 at B218 BMS NER E D CAPPY. Went with party of 20 men to support Sgt Nelson & later 30 B Battery. 2 officers from a 305 battery & further working party of 10 men went at 6pm to & Capart B Stewart & B. Nicholl went to reconnoitre on OK.	Rain - [?]
Oct 27th 15		
Oct 28th 15	Col Cameron went to interview [?] on matter	[?]

Army Form C. 2118.

WAR DIARY
or
INTELLIGENCE SUMMARY

364 Battery

(Erase heading not required.)

Instructions regarding War Diaries and Intelligence Summaries are contained in F. S. Regs., Part II. and the Staff Manual respectively. Title pages will be prepared in manuscript.

Hour, Date, Place	Summary of Events and Information	Remarks and references to Appendices
Sept. 29th 15.	Working party returned to 9 SIEGE B.S.R.	monthly returns
Sept. 30th 15.	Capt Cameron & 2nd Lieut. went to Ovillers to view position reconnaissance with a view to finding out a favourable front from which to the front to do this. Observer could the front to do this.	

1247 W 3299 200,000 (E) 8/14 J.B.C. & A. Forms/C. 2118/11.

27th Division

20 ter Bde: RFA Amm'n Coln

Vol I. 19.12 — 30.1.15

121/4/94

War Diary of the 20th Brigade Ammunition Col. R.F.A.

19.12.14. Column embarked at Southampton.
Officers:- Lieut. Fry. L. Commanding. Lieut Crewdson. R.
2/Lieut. Kydd. T. 2/Lieut Pitt. H.

20.12.14. Sailed at 4 p.m.

21.12.14. Arrived at Havre. Disembarked at 2 p.m.

22.12.14. Entrained at Gare Maritime 4 am.

23.12.14. Detrained at Arques at 7 p.m. and marched to Sercus. Billeted at Sercus until 6.1.15

6.1.15. Marched to Pradelles. Billeted at Pradelles the night of the 6th.

7.1.15 Marched to Reninghelst. Bivouaced the night of the 8th and marched into billets on the morning of the 9th.

9.1.15. The Brigade went into action.

10.1.15. Issued 35 Rounds shrapnell to 364th Bty and 114 Rounds to 99th Bty.

11.1.15. Issued 76 Rounds to 364th Bty. Captain Stanley. O.H. joined from Advanced Horse Transport Depôt.

12.1.15. 2/Lieut Pitt. H. transferred to 364th Bty. Issued 100 Rounds to 99th Bty.

13.1.15. Captain Fry. L. transferred to Royal Flying Corps. Issued 76 Rounds to 99th Bty and 71 to 364th Bty.

14.1.15. Issued 53 Rounds to 364th Bty and 38 to 99th Bty.

17.1.15. Brigade relieved by 19th Brigade. Column marched from Reninghelst to Boeschepe.

17.1.15 2/Lieut. Pitt. H.E. joined from Base.
25.1.15. No. 18791 Dr. Brooks. F.I. Died.
26.1.15 Issued with 50 Rounds H.E. from Divisional Column.

Column ordered to return to Reninghelst.
27.1.15. Order cancelled.
28.1.15 Issued 304 Rounds to 67th Bty.
30.1.15 Issued 68,000 Rounds S.A.A. and 300 Rounds Pistol Ammunition to the 1st Royal Irish Regiment.

31.1.15

P.W.Stanley Capt. R.F.A.
Cmdg 20th Bde Ammn. Col.

121/4634

27th Division

Ammn "C" a 20th Bde R+A.

Vol II. 2 – 28.2.15

121/4634

War Diary of the 20th Brigade Amm. Col. R.F.A.

2.2.15 Column marched from Boeschepe to ~~Dickebusch~~ Millekruis and billeted there.

7.2.15 Issued 12 Rounds 18 pr. to 364th Bty 7 Rounds H.E to 67th Bty and 76 Rounds 18 pr to 99th Bty. 2/Lieut Chown left to join 28th Division.

9.2.15 Column marched from Millekruis to ~~Dickebusch~~ near Ouderdom, and billeted there. Details from 15 Bde. A.C. joined. 13,000 Rounds S.A.A issued to 1st Royal Scots

10.2.15 Details from 14th Bde. A.C. joined. Issued 22,000 Rounds S.A.A. to 2nd D.C.L.I.

12.2.15 Issued 28 Rounds H.E to 67th Bty and 28 to 364th Bty.

13.2.15 Issued 26,000 Rounds S.A.A. to 2nd R.I.F. Issued 100 Rounds 18 pr to 11A Bty and 248 to 67th Bty.

14.2.15 Issued 532 Rounds 18 pr. to 99th Bty and 24,000 Rounds S.A.A. to 1st Leinster Regt.

14-15.2.15. Issued 1515 Rounds to 99th, 364th & 67th Bty. 48,000 Rounds S.A.A to 1st Royal Irish 15,000 Rounds to 1st Royal Scots, 276 Rounds Webley Ammunition to 3rd K.R.R. up to 8.40 am on the morning of the 15th.

15.2.15. Issued 304 Rounds 18 pr to 67th Bty and 24 Rounds to 11A. Bty.

16.2.15 Issued 85,000 Rds S.A.A. and 1 box Webley Pistol to 2nd. R.I.F.

17.2.15. Issued 45,900 Rounds S.A.A. to 4th R.B. 18,000. Rds to 2nd R.I.F. and 70,000. Rds to 1st A & S. Highlanders.

19.2.15 Issued 60,000. Rds S.A.A. to 4th K.R.R.

20.2.15. The C.O. Capt Hon. G.H Stanley went on leave to England. Issued 2 boxes Webley Pistol to 1st Royal Scots, 12000 Rds S.A.A. to 1st Royal Scots. & 29,000 Rds to 3rd K.R.R.

25.2.15. Issued 20,000 Rounds. S.A.A. to 1st Leinster. Regt. 14,000 Rds to 1st Royal. Irish. and 16,000 to 1st Argyll & Sutherlands.

26.2.15. Issued 12,000 Rds. S.A.A. to A.& S. High. and 38,000 Rds to P.P.C.L.I.

27.2.15 Issued 5,000 Rds. S.A.A. to 4th R.B. 2/Lieut. H. E. Pitt went on leave to England.

28.2.15. The C.O. Capt. Hon. G.H. Stanley returned from leave. Issued 16,000 Rds S.A.A. to 4th R.B., 52 Rds. 18 pr. Shrapnel and 24 Rds. H.E to 67th Bty.

G H Stanley Captain
Comdg 20th Bde A.C.

1.3.15